PERSPECTIVES ON STRATEGIC MANAGEMENT

PERSPECTIVES ON STRATEGIC MANAGEMENT

Edited by

JAMES W. FREDRICKSON

1817

HARPER BUSINESS

A Division of Harper & Row Publishers, New York

Grand Rapids, Philadelphia, St. Louis, San Francisco
London, Singapore, Sydney, Tokyo, Toronto

International Standard Book Number: 0-88730-357-9

Library of Congress Catalog Card Number: 90-4326

Printed in the United States of America

Library of Congress Cataloging-in-Publication Data

Perspectives on strategic management / edited by James W.
  Fredrickson.
       p.   cm.
  Includes bibliographical references.
  ISBN 0-88730-357-9 : $34.95
  1. Strategic planning. I. Fredrickson, James W.
HD30.28.P36 1990
658.4'012 — dc20
                                                      90-4326
                                                      CIP

90 91 92 93 MT/HC 9 8 7 6 5 4 3 2 1

CONTRIBUTING AUTHORS

Edward H. Bowman
Deputy Dean for Academic Affairs and
Reginald Jones Professor of Corporate Management
The Wharton School
University of Pennsylvania
Philadelphia, Pennsylvania

Victoria Buenger
Doctoral Candidate
Department of Management
College of Business Administration
Texas A & M University
College Station, Texas

Richard L. Daft
Ralph Owen Professor of Management
Owen Graduate School of Management
Vanderbilt University
Nashville, Tennessee

James W. Fredrickson
Associate Professor of Business and Gulf Oil Foundation
   Centennial Fellow
Graduate School of Business
University of Texas
Austin, Texas

Donald C. Hambrick
Samuel Bronfman Professor of Democratic Business Enterprise
Graduate School of Business
Columbia University
New York, New York

Henry Mintzberg
Bronfman Professor of Management
Faculty of Management
McGill University
Montreal, Canada

David J. Teece
Director, Center for Research in Management and
Mitsubishi Bank Professor of International Business and Finance
Walter A. Hass School of Business
University of California
Berkeley, California

CONTENTS

PERSPECTIVES ON STRATEGIC MANAGEMENT

1 INTRODUCTION
The Need for Perspectives

James W. Fredrickson

Strategic management is concerned with those issues faced by managers who run entire organizations, or their multifunctional units. As an academic field it has experienced unrivaled growth during the 1980s. That growth is evident in a wide variety of indicators: newly created journals, a dramatic increase in the volume of published research on strategy-related topics, new Ph.D. programs in strategic management, and an accompanying increase in the number of business school faculty positions earmarked for strategy.

But the increased interest in strategic management has not been confined to the halls of academe. On the contrary, a similar level of interest has been shown by the business community. Articles in the business press routinely address such issues as managing diversity and implementing strategic change, as well as concepts such as "strategic vision." Moreover, my experience in executive education indicates that more and more companies have concluded that they must develop more general managers than ever before. As a result, their employees are attending strategic management courses (in-house and university-based) in record numbers, and looking for solutions wherever they can find them.

So, what is the state of the strategic management field? Like many things, it depends on who you ask. Most scholars in the field tend to point to the volume of work being done as the best index of its inherent good health. Others acknowledge the volume of work, but question its quality and relevance. Some applaud the increased rigor of contemporary work as evidence that strategic management has become truly "scientific." They are countered by a minority who believe that attempts to be scientific have led the field away from theory development and true understanding. Moreover, there remains the issue of a paradigm. Most scholars would agree that strategic management lacks an overarching paradigm, but they do not agree on the implications of that. To some it is a major weakness, while others consider it an advantage and opportunity. Similarly, some scholars see strategic management as distinctive in its concern for understanding what is "real" to managers, but others see in it an underlying "logical positivism" that gets in the way of real understanding.

MOTIVE FOR THE BOOK

The present book is a direct outgrowth of a symposium I organized several years ago. Therefore, the logic underlying that symposium provides the logic for this book. In 1986 I submitted a proposal to the Business Policy and Planning Division of the Academy of Management, to be considered as a symposium session at the annual meeting in Chicago. The proposed symposium, titled "Evaluating the Last Five Years of Strategic Management Research," was motivated by my perception that the time had come for scholars in strategic management to take stock of what had happened in the 1980s. As noted earlier, anyone familiar with this field would recognize that there has been a tremendous increase in research (and theoretical writing) in the last ten years. My admittedly subjective assessment was that 70 to 80 percent of the "research" done in strategy has been published since 1980. Yet, there was no systematic questioning or introspection. No one seemed to be saying, "What do we think of the work that's being done? Is the promise of the field being realized?"

Armed with these perceptions, I asked four panelists—Ned Bowman, David Teece, Dick Daft, and Don Hambrick—to evaluate the strategic management research of the 1980s from their specific perspectives. I considered all of these people to be well-known and unusually thoughtful scholars. Moreover, they could bring to the symposium the contrasts I was looking for. Specifically, in selecting potential panelists I wanted them to bring diverse perspectives to their evaluations. By *diverse* I mean the views of a variety of academic disciplines and professional experiences, as well as the views of both strategy "insiders" and "outsiders." The charge that I gave the panelists was as follows: From the perspective of your own background and discipline, try to evaluate the field's research of the 1980s. Tell us (1) what you like about it, (2) what you don't like, and (3) what those evaluations mean for the future direction of strategic management research.

With regard to having diverse views represented in the symposium, several points are worth emphasizing. First, it was my perception that a useful, thought-provoking evaluation of strategy research required input from scholars who were interested observers of the area but who were also trained in, and aligned with, other fields. I recognized that some people would be put off by the presence of such "interlopers," but I felt their role was critical. Strategic management research often draws on the theory, concepts, and empirical conclusions of well-established disciplines. Second, I also wanted diversity among those panelists who were identified with the strategy area. It was my perception that panelists who differed substantially in age, professional training, and research orientation would likely provide the contrasting views that generate useful discussion and debate. With these criteria in mind, a few words about the panelists who have since become the authors of the chapters that follow.

I wanted the first speaker to provide a historical perspective on the recent changes in strategy research: not a traditional chronology, but a history "with a twist." I asked Ned Bowman to assume that role. Ned was trained first and foremost in management science and has been a staff executive in industry, as well as dean of the Business School at Ohio State. His work on risk and return is widely recognized in the strategy area. It was my hope that his unique combination of current position, training, and wide-ranging experience would bring uncommon insight.

In my view, industrial organization economics is one of the two disciplines most frequently used in strategy research. Therefore, David Teece, a Yale-trained economist whose work is familiar to strategy researchers, was asked to evaluate the work of the 1980s from his perspective. It was my hope that David's academic credibility and well-known candor would be a catalyst for discussion.

Strategic management scholars, particularly those who do strategic process research, draw heavily on the theoretical and empirical contributions of organization theory. Dick Daft, an active organization theorist who previously served as associate editor of *Administrative Science Quarterly*, was asked to evaluate the strategy research of the 1980s from that perspective. Again, he was recognized as an outsider, but one who was both an interested observer of the strategy area and an uncommonly thoughtful academic. I later learned that Dick had done extensive reading in expectation of writing a book on strategic management. The book was never written, but the preparation left Dick with strong opinions on the state of strategy research.

Finally, I wanted a panelist who had been a clear "insider" in contributions to the recent surge of strategy research. I asked my former Columbia colleague Don Hambrick to fill this role. Of all the panelists, Don was the only one whose Ph.D. training was in strategic management; he has also been one of the most active researchers in the field during the 1980s. Furthermore, I knew him to have strong views about the needs of the strategy field.

The goal of the symposium was to raise issues that would encourage debate and introspection by strategic management scholars. Therefore, the panelists were encouraged to provide their most provocative and controversial observations, which proved to be even more controversial than I expected. The reviewers who read the symposium proposal reacted very strongly to the three-page abstracts submitted by me and the panelists. One reviewer loved the proposal, one hated it, and a third disagreed with the panelists' positions but concluded that "people need to hear it." What struck me most was the second reviewer (the one long on hate) being particularly offended that outsiders were evaluating this field: "Who are they to evaluate strategy research? I would never think of going to an economics meeting and passing judgment on its research." Ever since my days as a strategic management doctoral student, I have been very sensitive myself to outsiders who condemn the field based on what I view as inaccurate perceptions. But I was still surprised by the strength of this reaction.

In spite of the best judgment of some of the reviewers, the symposium became part of the Centennial/Anniversary Program Track for the Academy's Chicago meeting. Moreover, even though it was scheduled for Saturday afternoon (the last day of the program), the session was "standing room only," with over 200 people attending.

Following the presentations, audience members offered a variety of strongly held opinions, and often pointed questions and observations, for the panelists. By the time the symposium ended, it was clear that we had struck a responsive cord (or among some, a nerve).

My interest in encouraging introspection and evaluation by strategic management scholars, in combination with the response (positive and negative) generated by the symposium, led to this book. It is important to emphasize, however, that the book is not a compendium of symposium papers. Rather, it builds on the general theme of the symposium—evaluating the current state of strategic management research and pointing new directions. In particular, we attempt to use the assessment of where the field is and where it has been as a basis for suggesting where research should go (i.e., what should characterize its research).

In writing the chapters included here, the panelists built on their symposium comments. In some cases that meant expanding and refining them, while in others it meant starting almost from scratch. To help in this task, one panelist took on a coauthor: Vicki Buenger joined Dick Daft in extending and refining his original thoughts.

In addition to the contributions by the original panelists and their coauthors, I was fortunate to get Henry Mintzberg to write a chapter. I was interested in expanding the topical coverage and practical appeal of the book and could think of no one better able to do both than Henry. He has been a dominant figure in the development and growth of strategic management over the past fifteen years, as an innovative investigator, a conceptual thinker, and an advocate. In his chapter, Henry characterizes and evaluates the ten models that he believes dominate work on strategy formation.

THE PERSPECTIVES

In the chapters that follow, the authors provide their perspectives on strategic management. In general, they describe what they like, what they dislike, and what should characterize future research. Readers will undoubtedly interpret the chapters from their own perspectives and will reach their own conclusions. As editor, however, I feel compelled to provide something of a "road map" to describe (beyond the earlier comments) what lies ahead in this volume.

In Chapter 2, Ned Bowman examines how strategy research has evolved over three decades. As a vehicle for this examination, he traces the changes that have taken place in two courses he has taught (one Ph.D. and one MBA) during that time. He concludes that the field still lacks a central paradigm, but that such an absence is not a problem. He ends with a call for, among other things, richer, more thorough research, the kind that must be published in book (versus article) form; for more "narrative," less "paradigmatic," work; for less logical positivism, higher order theory–building, and more work that is longitudinal and emphasizes the individual as the unit of analysis.

David Teece wrote the third chapter, where he identifies and evaluates the contributions of economic analysis to strategic management. In particular, he reviews five streams of economic analysis to determine their potential value to strategic management: (1) neoclassical price and production theory, (2) the structural approach to industrial economics, (3) the transactions cost approach, (4) the organizational economics approach, and (5) evolutionary economics. To set the stage, he outlines what he believes are the major questions facing strategic management and briefly describes the field's development. After arguing that the key issue facing strategic management is how to generate, augment, and protect "economic rents," David evaluates each of the five streams noted above. His conclusion is that economic analysis has provided some insight but has often added confusion to strategic management. In particular, he is highly critical of neoclassical price and production theory, which he sees as having little value to strategic management scholars or practitioners. He argues that, in contrast, recent work coming out of organizational-institutional economics is extremely valuable to strategic management. The chapter concludes with a summary of how the different literatures in economics might inform strategic management, particularly as they help in understanding how to generate, isolate, and capture rents.

As is obvious in the title of their chapter ("Hitching a Ride on a Fast Train to Nowhere"), Dick Daft and Vicki Buenger are very critical of the research being done in strategic management. To build support for their criticism, they contrast strategic management research with work being done in organization theory and behavioral accounting on their (1) social science assumptions, (2) theories and methods, and (3) management applications. They conclude that strategic management research is characterized by premature convergence on a single assumption set (logical positivism) premature rationalization of research methods and procedures, and premature adoption of norma-tive research approaches to achieve applied results. As a result, they go on to argue that more research in strategic management is actually producing less knowledge. Among other things, Dick and Vicki issue a call for greater diversity in strategic management thinking and re-search, greater attention to theory-building, and more flexibility in the choice of methods and techniques and in expressing ideas.

The fifth chapter, written by Henry Mintzberg, differs from the others in several respects. Most obviously, it is much longer. This is due to the fact that Henry took on a task that most of us would find daunting; it also reflects his strong feelings about the strategic man-agement field. Based on his review of the literature, he proposes ten schools of thought that have been used to describe the strategy for-mation process—the design, planning, positioning, entrepreneurial, cognitive, learning, political, cultural, environmental, and configura-tional schools. The underlying premises of each school are presented and critiqued, and each school's primary contributions to the field are identified. Readers familiar with his work will not be surprised to find that Henry favors the configuration school, for both its past contributions and its potential. The chapter eventually provides a matrix that summarizes each of the ten schools, allowing a com-parison of their underlying dimensions, such as historical evolution, origins, base discipline, current and future states, champions, in-tended and realized message, vocabulary, and central actor. Through-out, an analogy is drawn between these ten perspectives on strategy formation and the message conveyed in the well-known poem, "The Blind Men and the Elephant." To paraphrase Henry, strategic man-agement scholars are the blind men, and strategy formation is our elephant. No one has had the vision to see the whole beast, but everyone has grabbed hold of some part while remaining ignorant of the rest. But you do not create an elephant by simply adding the parts together—you need to understand the parts to understand the whole. And so it is with strategic management.

In the final chapter, Don Hambrick provides a perspective that differs markedly from those presented earlier. It is noteworthy that he attempts to be particularly objective in his characterization and evaluation of strategic management. He reviews the top journals in the field and identifies the fifty contributions that were most fre-quently cited (weighted by date of publication) between 1980 and 1985. These fifty contributions are then analyzed to determine whether recent attacks on the field are valid. Specifically, he attempts to determine whether strategic management research (1) has departed too far from its traditional roots; (2) has used increasingly sterile data, to the point of (3) aimless number-crunching; (4) has methods and models that are too static; (5) is based on restrictive and naive assumptions about managers; and finally, (6) is overly concerned with performance and prescription. Does the analysis support these criticisms? I will leave that for the reader to decide. But it clearly provides a unique and important perspective on the strategic management field and informs Don's recommendations for future research: a continuing commitment to "generalism," increased diversity of research methods, recognizing the value of theory-testing, building and testing more dynamics models, and employing more realistic assumptions about managers and organizations in our research.

Each of the following chapters presents a different perspective on the state of strategic management. As a result, they often consider different issues and reach different conclusions. Although there are some common themes that emerge (for example, the need for less logical positivism), I believe that the real value of this book lies in the *differences* in its contributors: in perspective, issues emphasized, recommended agendas, and so on. Our primary goal is to contribute to the constructive development of the strategic management field. To do that, I believe that we must (1) emphasize the need for periodic self-evaluation, (2) voice both satisfactions and dissatisfactions, (3) consider a wide range of perspectives, and (4) make the appropriate "course corrections." Given the highly personalized nature of scholars' interests and perspectives, their preferred solutions will be personalized as well. But if a volume such as this encourages more conscious and frequent introspection, more critical evaluation, and more awareness of alternative perspectives, we will have taken another step in the development of strategic management.

2 STRATEGY CHANGES
Possible Worlds and Actual Minds

Edward H. Bowman

> Once or twice she had peeped into the book her sister was reading,
> but it had no pictures or conversation in it, and "what is the use of
> a book," thought Alice, "without pictures or conversation?"
>
> —Lewis Carroll, *Alice in Wonderland* (p. 19)

> The thought crept in: it was probably more useful to go back than
> to go on. It was just faintly possible he might learn more from what
> he had left out of his forty years of reporting than to go on and add
> more observation.
>
> —Theodore White, *In Search of History* (p. 3)

This chapter examines strategy as it has changed over the past three
decades, primarily in several university courses but also in the "real
world." Part of the argument put forward will be that the courses
we teach are influenced by strategy thought in the industrial enterprise, and that this thought, in turn, is influenced by the secular state
of the economy. We shall look at two courses in order to discuss this
history and to explore the current state of strategy research. Comments about this research, how it is changing, and what changes we
might prefer, will end the chapter. I believe a discussion of the two
courses, one professional and the other research, offers a chance to
argue for what isn't available, based on what is.

The author wishes to thank Professors Kathleen Conner, Deborah Dougherty, and Paul
Tiffany for their helpful draft comments, and the Reginald H. Jones Center for its support.

EXPERIENCE IN TWO COURSES

The Professional Course

The academic field of policy/strategy went through a major shift, virtually a birth, in the 1960s and has subsequently gone through two minor shifts in the 1970s and 1980s. Before the sixties, many business schools required a business policy course as a capstone to graduate education in their MBA programs. The course was offered toward the end of the program and had the task of "tying together" all the functional courses previously taken in the program. The course was to be not only integrative but "professional"; that is, it was to correspond to the issues as faced by top management in the world of practice.

One unintended consequence of such a course design was that it became difficult to prepare young faculty for this task in their own graduate education. There was not a visible or cohesive field of research, published and available for study, and consequently, the road to promotion and tenure for young faculty was not an easy one. Though all of the above observations may still be relevant, it is clear that they have also started to become dated.

The strategy area started to change in the 1960s. It became more focused as a field of its own, not just an amalgam of other fields. As the field started to develop rapidly, new books and then other literature became available, more research started to appear, and elective, follow-on courses were added. Numerous doctoral programs in strategy were eventually a consequence of these changes. These programs, in turn, created markets in business schools for strategy faculty members. So far, the progression sounds quite good, but the story is not without problems. We will return to the earlier decade to understand those problems.

Three books became available in the 1960s, at the time I was introducing a new MBA course in business policy and strategy. I built the course around these books. Alfred Chandler's (1962) *Strategy and Structure*, written at MIT, is the exemplar of business history books. It explored the history of four large American corporations in the early part of this century as they grew in response to a changing economic environment, diversified, and changed their organizations. Chandler introduced a number of ideas about corporate strategy based, according to him, not on a priori theory but on his understanding of the stories as they unfolded. Though a historian, Chandler is also an empiricist in the following sense. Howard Gardner (1985: 8), in his recent book *The Mind's New Science*, discusses the history of philosophy: "In philosophy, I trace the perennial dispute between those of a rationalist persuasion (who view the mind as actively organizing experiences on the basis of pre-existing schemes), and those of an empiricist bent (who treat mental processes as a reflection of information obtained from the environment)." Hence, Chandler is a true empiricist. This distinction between rationalists and empiricists is an important one that will reappear again in this chapter.

The second book appearing in the 1960s was from the more rationalist school– it was certainly not empirical. Igor Ansoff at Carnegie-Mellon wrote the first book to be titled *Corporate Strategy* (1965). It took a programmatic approach to the topic and laid out an explicit sequence of issues to be considered. I think it is fair to call this work an engineering treatment– it certainly was written from an engineer's perspective. It took an analytic approach to the decisions embedded in corporate strategy: What would be the product/market? What would be the competitive advantage? What would be the synergy (the first use of this label)? What would be the "growth vector"? And what would be the make-or-buy choices? This book, as well as the Chandler book, placed substantial emphasis on diversification; we shall return to this point.

The third book of importance was more of a textbook than the first two. It was *Business Policy: Text and Cases* by Learned, Christensen, Andrews, and Guth (1965). In the style of the Harvard Business School, half of the book was cases. But the other half of the book, written largely by Ken Andrews, had chapters devoted to the issues of strategy formulation (Book I) and strategy implementation (Book II). As with Ansoff, *Business Policy* presented a rationalist view of the construction of corporate strategy, but the constructs presented were, according to the authors, "a simple practitioner's theory, a kind of Everyman's conceptual scheme" (p. viii). The business cases, of course, supply one form of empiricism. Again, many of the cases dealt with the issues of diversification, expansion, and growth.

History Parallels. I believe one can make the argument that the emphasis on growth, expansion, and diversification in the 1960s is, at least in part, a reflection of the American economy at that time. Opportunities seemed to be everywhere, and a firm could look at its own strengths and decide where the next move might be made. In contrast, little consideration had to be given to threats from foreign competition. To paraphrase an expression, the United States was the most favored nation. Therefore, American firms could, essentially, consider their own wishes and strengths and plan for future growth in a relatively unconstrained fashion.

Three partners at McKinsey wrote a paper some years later that captured the spirit of this argument. In "Strategic Management for Competitive Advantage," Gluck, Kaufman, and Walleck (1980) made the case that over time strategy thinking had gone through at least four stages—budgets, long-range planning, strategic planning, and strategic management. The stage in the 1960s was long-range planning. (By extension, budgeting would have been the stage in the 1940s and 1950s—and only the young would think that budgets were never new and didn't go through the classical diffusion process.)

Long-range planning considered the balanced development of all the functions of the business so that growth would not be constrained by the "logistics" of any element—people, equipment, technology, products, finances. But it was essentially, though not entirely, a look *within* the firm. *The New Yorker* (1987) made the same distinction concerning writers and poets. There, the distinction was between "mirror-writers" (for example, Emily Dickinson) and "window-writers" (Walt Whitman). In strategy, the emphasis in the 1960s was on the mirror.

The next stage in the McKinsey group's formulation is strategic planning, where the recommendation is to look outside the firm, that is, through the window, not in the mirror. The focus in this transition period (the 1970s) is on the specific industry. Industrial organization theory from economics deals almost entirely with this orientation, and Michael Porter's book *Competitive Strategy* (published in 1980, but preceded by his articles in the 1970s) is the exemplar for this period. My strategy course for MBA students made this transition comfortably.

The emphasis of this period was on the firm within its industry and on the important actors with whom it must cope—suppliers, competitors, potential entrants, substitute products, and customers.

As is traditional in economics, all of these actors were considered adversaries who tended to drive profits toward zero (at least with respect to "excess profits," or "rents"). Therefore, as the American economy offered expansion in the 1960s, so it offered stagnation (or "stagflation") in the 1970s, which change corresponded to the strategy field's emphasis on industry focus, industrial organization, and transition.

In the 1980s, we move into global competitiveness (balance-of-payments trauma) and a somewhat wider set of strategic considerations. In this period, the literature focus widens considerably (Porter 1985; Hayes and Wheelwright 1984; Rappaport 1986; Itami/Roehl 1987; Teece 1987), as do the strategic issues. We now see the McKinsey "strategic management" stage, which deals with a strategic treatment of all the elements of the firm—people, skills, technology, information, finance—to see if they are consistent with strategy and can be made more *competitive.* The industrial world sees "restructuring" on every hand, which is in part a response to the "market for corporate control." This shift acknowledges the pervasive nature of global competition.

Although some actors were identified as adversaries by industrial organization theory and economics, strategy now has more explicit input from sociology, and a resulting reconsideration of those actors in a potentially nonadversarial relationship. This is clearly the case in the sequence of suppliers, competitors, and customers; each and every one may be our partner. Early sourcing, technology sharing, quality cooperation, and just-in-time inventories are now the new look in suppliers. Customers may now be thought of as our best source of new product ideas, and they use our computers and information systems for logistics (and by extension, all of the previous ideas about suppliers hold because we are their suppliers). Even competitors may now be viewed as engaged in a cooperative (non–zero-sum game) relationship. For example, chemical industry firms share expertise on toxic spills and lobby Washington together; these firms even return to the old-fashioned idea of cooperative-mutual insurance underwriting for environmental risk because, for a while, the commercial insurance industry abandoned them (Bowman and Kunreuther 1988).

So the American economy, in the brief span of three decades since the birth of strategy as an academic endeavor (and since the beginning of my MBA course as well), has taken us from opportunities to transition to difficulty, from diversification to focus to global competitiveness, and from long-range planning to strategic planning to strategic management.

During the span of these three decades, the complex issue of the firm's performance measures has also shifted. While the issue of goals and performance may continue to be viewed from the standpoint not only of the firm itself but also of the firm in society (social welfare) and the top management in the firm (agency), the major performance concern for the firm may have shifted from growth to return on investment, to market over book value ratio (or Tobin's Q). The society, the firm, and the top-level manager continue to have interacting goals that are made more complex by the trade-off between short-term and long-term considerations. These complexities may reflect, in part, the shifts over the three decades mentioned earlier.

The industrial world, consulting practice, and even the professional literature seem to have followed the same path through the 1960s, 1970s, and 1980s. However, systematic and empirical strategy research has followed a less clear path. The "professional" course for MBAs that I have taught at three schools (Yale, MIT, and Wharton) during these three decades was relatively easy to map to the above pattern, using a combination of conceptual material and business cases, because the history of strategy practice has been followed reasonably closely in the professional literature of strategy. Research developments have not followed this history as closely.

The Research Course

A research course that I began fifteen years ago has been a somewhat more taxing exercise. In 1973 I decided to offer a research seminar in corporate strategy, essentially for doctoral students. I searched for two dozen articles for the seminar–two each for twelve or thirteen weeks–that were (1) published, (2) empirical, (3) research, and (4) about strategy–and this was fifteen years ago. I still teach the course, and for each reading, the students and I discuss "questions or topics, received theory and literature, methods of research, data sources, tests and treatments, alternative approaches, findings and conclusions, presentation style, problems and flaws, meaning to managers, and other comments."

It probably is no surprise that it took me quite a while to find the twenty-four papers that I was looking for from the journals that existed then. I wanted a course that was organized around what I thought was fairly interesting and good strategy research. In my judgment, there were no journals in strategy at that time. With a few odds and ends from elsewhere, the articles were pulled primarily from six, more general journals: *Administrative Science Quarterly*, *Management Science*, and *Bell Journal of Economics and Management Science* (since known as the *Bell Journal of Economics*, and now known as the *Rand Journal of Economics*); and three school journals—*Harvard Business Review*, *Sloan Management Review*, and *California Management Review*.

It has been possible since that time to greatly modify my collection of research articles, especially with the introduction of the *Strategic Management Journal* at the beginning of the 1980s. (Yet it may surprise today's professors that I still occasionally use some papers from that first set of selections, like Pfeffer's [1972] "Size and Composition of Corporate Boards of Directors," Fouraker and Stopford's [1968] "Organizational Structure and Multinational Strategy," and Altman's [1973] "Predicting Railroad Bankruptcies in America.") With two dozen research articles, it is possible to cover *many* kinds of problems, theoretical fields, methodologies, data sources, and presentation styles. Over the years it has become easier to find articles that touch on most major facets of our field of strategy.

Along with the research articles covered in this doctoral seminar, I always try to have book reports in the spirit of the articles. That is, I want each student to report on a research book—not a text, not a speculative book, but a *research* work for which some author/ researcher has gone out and looked at a particular problem, gathered descriptive material, applied some theory, and explained to the reader what it meant, in book form. Finding such books was even more difficult than finding the articles because I wanted about a dozen. Something that we really lack (to go to a conclusion before developing the argument) is good research books in strategy written by people who have done a big enough job that they can write books about their work. I will eventually mention five or six that I like, but there should be twenty or thirty available to us.

One positive difference from a decade ago that I see in strategy today, one which is manifest in my research seminar, is that we've brought in theories from a number of other domains. We are now doing fairly interesting strategy research based on half a dozen related theoretical fields—finance theory, industrial organization theory, population ecology theory, transaction costs theory, resource dependency theory, and behavioral decision theory. Ten years ago one would have had to stretch to find a single good study—which we would agree was a strategy study—that drew on the theories of these fields.

In my research seminar I have at least one paper from each of these six fields. In finance, I use a paper by Amihud and Lev (1981), who look at agency theory and diversification. They argue that firms diversify, if the manager controls the firm, to protect against employment risks of the top managers. This paper has the added advantage that its authors demonstrate their argument with two completely different types of data and analysis. In industrial organization, I use a chapter on the corn wet milling oligopoly from a book by Porter and Spence (1982); it is a very involved study using scenario analysis and simulation with corporate data. It has the attribute of "rational expectations" (about competitor behavior) as an important element of the analysis. (Note that all of these studies have data; I don't use papers that lack some kind of strong evidence. They may not all have the same kind of evidence, but they are all empirical works.) I also use a paper related to population ecology: Langton's (1984) work on Wedgwood Pottery and how it developed over an interesting fifty-year period two centuries ago. It is a combination of bureaucracy theory and social Darwinism, showing the interaction of internal and external developments. (It should be noted that Perrow [1985] wrote a scathing criticism of the article in the next journal issue from a power and welfare standpoint, and that Langton had a chance to respond.)

Intellectual exchanges or arguments like the one between Langton and Perrow are quite useful, but they are not as common in our field as they should be. Perhaps this is a sign of the immaturity of strategy literature. Laudan (1977: 46-47) makes an important point in this regard:

> If we look at the reception of Darwin's evolutionary biology, Freud's psycho-analytic theories, Skinner's behaviorism, or modern quantum mechanics, the same pattern repeats itself. Alongside of the rehearsal of empirical anomalies and solved empirical problems, both critics and proponents of a theory often invoke criteria of theoretical appraisal which have nothing whatever to do with a theory's capacity to solve the empirical problems of the relevant scien-

tific domain. . . . Rather than seeking to learn something about the complex nature of scientific rationality from such cases, philosophers (with regret) and sociologists (with delight) have generally taken them as tokens of the irrationality of science as actually practiced.

For transaction costs theory, I use a paper by Walker and Webber (1984) that examines organization boundaries and vertical integration, drawing on Williamson's (1975) work. It looks in a new way at external sourcing by the automobile industry. For resource dependency, I use a paper by Hirsch (1975) that compares the ability of the pharmaceutical and phonograph record industries to cope with important facets of their respective environments. It shows how important "gatekeepers" can be. For behavioral decision theory, I use my own paper (Bowman 1982) on risk seeking by troubled firms, which draws on Tversky and Kahneman's (1981) prospect theory. It moves beyond a standard financial view of corporate risk.

I offer the above articles as illustrations of the way that I think our field is changing by drawing on the best new theories from a wide variety of disciplines. We do this in part because we don't have our own central paradigm. But *even if we did*, these theories ought to be brought in; I feel that they enrich the strategy field.

OBSERVATIONS FROM RESEARCH

No Central Paradigm

The above discussion illustrates an often discussed characteristic of the strategy field— it has no central paradigm. The lack of a central paradigm in strategy will probably continue and is undoubtedly due to a number of factors. One reason is that the underlying social science fields on which strategy currently draws are economics and sociology— or to stretch just a bit, the rational and the natural (Scott 1981; Pfeffer 1982). These two perspectives are very different, yet they are both useful. The contrast between them on one issue— the purpose of the firm— highlights their differences. Though "maximization" (from economics) is sometimes utilized as a concept in strategy, purpose and performance are still at issue. Therefore, academics are still asking, "What is one to maximize?" and, "Who is the actor?" The sociologists' questions would be "Why and how should the firm survive?" and "For what function?"

Another reason for the continued absence of a central paradigm is that the interests represented in strategy are as disparate as those between physics and civil engineering, as between theory and practice. There is a big difference between positive science and professional design. (One meaning of *design*, as noted later, is Simon's [1969] process of changing *existing* situations into *preferred* ones. To oversimplify, it is the distinction between "what is" and "how to.") While they may be related to each other, their practitioners consider almost entirely different questions. One of the problems in graduate education for strategy is that one can make a reasonable case for including major elements from both positive science and professional design. Another problem is that most faculty specialize in only one of these areas and neither understand nor appreciate the other. It is a little bit like Adam Smith's pin makers, who specialize in either the heads or the points of the pins.

Because the problems of design are so broad—and one can consider strategy as an exercise in design—it is unlikely that either school will ever be dominant. This is particularly true when we consider the four levels of strategy now extant in the literature. I refer to institutional strategy, corporate strategy, business strategy, and functional strategy. To be brief, institutional strategy deals with fitting the firm comfortably into the legal, political, and social environments in which it operates; corporate strategy deals with the allocations, interactions, reinforcements, and economies of scale and scope among various business units of a firm, as well as choosing those units; business strategy deals with how a unit will position itself within a particular product market, considering the many dimensions available to it; and functional strategy deals with how a function (for example, marketing, R&D, or human resources) might seek to respond to the demands and opportunities it encounters. How could one central paradigm really cope with all these issues? What might result from attempts to provide a central paradigm is "reductionism," where much of the situation is assumed away by those constructing their preferred model. Reductionism in constructing a central paradigm is an ever present tendency and carries the risk of riding roughshod over the issues.

I generally believe that it is not bad that strategy does not have a central paradigm; we should continually bring in research work that is based on related areas (as I have illustrated). However, my research seminar continues to be based primarily on the mainstream of strategy work. Therefore, I should mention at least two articles out of the many that are somewhat closer to our central focus. I use the Woo and Cooper (1981) paper, "Strategies of Effective Low Share Businesses." They use Profitability Impact of Market Strategy (PIMS) data in a comparative analysis across types of industries of high share/low share and high profit/low profit businesses; they also cleverly analyze business strategy within these pseudo-industries. I also use Bourgeois' (1980) "Performance and Consensus," which investigates the relationships between top management teams' goals and strategy consensus on the one hand, and the performance of their firms on the other. Its empirical challenge to conventional planning wisdom is refreshing.

We are fortunate in strategy to have many research articles such as these to draw from. They present theoretical foundations, report analyses, provide evidence, draw conclusions, and ruminate on the import of their findings. Though these articles are unevenly distributed across the various levels of strategy (that is, institutional, corporate, business, and functional)—an issue to be discussed later—at least some are available as illustrations of each of the levels, and I am able to sample from each level for the research seminar.

Strategy Research Books. As mentioned earlier, my research seminar also incorporates a discussion of research books. The books that I offer as examples are Chandler (1962), Bower (1970), Allison (1971), Cohen and March (1974), Rumelt (1974), Miles and Snow (1978), and Miles and Cameron (1982). Each of these books actually takes a *detailed* look at an important problem. They all have data; they all draw some conclusions; and they are all written in the depth that allows you to really get a sense of what the authors are talking about. You can read some studies that leave you asking, "Did this author really tell me anything?" The people who wrote the above books found something important in their research. I will read them again, and I can tell you about these books after I have read them.

There are no doubt other books that I could use as illustration, but these few will serve the purposes of my argument. Chandler (1962), mentioned earlier as part of my professional course for MBAs, still qualifies in my mind as a research book. Similarly,

Bower's (1970) *Managing the Resource Allocation Process* gives us some sense of how large resource commitments are made within the diversified firm, how these are influenced by various levels of managers within the firm (with different roles), and how these commitments are derived from the developing strategy of the firm. Allison's (1971) *Essence of Decision*, though admittedly not about strategy, is a splendid empirical investigation of decision making in a crisis atmosphere (the Cuban Missile Crisis) and illustrates three very different modes of thought regarding organizational behavior.

As business educators we are dealing with two kinds of practitioners, the manager and the academic, both of whom can learn from examples. The manager typically learns from case studies, with which he or she can identify. The first, third, and fifth chapters of Allison's book present the models (and theories) that he wishes to explain. The second, fourth, and sixth chapters tell the story of the Cuban Missile Crisis, each chapter relying to *some* extent on the theory chapter preceding it. Over and over in my professional course in strategy, in which I also use this book, I have asked manager-students which set of chapters they appreciate most. The answer is always the story chapters. The story chapters are "peopled" and narrative. To quote Alice, they have both "pictures and conversations."

The academic practitioner also learns by example, even when it is theory that is being learned. I have found that one of the best kinds of comparative analysis (an extension here of Glaser and Strauss's [1967] arguments) is a Ph.D. student discussion comparing one published research piece with another. What did the different authors assume? What theories did they draw on? What were the differences in the constructs that they developed? How did they obtain their data? What statistical methodologies did they use (if any, if appropriate, and if powerful)? What conclusions did they reach? This "discovery of grounded theory" is itself a theory of practice.

The difference between the manager and the academic is, of course, the nature of their practice. Borrowing from Herbert Simon's (1969) ideas, one can argue that a, perhaps *the*, key element in research for the academic practitioner is the idea of design. How will this study be put together? For academics, a systematic investigation and group discussion of exemplars is perhaps the best kind of education. After such formal training, the academic must continue to learn from examples for the next forty or fifty years. The process can be discovered by the individual, but it should be enhanced with the appropriate treatment during the more formal education years.

To return to my identification of research books, the Cohen and March (1974) book *Leadership and Ambiguity*, which was reissued in 1986 with added appendixes, develops their "garbage can" theory of organizational decision making in the context of American college presidencies. The Rumelt (1974) book, *Strategy, Structure, and Economic Performance*, is an early study of the relationship between strategy, structure, and performance. Here the reader is offered a taxonomy of relative diversification, as well as the empirically grounded, apparent superiority of relatedness in diversification (something Ansoff [1965] had developed conceptually).

The Miles and Snow (1978) book, *Organization Strategy, Structure, and Process*, is a good example of a research book that has been extended with enough theory and commentary that some may use it as a textbook. Nevertheless, they investigated in some depth a series of industries, and companies within the industries, in order to develop (not unlike the "discovery of grounded theory" proposed by Glaser and Strauss) the theory of generic types of strategy, to understand their underlying rationale, and to describe the derivative behavior that one can anticipate with each generic type.

The Miles and Cameron (1982) book, *Coffin Nails and Corporate Strategy*, is also a splendid research book; it explored tobacco industry firms as they responded to the threat posed by the surgeon general's report on smoking. It is here that one sees generic strategies in use, as well as the stages in strategic response—domain defense (institutional strategy), domain offense (business strategy), and domain creation (corporate strategy). In addition, and beyond the usual industrial organization theory of competition, one observes cooperation with competitors and the important role of the government—something present in many of our industries.

CHANGES PREFERRED

Based on my view of the past three decades, there are a number of changes that I believe are needed in strategy research. They are offered as *additions* to our agenda; it is not subtractions from our present orientation but additions to future explorations that I prefer.

More Research Books

The first of my preferences is for more research books. One of the interesting and somewhat puzzling aspects of research books is that, although the field of strategy has many fewer than I would like, it has more than most of our sister fields in the business school. If one explores the fields of marketing and finance, for instance, one finds that they are prolific with research activity but seem to have few research books.

Research books in strategy offer many advantages over what we normally see in journal articles. For example, a topic can be investigated both more deeply and more richly. The theory, developed or received, can be full enough so that the constructs of interest can be well argued and justified by the author. Too often in a journal article the author must move too quickly from received theory, through surrogate variable and constructs, to measurement. Similarly, all too often the measurement is driven by the variables available, as in PIMS, and the constructs for which the measured variables are taken are not well thought out.

Books can also offer protection against reductionism, whereas a paper, apparently for reasons of space, must emphasize only a central argument. One especially common result of this problem appears in the concluding paragraphs of many papers, which offer normative statements for the manager. A classic ploy here is to take (a) a static analysis of (b) the correlation between/among variables, and then turn it into (c) a dynamic recommendation for (d) a causal chain between/among variables. While poorly written research books may also do this, fewer space limitations give book authors an opportunity to discuss at some length such suggestions for practice.

A further advantage of a research book, if the author has sought both theoretical patterns and empirical evidence, is that it offers the chance not only to inform the empirical story with the theoretical overlay but to use the empirical work to critique the theory. Though an article may do this as well, it is less likely to do so. In addition to comparing theory to evidence, a book may offer the opportunity to compare and contrast several theories in the context of a particular empirical problem (Kuhn 1970; Laudan 1977).

A fourth advantage of the research book is that the author can include in it much more institutional material than would fit in an article. For instance, a company, its product lines, its organization structure, its people, and its history can all be described in a book. "Other things being equal" is an argument that does not have to be made. Other things are really never equal, and the book offers an opportunity to show how and why.

Finally, research books seem to offer a better opportunity to break new ground than do articles. While admittedly I argue we have no central paradigm, if there is to be a paradigm shift a la Kuhn (1970), it is more likely to come in a book. A research book offers a forum for the iconoclast, whose ideas and position may not be well received by reviewers versed in the current state of the field.

It is important to emphasize that I do not bemoan the lack of research books for their own sake. It is my perception that such books are the best vehicle for conveying the richness of many strategy phenomena. Therefore, their continued absence prevents us from understanding important phenomena and answering important questions. Taken to its extreme, this trend will deprive the strategy area of much of the integrating effort that is needed to make sense of the increasingly specialized work that has come to dominate it.

Narrative Versus Paradigmatic

Jerome Bruner (1986), the dean of cognitive psychologists, has written a new book entitled *Actual Minds, Possible Worlds.* He talks about two modes of thought—the "narrative" and the "paradigmatic." The narrative mode tells the story; it shows meaning; you get a sense of what is going on. The paradigmatic mode is scientific; it has evidence of a different kind. It uses a method of science, but often it doesn't show the same kind of thing as the narrative mode. I believe that the field of strategy is drifting too far toward the paradigmatic mode. I will let Professor Bruner (1986: 11–14) make his own points:

> There are two modes of cognitive function . . . irreducible to one another. . . .
> Arguments convince one of their truth, stories of their lifelikeness. The one
> verifies by eventual appeal to procedure for establishing formal and empirical
> proof. The other establishes not truth but verisimilitude. . . . Perhaps Rich-
> ard Rorty (1979) is right in characterizing the mainstream of Anglo-American
> philosophy (which, on the whole he rejects) as preoccupied with the episte-
> mological question of how to know truth—which he contrasts with the
> broader question of how we come to endow experience with meaning, which

is the question that preoccupies the poet and the storyteller. . . . The logico-scientific mode (I shall call it paradigmatic hereafter) deals in general causes . . . [and] is driven by principled hypothesis. . . . Narrative mode . . . strives to put its timeless miracles into the particulars of experience, and to locate the experience in time and space. . . . [Scientists'] salvation is to wash the stories away when causes can be substituted for them. . . . Narrative deals with the vicissitudes of human intentions.

I am not a strong advocate of case studies and case presentations per se, but I would like to see some good studies on strategy that are "peopled"—that is, studies that have people with names, who are doing things, studies that help you think about why they are doing those things. I don't see much good strategy research of this kind. Research that deals with Bruner's "vicissitudes of human intentions" and presents Perrow's (1986) "feel" of the organization will have to be built around the behavior of individual people—real actors. Allison's book and Chandler's book are examples of this style of research. While academics may differ from practitioners, I believe that everyone's ability to remember and make sense out of an argument is often enhanced by this human perspective.

Research in strategy, as in most fields, may be characterized as deductive or inductive, although the labels don't always fit specific works very well. Nevertheless, Thomas Kuhn's (1970) idea can be used here: deductive work is largely normal science as it draws on an accepted theory or paradigm to explore some derivative issues. Inductive work is more akin to empiricism, as mentioned earlier. Glaser and Strauss (1967) developed an appreciation for this inductive type of work in their oft-cited book, *The Discovery of Grounded Theory*. Some of the current work in strategy falls in this category and deserves to be continued. However, the suggestions of Glaser and Strauss should be followed more closely. For example, the idea of comparative analysis drawing on multiple field studies is attractive, especially where theory is weak. The systematic development of formal theory from substantive theory—to the general from the specific— is also useful. None of this means that received theory, which would normally precede deductive work, should be ignored. However, it does mean that received theory should not strongly drive a strategy study.

This issue is further illustrated by Charles Perrow (1986: 164–176) in his book *Complex Organizations,* in which he develops a case for the "institutional school." He notes that "after the arid and dense forest of two-variable propositions . . . and the axiomatic edifice . . . it is a pleasure to read about a real organization confronting real problems in real time and space. . . . Above all, the descriptive and historical nature of this school gives us a 'feel' for how organizations operate." While Perrow is speaking of the institutional school in organization studies and sociology, Galbraith (1987: 129) commends the institutional school in economics: "In the United States . . . economics divides today as between classicists (the overwhelming number) and institutionalists, between those committed to the inevitable and constant equilibrium and those who, with much less claim to scientific precision, accept a world of evolution and continuing change."

For the study of strategy, I believe we need many more active institutionalists. Rich empirical work would increase our understanding of the many issues involved and may also be transformed or used directly for professional education purposes. There is always the risk that the professor would rather interact intellectually with other professors and doctoral students than with executives. While the first interaction is obviously worthwhile, to miss the second is folly. Most of us exist in professional business schools that, as with all professional schools, exist to help the professions–the worldly managers and managers-to-be.

Less Logical Positivism

Another change in strategy research would be directly related to the above and would be a move away from the overly strong emphasis on logical positivism. Several years ago, there was a review by Roger Evered of the Schendel and Hofer (1979) book. In his review, Evered (1980: 536–542) despaired over the drift he saw toward logical positivism:

> Positivism would be even more disastrous for policy/strategy than for other areas of social sciences. . . . The ideal research paradigm is presumed already known and important inquiry options are closed out too early. . . . Very little regard [is given] to the inherent epistemological assumptions of what is proposed in relation to the focal phenomena of the field.

Using a positivist perspective, an investigator can get data, make statements, and get results that are significant, but have quite modest

R squares. Often he or she is working with a large received data base accumulated by others for quite different purposes. With cluster analysis, factor analysis, and regression analysis, an investigator can feed in the data and get a small relationship. One wonders, "What really did they find out?" Maybe not much. Given the progress that statistics for the social sciences has made in the last three decades, one must offer criticism with some care. However, I am sometimes left with the impression that a kind of Gresham's law is at work. Is the bad money of statistical methodology driving out the good money of strategic substance? I am not saying we shouldn't do this kind of work; I simply hope that we don't continue down this road to the point where 90 percent of the empirical work in strategy can be described this way.

One of the potential problems of positivism mentioned earlier is the rapid journey made by an author/researcher from theory to construct, to surrogate variable, to measurement, to subsequent analysis. Often, but of course not always, we as authors do not give enough attention to the particular constructs that we are using. Do they really make sense? Have they been explored in all their relationships? Do they truly serve the purpose for which we use them? A different kind of criticism of positivism and its derivative work is that the issue may not really be very important; or at the extreme, it is trivial. While importance may be in the eye of the beholder, at least two groups might supply the straw vote. We should ask ourselves: Are other researchers interested in it? Are practitioners interested in it?

Donald Schon (1983: 39–46), in *The Reflective Practitioner*, develops a strong argument that questions the positivist school, especially when it comes to useful knowledge for practice:

Increasingly we have become aware of the importance to actual practice of phenomena—complexity, uncertainty, instability, uniqueness, and value-conflict—which do not fit the model of Technical Rationality. Now, in the light of the Positivist origins of Technical Rationality, we can more readily see why these phenomena are so troublesome. . . . From the perspective of Technical Rationality, professional practice is a process of problem *solving*. Problems of choice of decision are solved through the selection from available means, of the one best suited to established ends. But with the emphasis on problem solving, we ignore problem *setting*, the process by which we define the decision to be made, the ends to be achieved, the means which may be chosen. In real world practice, problems do not present themselves to the practitioners as given. . . . Herbert Simon, whose *The Sciences of the Arti-*

ficial has aroused a great deal of interest in professional circles . . . most clearly links the predicament of professional knowledge to the historical origins of the Positivist epistemology practice. Simon believes that all professional practice is centrally concerned with what he calls "design," that is, with the process of "changing existing situations into preferred ones" (Simon 1969: 55). But design in this sense is precisely what the professional schools do not teach. The older schools have a knowledge of design that is "intellectually soft, intuitive, informal and cookbooky," and the newer ones, more absorbed into the general culture of the modern university, have become schools of natural science.

While Schon, and to some extent Simon, are talking about professional education, I am arguing that these aspects of design (that is, changing existing situations to preferred ones) should be a component of a strategy research portfolio. We should study issues of design in an empirical context in order to describe them better. The practitioner and the researcher are doubly linked: the researcher supplies insights, relationships, and theory for the practitioner. But the practitioner supplies puzzles, ideas, judgments, and priorities for the researcher.

Higher Order Theory

An additional issue for strategy research is the need for a higher order of theoretical research. For example, where is the analogue for cognitive science at the level of the firm? Is it artificial intelligence? Is it a modern-day version of cybernetics (Steinbruner 1974)? Gardner (1985: 16) summarized how progress was made in another field by noting that "Wiener (1984) . . . concluded that there were important analogies between feedback aspects of engineering devices and the homeostatic process by which the human nervous system sustains purposive activity. These ideas of planning, purpose, and feedback, developed with mathematical precision, were directly antithetical to the behaviorist credo."

While there has been a healthy reaction to naive normative ideas in strategy by such prolific authors as Simon (1969), Cohen and March (1986), Mintzberg (1978), Pfeffer (1972), and Weick (1987), we may now have reached the point where we will have to move back and forth on an upward path of sophistication between the rational and the natural, between the normative and the positive (admittedly not quite the same polarity). New and more abstract theoretical work may be called for. What is unusually difficult in this regard will be an empirical grounding to help demonstrate the reality of this theoretical work.

Though a call for such work may seem antithetical to the reality of institutionalism, it does not run counter to the larger scheme that encourages pluralism. As I argued in an earlier piece on epistemology:

> At this stage in the development of managerial education and investigation, the mixed strategy of using all approaches is probably better than the reliance on only one or two, especially where students and managers may differ markedly in the ability to learn from the different approaches. A mixed strategy not only allows the possibility for reinforcement and/or a productive dialectic, but given the explicitly different perspectives, offers the chance for a future response to issues of corporate strategy which is *robust* (Bowman 1974: 49).

I believe research in strategy should become broader in its viewpoints, topics, methodologies, and theories—rather than narrower, as may be preferred by some. While science is a noble calling, it is not the only intellectual or academic approach to truth. Nor do I wish the world to believe that issues of strategy are only in some way derived from social science. At one time I felt that economics was the slighted aspect of strategy literature:

> The kinds of topics developed by economists which are of some interest are entrepreneurship, innovation and diffusion, portfolio selection and capital asset pricing, international trade, industrial organization and concentration, oligopoly and game theory, monopolistic competition, discretionary behavior, input-output analysis, capital budgeting and investment and the growth of the firm. . . . It can be noted with some interest that most of the literature and books addressed to corporate strategy directly . . . pay very little if any attention to the economics literature. If a single major criticism were to be leveled at the corporate strategy literature, this is perhaps the one (Bowman 1974: 40).

It is surprising, at least to me, how this situation has changed in fifteen years. The above epistemology paper was written in the same season that my research seminar was started. Certainly one would not make that comment today about the lack of connection between economic theories and strategy. What I believe may be missing today are more papers in areas like business history. While there are at least two polar views of history, each can contribute to our understanding of this field. Those of the Annales school, as exemplified by Fernard Braudel (1986), argue that it is the major underlying forces (geography, politics, economics, technology) that determine history. Contrarily, those adherents of what some call the Schumpeterian school of business history argue that it is particular actors (for example, entrepreneurs) who shape historical outcomes. An example of *both* schools of thought, perhaps classified as sociology by some, is Langton's (1984) study of the development of the Wedgwood Potteries in the last half of the eighteenth century. Here one reads not only about the specific actions and decisions of Josiah Wedgwood but also about the growing British transportation system, which opened up national markets. Alfred Chandler's *Strategy and Structure* is another, more extended example, from a period 150 years later.

It should be emphasized that we need not choose between the old and the new history; battle lines do not need to be drawn, as they recently were in the *New York Times Book Review*. In "The Ugly Historians," Neil McKendrick (1988: 14) notes that "when the new historian cannot conceal his contempt for a history that persists in studying important people, significant events, and successful historical movements, it is hardly surprising that the old historian will take delight in making mock of statements such as one writer's observation that 'Mickey Mouse may be in fact more important to an understanding of the 1930's than Franklin Roosevelt!'" Both the old and the new history make useful contributions to our understanding of strategy; good history is good research.

More Longitudinal and Individual Work

Professor Ed Zajac and I have done a study (Zajac and Bowman 1985) on the publications of the last five years in the *Strategic Management Management Journal*. We specified characteristics *a*, *b*, *c*, *d*, and *e* of empirical research and classified each paper according to those characteristics. We were able to draw some conclusions and provide some observations. But two characteristics were dropped because we didn't get enough variance—"individual versus organization," and "longitudinal versus cross-sectional." Less than 10 percent of the articles focused on the individual level of decision making vis-à-vis strategy, so we couldn't use it because the remaining 90 percent had to do with the organization as a unit. Similarly, less than 10 percent of the studies were really longitudinal, and 90 percent were essentially cross-sectional; so we couldn't use that characteristic either. I think that both of these findings are disheartening. That is, I would encourage strategy researchers to do more work on individual people making strategic decisions, in truly longitudinal studies.

When we do not do longitudinal studies, we are likely to miss phenomena such as retrospective rationality, learning, escalation, and most elements of a game theoretic nature. If we miss the individual decision maker, we are likely to miss issues of cognition, bounded rationality, heuristics, and image and representation. There is general agreement on the complexity and uncertainty associated with strategic decision making. However, research programs in strategy that explicitly deal with issues of bounded rationality are strangely lacking in the academy.

More Levels of Strategy

Of the four levels of strategy currently found in our literature—from top to bottom: institutional, corporate, business, and functional—we see a lot of work on the corporate strategy and business strategy levels. I think to some extent we slight the institutional level; we should be interested in the issues of how a corporation fits itself comfortably into the social environment and the body politic. For instance, problems of hazardous waste in the chemical industry are enormously important to that industry (Bowman and Kunreuther 1988). This is an institutional problem of the kind that strategy research typically ignores.

Many problems or issues in institutional strategy point toward the sociological notions contained in resource dependency. Strategy research, for instance, rarely gives explicit consideration to the government, its laws, and its agencies as a crucial part of the firm's environment. Likewise, we are only now starting to look at the functional correspondence to strategy of the firm. Marketing, R&D, manufacturing, and finance, even if they have their own research, should be a part of our research endeavor. And at all levels of strategy, though we are doing some, we are not doing enough internationally focused research.

Foreground Versus Background

"Figure versus ground," or "foreground versus background" (contrasts drawn from both art and psychology), are terms that people like Jim March use. A connected issue for strategy, which has not been well enough developed in either the general/theoretical literature or in specific research studies, is "today versus tomorrow." I am not referring to the common cry (Hayes and Abernathy 1980) that finance theory, investment analysts, and mobile managers shortchange the future. I am referring to the fact that most students of strategy focus on today's strategy problems and on ways of coping with them. Surely I agree that one must survive today in order to fight tomorrow. But to focus on today's problems may miss the nuances of tomorrow's world. Some of the work on strategy should be concerned with how managers address this trade-off. For example, how do you develop talent that can make strategic decisions in the future when you can't spend money today on future strategies because you hardly know what the problems are?

My colleague Aron Katsenelinboigen (1984) writes that a major difference in chess styles between nineteenth- and twentieth-century masters is that one searched for material advantage while the other searches for positional advantage. The former weights the independent value of each piece in an exchange. The latter considers the relational arrangement of the pieces for a particular game and "his chances to parry his opponent's future moves" (p. 10). This metaphor correlates directly to the concern for foreground versus background, or for either today's strategies or tomorrow's.

Even in the planning literature a similar distinction exists—between "Cooks-Tour" planning and "Lewis-and-Clark" planning. James Schlesinger (1966: 7, 8), cabinet officer under several U.S. presidents, writes that "Cooks-Tour planning . . . rests, implicitly or explicitly, on the supposition that the future is sufficiently certain that we can chart a straight course years in advance. In it, direction, speed, size of commitment, and achievement milestones (not decision points) are indicated at least with rough precision." By contrast, what he terms "Lewis-and-Clark planning . . . acknowledges that many alternative courses of action and forks in the road will appear, but their precise character and timing cannot be anticipated. . . . The planning function . . . is to prepare to cope with [the] uncertain terrain of the future." He adds that the cost of acquiescence to the organization pressures for precise planning "is neglect of uncertainties, lost flexibility, neglected and suppressed options, and less-than-optimal adjustment to changing opportunities and threats existing in the external environment."

The ideas of Katsenelinboigen and Schlesinger highlight the difference between the particular focus on efficiency and the general/contingency focus on survival. Strategy research looks too much at the first and not enough at the second.

A recent piece of research I undertook, published as "The Concerns of the CEO" (Bowman 1986), further illustrates my point. By far the most salient concern of the twenty-six CEOs interviewed was "management development." They were strongly concerned with whether and/or how their associates would be prepared to deal with the problems of the firm. Upon reflection, I believe this concern can be interpreted as addressing tomorrow's strategy problems. One can sensibly allocate resources today to deal with today's strategy problems. But as previously asked, how can you deal with tomorrow's problems when you don't even know what they will be? I believe that one of the only ways to deal with tomorrow's problems is to work on the robustness of the organization and on the protection of its core skills. This, I feel, is largely in the hands of the many top and middle managers who have to cope with these problems.

Nelson and Winter (1982) discuss the skills of the organization and how these core skills, largely tacit, become the competitive advantage of the firm. They comprise in large part the "invisible assets" that Itami/Roehl (1987) argue must be mobilized. Strategy researchers pay little attention to these skills. Perhaps the main concern of corporate strategy (as distinct from business strategy) should be with the development of these organizational skills, this tacit knowledge that provides for and protects against the future. Nobel laureate Robert Solow (1988: 10) suggests that "the major source of economic growth in modern industrial economies is the advance of knowledge." I argue that this is analogous to the future prosperity of the individual firm. Strategy research must reflect this knowledge-building for the future.

OVERALL AGENDA

If we wish to encourage pluralism in both theory and research methods, as well as in the style of presentation and in discourse, it may take some changes in the academy. Those of us who have lived there for a long time know this is problematic. Tenure is, I suppose, both the problem and the solution. How can we expect untenured faculty to pursue the long-term course outlined above? For example, while senior faculty in strategy can argue the benefits, the quality, and the contribution of publications (articles, essays, chapters, monographs, and books) that go beyond a logical positivist perspective, it is not clear how well received these arguments will be in many business schools. One solution for the younger professor going through this process would be the support of a group—an invisible college—of faculty at good schools who understand and appreciate such work. However, for this "college" to be built, more faculty must recognize the limits of positivism and become advocates for an enlarged perspective.

What will probably be even more difficult will be strategy research taking on the coloration of history, philosophy, and design. These are all accepted parts of the modern university, but they have not yet been accepted in the "modern" business school. The idea that tenure can be both the problem and the solution encompasses the possibility that more senior faculty, once they have tenure, can devote their efforts to these broader forms of research. Unless the young faculty member is unusually creative and lucky and the institution is broadminded, the research efforts I speak for here may have to come from those further along in their careers. Interestingly enough, I can think of examples of both young iconoclasts and older reformists; we need to value both.

My argument for research in strategy has been for broadening rather than narrowing. It has been geared toward including more fields of related theory, and even new theories, rather than toward a primary search for a central paradigm; toward the uncertainties of the future rather than the complexities of the present; toward the skills of the background that go beyond the choices of the foreground; toward the narrative to complement the paradigmatic; toward institutional and functional strategies, to add to the corporate and business strategies; and toward the individual and longitudinal studies rather than the solely organizational and cross-sectional. I argue for inclusion of the historian, the institutionalist, and the empiricist, rather than for their exclusion.

Many of the above choices can be reflected in research regardless of its forum. However, I believe that research books offer the best hope of satisfying these wishes. Therefore, as a group of academics we should encourage colleagues, at various stages of their careers, who have not considered a research project culminating in a book, to undertake one.

REFERENCES

Allison, G. T. 1971. *Essence of Decision: Explaining the Cuban Missile Crisis.* Boston: Little, Brown and Company.

Altman, E. 1973. "Predicting Railroad Bankruptcies in America." *Bell Journal of Economics and Management Science* 4, no. 1 (Spring): 184–211.

Amihud, Y., and B. Lev. 1981. "Risk Reduction as a Managerial Motive for Conglomerate Mergers." *Bell Journal of Economics* 12, no. 2 (Fall): 605–617.

Ansoff, H. I. 1965. *Corporate Strategy: An Analytic Approach to Business Policy for Growth and Expansion.* New York: McGraw-Hill Book Company.

Bourgeois, L. J., III. 1980. "Performance and Consensus." *Strategic Management Journal* 1, no. 2 (July–August): 227–248.

Bower, J. L. 1970. *Managing the Resource Allocation Process.* Boston: Harvard Business School, Division of Research.

Bowman, E. H. 1974. "Epistemology, Corporate Strategy, and Academe." *Sloan Management Review* 15, no. 2 (Winter): 35–50.

_____. 1982. "Risk Seeking by Troubled Firms." *Sloan Management Review* 23, no. 4 (Summer): 33–42.

_____. 1986. "Concerns of the CEO." *Human Resource Management* 25, no. 2 (Summer): 267–286.

_____, and H. Kunreuther. 1988. "Post-Bhopal Behavior at a Chemical Company." *Journal of Management Studies* 25, no. 4 (July): 387–401.

Braudel, F. 1986. *The Wheels of Commerce.* Civilization and Capitalism, 15th-18th Century, Vol. 2. New York: Harper & Row.

Bruner, J. 1986. *Actual Minds, Possible Worlds.* Cambridge, Mass.: Harvard University Press.

Carroll, L. 1865. Reprint. *Alice's Adventures in Wonderland.* London: Octopus Books, 1978.

Chandler, A. D., Jr. 1962. *Strategy and Structure: Chapters in the History of American Enterprise.* Cambridge, Mass.: MIT Press.

Cohen, M. D., and J. G. March. 1986. *Leadership and Ambiguity: The American College President.* 2d ed. Boston: Harvard Business School Press.

Evered, R. 1980. Review of *Strategic Management: A New View of Business Policy and Planning,* edited by D. E. Schendel and C. W. Hofer. *Administrative Science Quarterly* 25, no. 3 (September): 536–542.

Fouraker, L. E., and J. M. Stopford. 1968. "Organizational Structure and Multinational Strategy." *Administrative Science Quarterly* 13, no. 1 (June): 47–64.

Galbraith, J. K. 1987. *Economics in Perspective: A Critical History.* Boston: Houghton Mifflin Company.

Gardner, H. 1985. *The Mind's New Science: A History of the Cognitive Revolution.* New York: Basic Books.

Glaser, B. G., and A. L. Strauss. 1967. *The Discovery of Grounded Theory: Strategies for Qualitative Research.* New York: Aldine de Gruyter.

Gluck, F. W., S. P. Kaufman, and A. S. Walleck. 1980. "Strategic Management for Competitive Advantage." *Harvard Business Review* 58, no. 4 (July-August): 154–161.

Hayes, R. H., and W. J. Abernathy. 1980. "Managing Our Way to Economic Decline." *Harvard Business Review* (July-August): 67–77.

Hayes, R. H., and S. C. Wheelwright. 1984. *Restoring Our Competitive Edge: Competing Through Manufacturing.* New York: John Wiley & Sons.

Hirsch, P. M. 1975. "Organizational Effectiveness and the Institutional Environment." *Administrative Science Quarterly* 20, no. 3 (September): 327–344.

Itami, H. with T. W. Roehl. 1987. *Mobilizing Invisible Assets.* Cambridge, Mass.: Harvard University Press.

Katsenelinboigen, A. 1984. *Some New Trends in Systems Theory.* Intersystems Publications.

Kuhn, T. S. 1970. *The Structure of Scientific Revolutions.* 2d ed. Chicago: University of Chicago Press.

Langton, J. 1984. "The Ecological Theory of Bureaucracy: The Case of Josiah Wedgwood Pottery Industry." *Administrative Science Quarterly* 29, no. 3 (September): 330–354.

Laudan, L. 1977. *Progress and Its Problems: Toward a Theory of Scientific Growth.* Berkeley: University of California Press.

Learned, E. A.; C. R. Christensen; K. R. Andrews; and W. D. Guth. 1965. *Business Policy: Text and Cases.* Homewood, Ill.: Richard D. Irwin.

McKendrick, N. 1988. "The Ugly Historians" (A review of T. S. Hamerow, *Reflections on History and Historians* [Madison: University of Wisconsin Press, 1987] and Gertrude Himmelfarb, *The New History and the Old* [Cambridge, Mass.: Harvard University Press, The Belknap Press, 1987]). *New York Times* (7 February): 14.

Miles, R. E., and C. C. Snow. 1978. *Organization Strategy, Structure, and Process.* New York: McGraw-Hill Book Company.

Miles, R. H., and K. S. Cameron. 1982. *Coffin Nails and Corporate Strategy.* Englewood Cliffs, N. J.: Prentice-Hall.

Mintzberg, H. 1978. "Patterns in Strategy Formation." *Management Science* 16, no. 2, pp. 44–53.

Nelson, R. R., and S. G. Winter. 1982. *An Evolutionary Theory of Economic Change.* Cambridge, Mass.: Harvard University Press.

The New Yorker. 1987. "Briefly Noted," October 5.

Perrow, C. 1985. "Comment on Langton's Ecological Theory of Bureaucracy." *Administrative Science Quarterly* 30: 278–288.

———. 1986. *Complex Organizations: A Critical Essay.* 3d ed. New York: Random House.

Pfeffer, J. 1972. "Size and Composition of Corporate Boards of Directors: The Organization and Its Environment." *Administrative Science Quarterly* 17, no. 2 (June): 218–228.

———. 1982. *Organizations and Organization Theory.* Marshfield, Mass.: Pitman.

Porter, M. 1980. *Competitive Strategy.* New York: Free Press.

———. 1985. *Competitive Advantage.* New York: Free Press.

———, and A.M. Spence. 1982. "The Capacity Expansion Process in a Growing Oligopoly: The Case of Corn Wet Milling." In *The Economics of Information and Uncertainty*, edited by J. McCall, ch. 8, pp. 259–309. Chicago: University of Chicago Press.

Rappaport, A. 1986. *Creating Shareholder Value: The New Standard for Business Performance.* New York: Free Press.

Rorty, R. 1979. *Philosophy and the Mirror of Nature.* Princeton, N. J.: Princeton University Press.

Rumelt, R. P. 1974. *Strategy, Structure, and Economic Performance.* Boston: Harvard Business School, Division of Research.

Schendel, D. E., and C. W. Hofer, eds. 1979. *Strategic Management: A New View of Business Policy and Planning.* Boston: Little, Brown and Company.

Schlesinger, J. 1966. "Organization Structures and Planning." Rand Paper, P-3316 (25 February).

Schon, D. A. 1983. *The Reflective Practitioner: How Professionals Think in Action.* New York: Basic Books.

Scott, W. R. 1981. *Organizations: Rational, Natural, and Open Systems.* Englewood Cliffs, N. J.: Prentice-Hall.

Simon, H. A. 1969. *The Sciences of the Artificial.* Cambridge, Mass.: MIT Press.

Solow, R. 1988. "Short-Run Gain or Long-Run Health." *Technology Review* 91, no. 2 (February/March): 10 (MIT insert).

Steinbruner, J. D. 1974. *The Cybernetic Theory of Decision: New Dimensions of Political Analysis.* Princeton, N. J.: Princeton University Press.

Teece, D. J., ed. 1987. *The Competitive Challenge: Strategies for Industrial Innovation and Renewal.* Cambridge, Mass.: Ballinger Publishing Company.

Tversky, A., and D. Kahneman. 1981. "The Framing of Decisions and the Psychology of Choice." *Science* 211, no. 4481 (30 January): 453–458.

Walker, G., and D. Webber. 1984. "A Transaction Cost Approach to Make-or-Buy Decisions." *Administrative Science Quarterly* 29, no. 3 (September): 373–391.

Weick, K. E. 1987. "Substitutes for Strategy." In *The Competitive Challenge: Strategies for Industrial Innovation and Renewal*, edited by D. J. Teece, ch. 10, pp. 221–234. Cambridge, Mass.: Ballinger Publishing Company.

White, T. H. 1978. *In Search of History: A Personal Adventure.* New York: Warner Books.

Wiener, N. 1948. *Cybernetics, or, Control and Communication in the Animal and the Machine.* New York: MIT Press.

Williamson, O. 1975. *Markets and Hierarchies: Analysis and Antitrust Implications.* New York: Free Press.

Woo, C. Y. Y., and A. C. Cooper. 1981. "Strategies of Effective Low Share Businesses." *Strategic Management Journal* 2, no. 3 (July-September): 301–318.

Zajac, E. J., and E. H. Bowman. 1985. "Perspectives and Choices in Strategy Research." Reginald H. Jones Center Working Paper 85–15.

3 CONTRIBUTIONS AND IMPEDIMENTS OF ECONOMIC ANALYSIS TO THE STUDY OF STRATEGIC MANAGEMENT

David J. Teece

INTRODUCTION

This chapter attempts to identify, relate, and balance concepts from economic analysis that might assist in the development of the nascent field of strategic management. In particular, five streams of economic analysis are reviewed for their potential importance to strategic management: (1) neoclassical price and production theory, (2) the structuralist approach to industrial economics, (3) the transactions cost approach to industrial economics, (4) the organizational economics approach to industrial economics, and (5) evolutionary economics. An effort is then made to provide an integrative paradigm that shows where different types of economic analysis can be helpful, and how other disciplines and subject matters relate to each other and to the field of strategic management. Relatedly, the chapter contends that especially useful contributions to strategic management from economists are at present originating from recent work in organizational-institutional economics. Indeed, the standard neoclassical textbook approach to economic analysis often obscures more than it reveals; it is, moreover, not especially accommodating

This chapter builds on Teece and Winter (1984) and Teece (1984). I am very grateful to Robert G. Harris for his trenchant comments and helpful suggestions. I am also indebted to Richard Rumelt for his provocative comments and deep insights into what strategic management is all about.

and sometimes even hostile to the intellectual approaches that must be assembled if one is to come to grips with key issues in strategic management.

STRATEGIC MANAGEMENT AND ITS INTELLECTUAL ANTECEDENTS

Strategic management can be defined as the formulation, implementation, and evaluation of managerial actions that enhance the value of a business enterprise.[1] *Strategy formulation* includes identifying an organization's competitive strengths and weaknesses, determining the firm's external opportunities and threats, establishing operational goals aligned with value creation, developing and analyzing alternative strategic paths, and selecting among them. One must acknowledge, however, as Mintzberg (1987) and Weick (1987) emphasize, that strategies are formed as well as formulated. While strategy "formulation" might appear to imply deliberate planning and action, it can also emerge (or be inferred) from a pattern of actions not deliberately conceived as a "strategy." *Strategy implementation* requires the enterprise to devise policies, common values, and incentives to motivate employees appropriately and to allocate organizational, technical, and financial resources in a manner that will allow identified strategies to be pursued successfully.

The strategic management process can be described as an objective, systematic approach for making major decisions in a business enterprise. Hence, it is the hallmark of professional management today. It is more art than science.

The field of strategic management is an area of inquiry developed in most business schools in the United States, Europe, and Japan, as well as in some corporations. It is my view that the field seeks to provide an intellectual foundation to inform an established arena of practice in the modern business enterprise. In recent years, the field has both informed and been informed by practice. The field has a quality journal—*The Strategic Management Journal*—and an active society. Yet it is still searching for its intellectual roots.

While strategic management appears to be primarily concerned with normative questions of interest to top management, there are a number of key issues that scholars who do research in the area of strategic management seem to think of as fundamental. It is their focus on these issues that separates, or ought to separate, the study of strategic management from related fields.[2] However, discussions of these questions is rarely explicit. As a corollary, the assumptions used by theorists and practitioners are also often obscure and may require much probing before they are revealed, if they ever are. While not everyone would agree, key issues appear to include the following:[3]

1. What is the source of economic rents and differential performance for individual firms? How can the source of these rents be protected from competitors? (This issue is not typically addressed by other fields. Economists explore rent creation and protection at the industry level, but not at the firm level.) Why are intraindustry differences in profitability so large?

2. Are there limits to how large an organization can become and still remain innovative and efficient? How must organizations be structured and managed to be efficient and innovative? To what degree are efficiency and innovativeness in conflict?

3. What are the significant differences between contracting arrangements and internal organizations? How do the boundaries of the firm—lateral and vertical—affect performance? When is cooperation—upstream, downstream, later, or horizontal—with other enterprises superior to integration? How does institutional context (for example, United States vs. Japan) matter?

4. How does the degree of corporate "coherence" (that is, relatedness among product lines) affect performance? When do firms that show tight coherence outperform conglomerates, and why?

5. What constitutes corporate capabilities? What configuration of assets constitutes a capability? How, if at all, are capabilities transferred? Is it possible to identify a "core business"?[4]

6. Can a firm's knowledge assets be managed strategically? If so, how can knowledge assets be characterized?

7. What is a business? Is it a meaningful concept? How can a business be identified? How do boundaries of markets differ from those of businesses?

8. Do firms and industries evolve in predictable ways?

9. Are there distinctive models of decision making that are strategic? Are strategic decisions separated from others just by domain (as in Chandler's distinction between operating and strategic decisions), or is the mode of decision making different too?

How large is the opportunity for strategically directing or re-directing a business enterprise?

10. What is needed to implement clever strategies, and how much difference does good strategic management really make?

These questions are by no means exhaustive, but they are certainly challenging. No other field or discipline accepts them as mainstream issues. No field tackles them effectively, although progress is being made through interdisciplinary efforts.

The field of strategic management is defined not by methodology, discipline-based theories, or paradigms, but by a set of questions, the answers to which have tremendous implications for management practice. The field is interdisciplinary at present; the scholars are intrigued by the questions the field raises, and are well aware of the limited answers afforded by more established disciplines.

Because the fundamental issues in strategic management are big and important, and our understanding of them so very limited, the field is simultaneously much less satisfactory and more intellectually challenging than established disciplines like economics, or other fields of business inquiry such as accounting, finance, and marketing. To practice the art of strategic management well requires an understanding of all the key business functions and their integration, as well as of the global business environment, and human resource and technological management. To research the field likewise requires a broad-based interdisciplinary framework. It is perhaps because strategic management problems cannot be conquered by breaking them down into their most microcosmic parts (doing so eliminates the field's inherent integrative perspective), that the field has yet to be tamed by the mainstream theoretical techniques of the basic social science disciplines.

Relatedly, while numerous "single variable" theories of strategy ("market share," "focus," "culture") are always being propounded, particularly by management consultants, strategic management is far too complicated to be understood in these terms. To improve understanding, the next section provides a cursory sketch of the history of the field. It can be usefully divided into what might be called the preanalytic and the analytic periods. Mel Horwitch (1988) has provided the most insightful treatment to date, and what follows has benefited from his insights and capabilities.

Preanalytic Era (up to 1970)

The study of what is now called "strategic management" (formerly called "business policy") began at the Harvard Business School with a case study approach that emphasized the role of the general manager, the importance of leadership, and a top-down view.[5] The case study approach was useful not only as a pedagogic mechanism but also because it immediately made it apparent to the professor, if not to the student, that firms engaged in the same activity and using the same technology, in stark contrast to predictions from models of perfect competition, often performed differently. Firms in the same industry could also be shown to have different product approaches, different approaches to distribution, and different organizational structures (Chandler 1962). These differences in approach in similar market environments came to be called "strategies." In this first era of strategic management—the "preanalytic era"—there was little if any role for economic analysis and for strategic planning techniques. The focus was on the CEO and how he or she could and should direct the enterprise.

During this era, most large companies were organized along functional lines. Most of the study and teaching of management was, accordingly, functionally oriented. Strategic management, or business policy as it was then still called, was concerned principally with *general* management, that is, with decisions, actions, structures, and systems that integrated functional activities or, at a minimum, were conducted at levels *above* functional management. The emergence of multidivisional and diversified forms of corporate organization based on disparate lines of business heightened awareness of the explicit need for *strategic*, as opposed to *operational*, management. It also made apparent the differences between business strategy and corporate strategy.

Analytic Era (late 1960s to 1980)

A second era, which began in the late 1960s, is what Horwitch (1988) has called the "golden age" of strategic planning. This epoch saw the development and utilization of tools—particularly product-portfolio analysis and the experience curve—and the rise of a staff-oriented strategic planning function in the business enterprise. Management consulting firms selling sets of techniques that had limited empirical or theoretical foundations blossomed at about the same time.

It was in this second era that economic analysis came to play a more significant role in strategic management. Empirical studies in industrial organization led to the identification of significant intra-industry differences in profitability. This in turn induced Caves and Porter (1977) to develop the concept of mobility barriers as an intra-industry analogue to Bain's (1956) concept of entry barriers at the interindustry level. Armed with these concepts and others from industrial organization, Michael Porter (1980) articulated an extensive compendium of concepts for analyzing industries and competitors. These concepts were presented in clear, forceful language and have subsequently become widely adopted by practitioners in the United States and abroad. They revolutionized the field.

New Questions (the 1980s)

The 1980s have seen a reaction to some of the overselling of analytic techniques during the 1960s and 1970s. Probably the most oversold technique was that of the learning curve. The Boston Consulting Group (BCG) in particular advanced learning economies at certain times to explain just about everything. This led to the recommendation that firms should obtain market dominance, almost no matter what the cost.

The field of strategic management and the practice of management consulting are still growth industries, but rigid and stupefying adherence to particular analytical tools is on the decline. Nevertheless, it is my view that the field remains, unfortunately, theoretically unsatisfactory. It purports to be normative, but the foundations for particular policies or strategies are rarely articulated in ways that are likely to satisfy the inquiring minds of either academics or executives. There is a tendency to overuse contingency tables, which implicitly contain special theories with unspecified assumptions. The field still employs many anecdotes and war stories; only a small body of careful empirical and theoretical work has emerged. As discussed earlier, there is also no generally accepted paradigm to pull together the many valid components of strategic management work.

When theoretical propositions are put forward, it is often without attention to underlying theoretical constructs. For example, concepts as basic as mobility barriers and entry barriers imply certain investment irreversibilities that are not spelled out. Why cannot firms instantaneously change strategic direction? What are the underlying organizational processes that render change difficult? When and under what circumstances is strategic change possible? Correct answers to such questions probably depend on issues in organizational and institutional economics that have themselves received scant theoretical attention. Until an empirically valid theory emerges, the field of strategic management will remain confused and contentious and will present normative principles of dubious value.

In order to prepare the subject matter of strategic management for theoretical development, it is useful to specify a fundamental problem or question. Namely, what is the big question that strategic management scholars are trying to answer? What outcome does one want to attain through the creation of a body of theory and the derivation of normative principles of strategic management? Fundamental as it may appear to be, this question is rarely addressed in the literature. The approach offered here is to view the fundamental problem of strategic management as the derivation and implementation of strategies to enhance the value of the enterprise. This is not the only possible approach, but it is one that is likely to yield insightful answers.

STRATEGIC MANAGEMENT AS RENT-SEEKING HEURISTICS FOR TOP MANAGEMENT

Many scholars of strategic management might agree—though they often do not say so—that a key, if not *the* key, issue is one of how to position and manage the firm so as to generate, augment, and protect "economic rents." Economic rents are the returns above those necessary to keep the underlying assets available to the firm in the long run.[6] Rent-seeking is not just the search for static efficiencies, because even the most efficient internal activities supporting the wrong products or markets will generate losses. Nor is it just market share acquisition, as sales or market shares do not automatically translate into profits. It is—or can and should be—what economists refer to as the "study of rent-seeking by the enterprise." (This leaves to one side just how corporate profits are distributed among stockholders, managers, workers, and other stakeholders.) My contention is that a rent-seeking orientation is useful in the field of strategic management because there is a chance that a viable paradigm can be crafted with such a focus.

As an alternative, however, the goals of strategic management could be defined in process terms. For instance, a recent textbook defines the ultimate objective of strategic management as "the development of corporate values, managerial capabilities, organizational responsibilities, and administrative systems that link strategic and operational decision making at all hierarchical levels, across all businesses, and across functional lines of authority in a firm" (Hax and Majhuf 1984: 71). The approach I am advocating, by contrast, looks at how strategic management enhances the difference between the market value of the firm and the capital its owners have invested.[7] It is important to recognize at the outset that rents are fundamentally derived from some unique or idiosyncratic asset owned or controlled by the firm. For if the supply of the asset—whether human, physical, locational, organizational, or legal capital—that is the source of the rent stream could be expanded by competitors, the returns to market participants would be brought down to competitive levels.

Needless to say, the art of identifying and creating new rent streams constitutes what might be thought of as entrepreneurship. Enhancing and protecting the rent stream from an existing product or process is not, of course, just a function of strategic management: it is what management, organization, and planning are all about. But certain key decision variables are usually the responsibility of the top management team. It is that subset of decisions that can be thought of as strategic decisions.

CONTRIBUTIONS (AND IMPEDIMENTS) MADE BY ECONOMIC ANALYSIS TO THE STUDY OF STRATEGIC MANAGEMENT

In recent years, economic analysis has made and continues to make contributions to the emerging field of strategic management. The contention advanced in this chapter is that some branches of economic analysis have illuminated while other branches have obfuscated the

Figure 3-1. Taxonomy of Economic Theories Pertinent
to Strategic Management.

Focal Concern:	Production	Exchange	Production and Exchange
Hyper	☐1 Neoclassical economics (textbook orthodoxy)	☐2 Neoclassical economics (working paper orthodoxy)	☐3 0
Bounded	☐4 Evolutionary economics	☐5 Industrial economics (structural and transactions cost perspectives)	☐6 Organizational economics

(Rationality Assumptions)

Source: Based in part on Winter (1988).

study of strategic management. Noneconomists may see economics
as a monolithic body of theory and all economists as believing in the
same creed and adopting the same deductive method; that is not the
case. Economics is becoming increasingly heterodox, although this is
more the case in Europe and Japan than in the United States. Indeed,
in the language of Kuhn (1962), the "protective belt" around the
basic mainstream paradigm has been drawn rather tight in the United
States. Interestingly, the belt is beginning to loosen as it becomes increasingly clear that received theory has been unable to comprehend
economic reality in many areas. Figure 3-1 illustrates some of the
variety that exists in the economic approaches that are pertinent to
strategic management.

   As noted in the figure, these approaches differ not only in their
focal concerns (production, exchange, or both), but also in the
rationality assumptions employed (bounded or hyper). Production
theory addresses how goods are produced, while exchange theory
addresses how goods are traded and priced. Under the assumption
of bounded rationality, individuals are assumed to have limited cognitive capacities to store, retrieve, and compute information. Under

the assumption of hyper rationality, no such constraints are assumed. Thus, economic models that assume hyper rationality impute godlike characteristics to economic agents.

In the discussion that follows, all the cells (except 3) will be covered approximately in the order in which they have developed historically. Cell 3 is, for practical purposes, an empty set. Neoclassical economists have very little to say about the boundaries of the firm and how they relate to changing technologies. What does exist comes out of monopoly and conspiracy theory and has not been satisfactorily verified.

Neoclassical Price and Production Theory

Modern post-Marshallian microeconomics is nicely laid out in all the standard microeconomic texts. This body of learning provides the intellectual foundations for most academic economists and is useful for understanding price determination in simplified auction markets (for example, stocks, bonds, wheat, corn, crude oil, cotton). Indeed, most examples in the texts are from such simplified markets. These texts also provide clear expositions of the theory of perfect competition and the pure theory of monopoly. The concepts of competition and monopoly are valuable constructs that should be understood—and typically they are, by managers, academics, and consultants interested in strategic management. However, the underlying model of markets, and especially of the firm, is severely limited and sometimes obscures more than it reveals.

In neoclassical analysis, economic systems are conceived in terms of firms (producers) facing households (consumers) and exchanging commodities and factor services in markets that express the forces of supply and demand. Markets are always predisposed to "clear" since prices will *equilibriate* at precisely that point at which there is no excess supply or demand. (When markets are characterized by neither excess demand nor excess supply, they are often said to have cleared.) Moreover, it is assumed that prices provide all the information necessary to allow all entities to behave optimally. Markets are assumed to be complete and to clear instantly with zero transaction costs, and future states of nature have probabilities of occurrence assigned to them. There is no role for organizations or institutions (other than markets and governments), nor is there typically an endogenous treatment of technological change or changing consumer tastes.

Neoclassical analysis is extremely limited in its usefulness to the manager—not because it involves abstraction, but because the abstraction so often caricatures economic reality. Without doubting the legitimacy, concerns, and objectives that have shaped mainstream economics, one can doubt very seriously that a discipline thus shaped makes a wholly constructive contribution to strategic management. The following paragraphs examine some areas where such doubt seems particularly well justified.[8]

Treatment of Know-how.   The production and utilization of technological and organizational knowledge is a central economic activity. Yet it is handled in a most cavalier way in neoclassical economic theory. By far the most common theoretical approach is simply to take technology as given, ignoring the fact that the options open to a manager almost always include some degree of innovative improvement in existing ways of doing things. On the occasions when this pattern is broken by explicit attention to technology change, the treatment of states of knowledge and the changes therein is often simplistic and undifferentiated. For example, it is common to assume that technology is uniformly available to all. Or, if technology is proprietary, then it is information that can be embedded in a "book of blueprints." In reality, however, know-how is commonly not of this form. Know-how is often tacit, in that those practicing a technique can do so with great facility but they may not be able to transfer the skill to others without demonstration and involvement (Teece 1981). To assume otherwise obscures issues relating to the generation and transfer of know-how. In general, the fact that technological and organizational change is such an important and pervasive aspect of reality, and yet so peripheral in economic theory, may be the single most important factor that limits the contribution of orthodox economics to strategic management.

Focus on Static Analysis.   Strategic management issues are centrally concerned with dynamics. Economic theory, on the other hand, deals almost exclusively with equilibrium analyses, which are very often static. In recent years, much greater attention has been given to theoretical formulations that are dynamic in nature, but formal modeling endeavors of this kind are often exceedingly difficult to perform. Accordingly, only very simple problems can be dealt with mathematically, and these are certainly not the kinds of problems that concern top-level managers. While comparative statics is one way to get at dynamic issues, it suffers from inattention to the path of equilibrium. Yet these matters are usually exceedingly important. When industries and markets are being transformed, top management must be as concerned with the journey as with the destination.

Focus on Equilibrium. Economic analysis makes wide use of equilibrium analysis. An equilibrium is a state where the intended actions of rational economic agents are mutually consistent and can therefore be implemented. In fact, almost all of the central propositions of economics rely on the assumption that markets are in equilibrium. But equilibrium is clearly a fictitious state. The justification for its use is the supposed tendency toward equilibrium, which is, however, an empirical rather than a theoretical proposition. Indeed, G. B. Richardson (1960: 1-2) argues that "the general equilibrium of production and exchange . . . cannot properly be regarded as a configuration toward which a hypothetical, perfectly competitive economy would gravitate or at which it would remain at rest." His argument is the obvious one: that for equilibrium to be attained, firms need information about each other's investment plans. In the absence of collusion or a complete set of forward markets, however, such plans are not going to be fully and accurately revealed. Accordingly, "it is difficult to see what but an act of faith can enable us to believe that equilibrium would be reached" (Richardson 1960: 11). Indeed, as Hahn (1973: 4) has pointed out, the basic purpose of the famous Arrow-Debreu model of equilibrium is "to show why the economy cannot be in this state." While equilibrium analysis yields valuable insights into certain public policy issues, it is of limited use to managers of the strategic process. Indeed, it obscures more than it clarifies. It certainly distracts attention from process issues.

Inadequacy of the Theory of the Firm. With little exaggeration, one can assert that until very recently, economics lacked a theory of the firm. To be sure, textbooks often contain the chapter heading for "The Theory of the Firm." But on closer examination, one finds a theory of production masquerading as a theory of the firm. Firms are typically represented as production functions or, in some formulations, as production sets. These constructs relate a firm's inputs to its outputs. The firm is a "black box" that transforms the factors of production into usually just one output. Therefore, firms are single-product in their focus. If multiproduct firms exist, then they are flukes in that they have no distinct efficiency dimensions (Teece 1982). The boundaries of the firm—the appropriate degree of vertical, lateral, or horizontal integration—thus cannot be explained by traditional economic analysis. Moreover, the theory is completely silent with respect to the internal structure of the firm. In short, the firm is an entity that barely exists in the received neoclassical theory. The only dimensions of its activities that are given much play are the volume of its output and the price at which that output is sold. Yet this limited scope is clearly inadequate for the problems of strategic management.

Suppression of Entrepreneurship. Because equilibrium analysis has such a dominant position in received economic theory, and because change is so often modeled as a movement from one equilibrium condition to another, the role of entrepreneurship (used here to mean the process of effectuating change) tends to be downplayed, if not outrightly suppressed. In fact, "it may be said quite categorically that at present there is no established economic theory of the entrepreneur. The subject area has been surrendered by economists to sociologists, psychologists, and political scientists. Indeed, almost all the social sciences have a theory of the entrepreneur, except economics" (Casson 1982: 9).

Casson goes on to identify two villains. One is "the very extreme assumptions about access to information which are implicit in orthodox economics. . . . Simple neoclassical models assume that everyone has free access to all the information they require for making decisions" (p. 9). Such an assumption reduces decision making to the mechanical application of mathematical rules for optimization. This trivializes decision making and makes it impossible to analyze the role of entrepreneurs. Moreover, even the Austrian school (for example, Hayek or Mises), which does take the entrepreneur more seriously, is often trapped by subjectivism, rendering predictive theory-building difficult. A predictive theory of the entrepreneur is impossible for the Austrian school because "anyone who has the sort of information necessary to predict the behavior of entrepreneurs has a strong incentive to stop theorizing and become an entrepreneur himself" (p. 9). The need for a theory of entrepreneurship—or at least a theory that does not suppress the process of entrepreneurship—is of considerable importance to strategic management. And it is not likely to be provided by neoclassical economics.

Stylized Markets.   In neoclassical theory, transactions are performed by faceless economic agents operating in impersonal markets. However, markets are not nearly so anonymous. Even traders on the New York Stock Exchange—supposedly the most "objective" of all markets—know a good deal about each other. Reputation, experience ratings, and the like are the very stuff that permits markets to operate. To strip such considerations from the theory—or to try and add them just one at a time—renders economic theory impotent before many strategic management problems. Where managers know each other, trust relationships abound, and fly-by-night operators can generally be exposed.

Real-world markets are characterized not only by a variety of information conditions; they also differ widely in the frequency with which transactions and the opportunities for, and costs of, disruption occur. (For instance, compare the sale of a nuclear power plant with the sale of a bushel of wheat.) Yet the analysis of intermediate markets and relational contracting (Williamson 1979) is virtually absent from the neoclassical textbooks and most advanced theorizing. By neglecting the institutional foundations of market structure, therefore, the conventional tools of economic analysis are rendered of little use in most strategic management problems.

Assumptions about Decision Makers.   Economic analysis commonly assumes a form of behavior that has been referred to as "super-rational," or "hyperrational" (Simon 1978). Decision makers are supersmart, do not have problems with memory loss or memory recall, and can instantly formulate and solve problems of great complexity. Even their expectations are assumed to be rational. This is not an abstraction but a caricature of the business decision maker. It is clear that hyperrationality is simply not an adequate characterization of individual behavior, much less of organizational behavior. It is equally clear that strategic management can learn little from abstractions of this kind.

Behavior of Cost.   In microeconomic theory, and in practically all textbook treatments, short-run costs are considered to rise with increasing output because of the law of diminishing returns. While the empirical evidence generally contradicts the assumption of increasing short-run marginal cost, the rising marginal-cost curve persists in the textbooks. This is because it must, if much of the rest of the paraphernalia of neoclassical microeconomic theory and welfare economics is to survive. Without the rising marginal-cost curve, it is often harder to derive industry equilibriums and to arrive at normative conclusions—hence the reluctance to push it into the appendixes, where it might well belong.

The above point is not meant to suggest that economists have not been involved in an important stream of research on alternative cost structures, such as the progress function (Alchian 1959). In the 1960s, the concept was applied (and sometimes misapplied) to strategic management by BCG and others. Indeed, the progress function and various derivative concepts have proved quite valuable in linking cost behavior to strategic choices. But the economics literature on it remains somewhat enigmatic, as well as detached from mainstream treatments of cost.

Yet the concept has become an important, possibly overused, concept in strategy management. In fact, Richard Pascale has invented the term "Honda effect" to describe how consultants, academics, and executives have tended to squeeze reality into the straightjacket of the experience curve and other parables, "to the neglect of the process through which organizations experience, adapt, and learn" (Pascale 1984: 3). Pascale juxtaposes BCG's parable of Honda's entry into the British and American motorcycle industry with reality as seen by Honda's management team. The BCG paradigm imputes coherence and purposive rationality when, in Pascale's view, the opposite was closer to the truth.

The previous discussion suggests that orthodox microeconomic theory, useful as it is for understanding many important economic and public policy issues, is of little value to the strategic manager. In fact, received theory tends to saddle the practitioner with perceptual blinders that block peripheral vision. Oddly enough, it appears that the strong bias in neoclassical thinking toward equilibrium and reductionism may be due to economists imitating the discipline of physics. (Unfortunately, this imitation does not extend to the principle of empirical verification. In physics, theories must undergo and survive empirical verification before being accepted as scientific knowledge. This does not appear to be the case in many branches of economics, where theories that are at odds with the empirical evidence often seem to have a life of their own.) But while physics began to change course during the nineteenth century—toward a more organic, indeterminate perspective on natural events—neoclassical economics has tended to reinforce its addiction to the style of Newtonian physics. Neoclassical economics remains strongly mechanistic, not adaptive. Technological change, so critical to the understanding of today's global economy, remains exogenous in practically all neoclassical economic models, if it is included in them at all. Accordingly, it is difficult to see how neoclassical economics could provide the starting point for serious forays into the intellectual problems staked out by scholars and practitioners in the field of strategic management.

Needless to say, the neoclassical textbook approach (cell 1 in figure 3-1) is being rapidly supplemented by numerous working papers and journal articles—what is referred to as "working paper orthodoxy" (cell 2 in figure 3-1)—which attempt to shore up the neoclassical deficiencies, but typically only one at a time! This means that on just about every issue and proposition in economics, theorists—and in particular, game theorists—almost always have at least one special theory to offer. However, this burgeoning class of special theories is decidedly unrobust and is rarely exposed to the chill of empirical verification. Consequently, it is not reviewed here, as it has almost nothing to offer at this time to key issues in strategic management. By explaining everything, it explains nothing. I challenge proponents of game theory to demonstrate otherwise. Unfortunately, this last wave in the 1980s was itself preceded by an earlier wave in the 1960s which turned out to be almost equally as barren. Given the significant intellectual investment in these activities, the outcomes are quite pathetic—at least in terms of their utility to students of the field of strategic management.

Industrial Economics: The Structuralist Perspective

As mentioned earlier, Michael Porter (1980) revolutionized the study of strategy by demonstrating the utility of industrial economics to the formulation of business strategy. Inasmuch as his work draws heavily on the received industrial organization literature circa 1970, it is instructive to review the basic approach underlying Porter's "five forces" model (see figure 3-2) and its usefulness to strategic

Figure 3-2. Forces Driving Industry Competition.

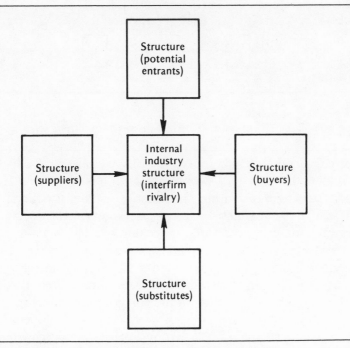

Source: Adapted from Porter (1980: 4).

management. The basic idea is that each set of forces conditions the level of rents. This approach has its roots in the structure-conduct-performance paradigm. Indeed, the four "parameter" forces (substitutes, suppliers, buyers, and potential entrants) are all elements of market structure, while the fifth (intraindustry competition) captures the concept of "conduct." As Porter (1980: 3) notes, competition in an industry is rooted in its underlying economic structure.

The structure-conduct-performance paradigm was developed by Ed Mason at Harvard in the 1930s and Joe Bain at Berkeley in the 1940s. A highly stylized version is represented in figure 3-3. According to this model, the conduct (C) of firms is somehow determined out of market structure (S). Conduct refers to the degree of collusiveness, R&D behavior, price-output policies, advertising, and so forth. Market performance (P) ultimately depends on structure alone, since conduct is seen as uniquely related to structure. Cournot (1938) was perhaps the first to employ this paradigm, and Stigler's (1963) theory of oligopoly also relied on it; structure determines the

Figure 3–3. Structure-Conduct-Performance Paradigm.

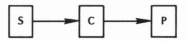

extent to which firms collude, and hence the performance of firms in the market.

Porter's model, while rooted in this paradigm, is considerably richer than the industrial economics textbook approach. He recognizes strategic groups within an industry, market signaling, commitment, and the dynamics of structural evolution. Moreover, he observes that industry structures are segregated and strategy is formulated according to whether industries are fragmented, emerging, mature, or declining. In fragmented industries, for instance, various ways of coping with fragmentation are outlined, such as specialization by customer type, order type, or geographical area. Strategic traps, such as attempting to seek dominance in an inherently fragmented structure, are also flagged by Porter. In emerging industries, various strategic decisions are outlined (such as timing). As with the other structural types, a contour map is drawn and obstacles are flagged, but no clear pathway towards higher profits is identified. However, useful lists of what to look for and what to avoid are provided.

What Porter encounters in *Competitive Strategy* is the limits of the structure-conduct-performance paradigm that he so successfully employed. The utility of this framework is to be found in formulating business unit strategy, not corporate strategy. There is no theory of the enterprise embedded in his analysis, nor is there a theory of organizational economics or organizational behavior. The reason for this is obvious. What Porter has to work with in the structure-conduct-performance paradigm is a theory of market structure and industry performance, not a theory of organization, of institutions, or of firm-level performance. While Porter does make efforts to focus on individual firm performance issues, there is no intellectual framework available for him to employ. Porter's second book, *Competitive Advantage* (1985), contends with these same deficiencies.

Figure 3–4. Corporate-Level Strategies.

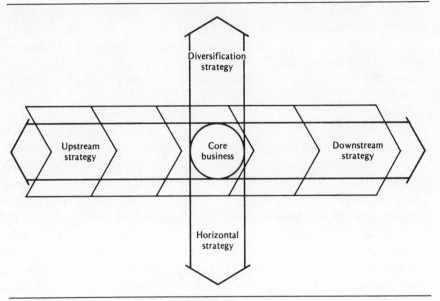

Source: Adapted from a slide presentation by Torger Reve at the meeting of the Strategic Management Society, Singapore, October 1986.

Industrial Economics: The Transaction Cost Approach

Until recently, strategic management lacked a plausible paradigm for thinking about corporate-level strategy as compared to business unit strategy. Corporate-level strategy engages such critical issues as diversification and vertical and horizontal integration. These issues are mapped in figure 3–4.

The fundamental question here is whether rents can be generated by combining businesses (vertically, horizontally, laterally, and so forth), using hierarchical methods (integration), market methods (contracts), or hybrid forms (for example, joint ventures). Such rents are to be expected if integration economies exist, and if these economies have not already been fully captured. The strategic question is not just whether a firm should move into related businesses (lateral, backward, forward, horizontal), but *how* it should do so. There are a number of organizational choices, including contracts, franchises, joint ventures, "alliances," and integration.

To ascertain whether institutional/organizational or contractual methods should be used to mediate these transactions, transaction cost analysis can be profitably employed. The basic approach is as follows: Suppose amalgamation economies exist through the establishment of organizational linkages. The choice of governance structure ought to evolve around the relative efficiency properties of the alternatives. To start the analysis, the a priori assumption can be that arm's-length contractual relationships are the most efficient, since they require the least organizational overhead. However, the presumption can be easily overturned if, in order to obtain the amalgamation economies in question, one or both parties must dedicate specialized (irreversible) investments to the relationship. Then, in the absence of safeguards, one or both parties are likely to prefer common ownership of the amalgamated activities. Otherwise, they will be exposed to "recontracting" hazards (that is, one party may take advantage of contractual ambiguities). In the absence of adequate safeguards, such exposure can cripple incentives to cooperate, or at least change the terms upon which cooperation proceeds. In short, *transaction costs* of one kind or another will arise when *specialized assets* (equipment, know-how, and so on) need to be deployed. Depending on the nature of the specialized assets, *integration* can turn out to be the most efficient strategy for the economic units in question. These matters have now been afforded extensive treatment in the literature (Williamson 1975, 1979, 1981, 1985; Teece 1982, 1986; Monteverde and Teece 1982a, 1982b), and so they are not delved into further here. But they are ripe for further incorporation into the strategic management literature.

Transaction cost economics also provides certain insights into the internal structures needed to support specific strategies. Oliver Williamson, the leading contributor, has developed theories, and others have provided evidence to support some of the following conclusions:

1. There are basically only two fundamental internal forms: the unitary and the multidivisional.
2. The unitary form works adequately for small organizations, but with radial expansion it is exposed to control problems and a confounding of operating and strategic decisions.
3. The multidivisional form is ideal for multiproduct activity.[9]

But beyond such conclusions, economists of practically all persuasions have little to say about internal organization, or about related issues such as corporate culture.

In order to fully develop its capabilities, transaction cost economics must be joined with a theory of knowledge and production. This is because the corporation is not just an instrument for organizing transactions; it is also an instrument for learning. Important characteristics of this learning are: (1) it involves organizational as well as individual skill, (2) it is cumulative activity (as discussed below), (3) it is path dependent, and (4) the knowledge generated lies somewhere in organizational methods or routines. As transaction cost economics begins to incorporate such notions into its core, it will provide powerful insights into an additional set of strategic management issues.[10]

Evolutionary Economics and Related Approaches

For want of a better label, I refer to an emerging branch of analysis, one that has technological change as its core, as "evolutionary economics." Sidney Winter (1988: 173) points out that evolutionary economics

> emphasizes the inevitability of mistaken decisions in an uncertain world, and the active, observable role of the economic environment in defining "mistakes" and suppressing the mistakes it defines. Relatedly, the sort of explanation it offers for states of affairs is an evolutionary explanation—some antecedent condition existed, and the state of affairs now observable reflects the cumulative effect of the laws of change operating on that antecedent condition. In other words, the focus of explanatory effort is on dynamics. Like transaction cost economics, evolutionary economics tends to direct attention to observed economic behavior rather than hypothetical sets of alternatives. Like evolutionary biology, it is much concerned with how patterns are reproduced through time in the face of continuing turnover in the population of individuals displaying the pattern. Finally, it regards understanding of the ongoing, interrelated processes of change in technology and organization as the central intellectual problem to be confronted by a theory of the firm.

There has been a recent burst of writings in evolutionary economics and related approaches, and a remarkable convergence of thinking on many important issues. Yet there has been practically no carry-over to strategic management. The opportunities, however, exist. Admittedly, strong ecological positions that see firms as being unable to engage in significant change and as not having any choices available other than possibly their birth dates, obviously do not provide foundations for thinking about strategy; they only serve to suggest that strategy cannot matter, or that it is "all in the timing."[11]

The utility of less extreme evolutionary approaches to strategic management stems from the focus of evolutionary theories on three concerns. First, they are concerned with technological change and its implications for economic processes, and they focus attention on key issues of interest to management in industries experiencing, or exposed to, rapid technological change. Second, evolutionary approaches take into account production processes, learning, and innovation. These issues are of great significance to both strategy formulation and implementation. And third, these approaches examine dynamics and change processes, which are, of course, the very stuff that strategic management is all about.

Certain elements of evolutionary economics were developed by Schumpeter (1934) decades ago. In doing so, Schumpeter questioned the static underpinnings of neoclassical economics and at the same time suggested an alternative approach. He adopted an evolutionary model in which technological change and the efficacy of the entrepreneur as an innovative agent played the most significant roles; processes of industrial mutation increasingly revolutionize the economic structure from within. Schumpeter saw this "creative destruction" as the essential fact of capitalism.

But the evolutionary economics described here is much more. Schumpeter attempted to place technical change at the heart of his system and also addressed problems of social, institutional, and political change. He consistently emphasized innovation as the main source of dynamism and competition in capitalist development. Schumpeter sometimes emphasized the role of the small firm as the driver of innovation and change, but at other times described large firms with market power as the principal contributors. Schumpeter had almost nothing to say, however, about issues of strategy and public policy, as these were not his concerns. His purpose was to explain capitalism, not to suggest how it could be invigorated or what corporate and business strategies had the best chance of being profitable in a world where the leitmotiv was creative destruction.

Nevertheless, those economists who have taken their cue from Schumpeter have, half a century later, created a field of innovation studies that can inform the field of strategic management. Key concepts that can be associated with the evolutionary school and appear to have relevance to strategic management include the six discussed below.

Technological Regimes. Whereas research on innovation a decade ago tended to focus on particular innovations, innovations are now commonly viewed as connected, and attention has been shifted from the individual innovation to the connecting structure. The basic idea is that innovation must be understood as an evolutionary process, punctuated by periods of rapid change. Nelson and Winter (1977, 1982) have used the term "technological regimes," and Rosenberg (1976) has referred to "technological trajectories," to describe the underlying technical and learning structures guiding technical change at any time.

The application of the paradigm concept has affected thinking about technology policy, both public and private. This concept causes the focus to shift from particular innovations to classes of innovations, where a cumulative effect can be felt. DNA and monoclonal antibodies in biotechnology are examples of technology paradigms, as is solid-state, silicon-based memories in microelectronics.

The notion of a paradigm or trajectory for technology undercuts the view that industry structure is a key to the process. The notion of trajectory suggests a certain technological determinacy and the need for firms to adjust to it, and propel it, if possible. Paradigm shifts have obvious implications for entry barriers and entry timing, key issues in strategic management.

Path Dependencies. Closely related to the paradigm concept are path dependencies. Technology sometimes evolves with significant irreversibilities, as well as forward constraints. That is, the path along which the technology can evolve in the future is often highly constrained—as well as cumulative, with one improvement building on the next in serial fashion. The development of dynamic random-access memories (DRAMS), from 64 through 256 to one megabyte and beyond, is a case in point. A firm that did not participate in the development and production of one vintage had a slim chance of participating in the next. Technological paradigms may afford one or more paths, each of which is characterized by path dependency. This can create a kind of dynamic "lock-in" phenomenon with powerful implications for industry and firm development.

Selection.   The level of competition, the frequency of technological discontinuities, and the nature of government policy (for example, antitrust or trade policy) govern the strength of a *firm's* selection environment. The selection environment for a *business* may be more or less demanding, depending upon the policies and practices of the enterprise within which the business is embedded. In weak selection environments—that is, where lackluster performers are not quickly weeded out—inefficiency can live on in some business units for decades, particularly if the firm's selection environment is also weak, as may be the case in some regulated industries.

Technological Opportunities.   An important characterization of an industry is the technological opportunity available to it. Technological opportunities are determined in part by discoveries in basic science and the degree to which they open up fruitful avenues for new applications. In biotechnology, for instance, scientific discoveries that enabled the genetic structure of microorganisms to be modified (for example, Watson and Cricks' 1956 discovery of the double helix structure of DNA), augmented by the discovery of techniques such as recombinant DNA (a technique for removing specific genes from one organism and implanting them into the DNA structure of another), have provided enormous commercial opportunities for both incumbent firms and new entrants in many industries. These include pharmaceuticals, agricultural chemicals, materials, and electronics. The number and diversity of technological opportunities that exist in an industry are important characteristics likely to have a marked impact on industry dynamics. Therefore, they should be part of the analytic apparatus employed by strategic management.

Appropriability Regime.   The availability, or lack thereof, and scope of enforceable intellectual property rights are important features of industrial dynamics. If an industry is one in which intellectual property protection (patents, trade secrets, and so on) is effective, as in pharmaceuticals and organic and inorganic chemicals, then the manner in which competition will play itself out is markedly different from competition in other industries, such as financial services or semiconductors. The intellectual property protection afforded in these last two industries is intrinsically weak. Indeed, one writer recently noted that "in a world where there are no secrets, where innovations are quickly imitated or become obsolete, the theory of competitive advantage may have had its day. . . . Nowhere are the limits of the big play better demonstrated than in financial service industries" (Bhide 1986: 59). My contention here is that these statements reflect a failure of the strategic management literature to partition industry environments according to the nature of the intellectual property regime. This is a critical factor in all industries.

A second characteristic of the intellectual property regime, which is analytically separate from the first, is the distance that exists between the proprietary and the public knowledge bases. If the public knowledge base is on a par with the proprietary, as when university research opens up a new technological paradigm, or if elements of the public research enterprise outpace private efforts, then entry costs are drastically lowered. The asymmetry between new entrants and incumbents is of critical importance to the way in which competition plays itself out.

The above and other related issues can be developed much more fully; at present, they are not discussed in either the industrial organization literature or the strategic management literature. The implicit assumptions in neoclassical economics are that all industries have the same intellectual property protection and that new technology can be protected through the mechanism of intellectual property law. This is rarely the case, and both innovation strategy and business strategy must be adjusted accordingly.

Dominant Designs and Lock-in by Small Events. Abernathy and Utterback (1978) have postulated a life cycle model of industry development. That model is instructive because it highlights the impact that the emergence of a dominant design can have on industry structure and firm profitability. A related literature on competing technologies highlights the phenomenon of market "lock-in" and the implications for firm performance. Each will be briefly reviewed.

According to the Abernathy-Utterback model, the evolution of an industry is often characterized by early focus on product innovation and a neglect of process innovation. The latter occurs because in the early stages of a product life cycle, competition is on the basis of product performance, design changes are still occurring, and there is little incentive or need to manufacture in volume at low cost. Production processes remain unspecialized, and general purpose equipment and job shop production methods characterize production. Once a dominant design emerges from this competition among alternative designs, the terms of competition switch, and price becomes critical.

The implicit assumption in the above argument is that the industry in question is in a regime of weak appropriability, so that rivals can copy the designs that users appear to favor. With product imitation, competition thus switches to cost; access to, or possession of, a low-cost product delivery capacity becomes critical. Process technology is usually the key to achieving such low cost: competitors usually have similar factor costs because they are free to locate facilities wherever costs are lowest. Process technology also becomes critical because it is much harder to copy than product technology and it does not have to be released in order to yield benefits to its owners. Moreover, process technology can be protected by trade secret law, a form of intellectual property protection that is often stronger than patent protection.

The concept of the dominant design reinforces the importance to industry dynamics and individual firm performance of timing and the possession by innovators and imitators of relevant cospecialized assets. Thus, early success in pioneering a new product concept is often for naught if a firm exits before the dominant design has emerged. Witness AMPEX's inability to profitably participate in the home videocassette recorder (VCR) market. Product pioneering is also for naught if the innovating firm fails to assemble the relevant cospecialized assets (Teece 1986). Indeed, Flaherty's (1983) methodologically appealing empirical study of market share determination in the U.S. semiconductor industry confirms the importance of technological leadership; but it also highlights the importance of applications engineering, as well as sales and service support. Likewise, Hartman and Teece (1988) establish the performance impact of manufacturer reputation and the size of the installed base on firm performance in the minicomputer business.

It should be recognized that the design that dominates is not always that which is intrinsically, or ultimately would be, the best. In an insightful treatment of competing technologies, Brian Arthur (1988) explains how technologies become more attractive the more they are adopted, so much so that competition among technologies usually becomes a competition between bandwagons. Increasing returns to adoption can arise from several sources, including learning by using, network externalities, production scale economies, informational increasing returns, and technological interrelatedness. Arthur points out that in a world in which consumers are ignorant about future paths of technological activity, inferior designs that provide initial appeal can sometimes get selected over long-term superior designs. This lock-in can be triggered by small, chance events. For example, the selection by electric utilities of light-water reactors over what would have been (given equal development efforts) superior, gas-cooled designs is probably due to the U.S. Navy's selection (in the early 1950s) of light-water reactors to power submarines. The gains in learning and construction experience locked the market into this technology by the mid-1960s.

It should be apparent that evolutionary and ecological views provide fewer opportunities for adaptive behavior than do other approaches. Pure ecological perspectives reject the feasibility of adaptation and rely instead on selection. But more balanced views recognize that although organizations are characterized by strong inertial forces that severely limit change, they do not make it impossible. "Genetic engineering" is possible with organizations, but as with biological systems, it is not easy. In spite of such limitations, the evolutionary perspective is likely to make the strategy manager more keenly aware of aspects of the enterprise that cannot be changed, thereby directing attention to feasible "organizational engineering." Organizational engineering is likely to be "frame-breaking" in its impact, as when the whole top management team is replaced, or where poor performance leads to a crisis and the imposition of severe constraints by the company bank. It is also likely to cause management to focus on the buying and selling of organizational units as the only way to quickly reconfigure an enterprise—although what is changing might be simply what lies inside the firm's boundaries, rather than the subunits themselves. In short, an evolutionary perspective is likely to cause a keener awareness of: (1) constraints in implementing strategy, (2) the influence of timing, (3) the importance and the ramifications of setting strategic direction early in the life of the enterprise, and (4) the need to engage in mergers and acquisitions to effectuate strategy. Just how all of this plays out has yet to be addressed in ways likely to assist managers, but the possibilities are apparent. The next section elaborates.

Organizational Economics

The term "organizational economics" was coined by Barney and Ouchi (1986). For them, it denotes the study of organizations and organizational phenomena using concepts taken from contemporary organization theory, organization behavior, and microeconomics. Moreover, a small but growing body of work in the strategy area is being built through a melding of transaction cost economics and evolutionary economics. The organizational economics approach contends that firms need to be understood, and their boundaries explained, in terms of learning, path dependencies, selection, and transaction costs. (This contention has not been previously articulated in the literature, but appears to follow from a joining of the various concepts introduced earlier.) The organizational economics approach embeds a theory of production and enterprise development inside the transaction cost paradigm. It purports to provide a framework to explain corporate coherence and corporate diversification by developing the concept of a firm's "core business," which in turn is the set of competencies that define a firm's distinctive advantage.

A firm's core business, according to the organizational economics approach, stems from the underlying, natural trajectory embedded in the firm's knowledge base. Thus, new product development usually proceeds along the lines of previous successes. A wave of improvements, often dramatic in their significance, may follow the introduction of a major new technology. Of course, the desirability of seeking further improvement depends upon the commercial promise that market entry may have yielded, or at least signaled. The history of prior commercialization efforts may indicate the most promising technological neighborhoods to explore for market acceptance. However, sometimes there may be a kind of inevitability to the direction of search, driven by what was referred to earlier as "technological imperatives." A change in technological regime—where regime is defined by the convergence of engineering beliefs about what is feasible, or at least worth attempting—or the simultaneous coexistence of several related technological regimes (as with both [CMOS] and [NMOS] technologies in semiconductors) may soften technological imperatives, making them less path-dependent. Of course, technological discontinuities may blow path dependencies asunder.

There are important implications in the above concept for economic theory, for strategic management, and for the organization of economic activity more generally. First, because promising areas of research inquiry lie close to the firm's existing knowledge base, and because a set of production/manufacturing activities are typically implied by a particular research focus, a firm's core business (or possibly core businesses) can be expected to display a certain stability and coherence. Path dependencies inherent in technological progress and business development can be expected, at least partially, to drive the definition of a firm's capabilities, and therefore the business in which it has a comparative advantage.

Path dependency is reinforced as a limiting factor by a set of organizational routines that develop once a particular research endeavor bears fruit. Whereas the creative part of research is at least partly ad hoc, routines characterize efficient postdevelopment behavior in production, marketing, distribution, and sales. A routine is defined by repeatedly putting a skill, or set of skills, to use in a particular or distinctive environment. As mentioned earlier, path dependencies define the neighborhoods/environments in which skills can be most productively applied. Hence, a firm's initial point of entry in a technological regime, and the trajectories/paths that it initially selects, will define in large measure the kinds of competencies that the firm will generate, as well as the products it will develop and commercialize. After first commercialization, a set of routines will develop that will lead to stronger competencies in certain areas.

The skillful performance of organizational routines provides the underpinnings for what is commonly thought of as the firm's distinctive competency. The competencies, coupled with a modicum of strategic vision, will in turn help define a firm's core business. A firm's core business is necessarily bounded by particularized competencies in production, marketing, and R&D. Employees will tend to form natural teams that do not regroup or absorb new members easily.

Since routines cannot be codified, they must be constantly practiced to achieve high performance. This in turn suggests that the firm must remain in certain activities even though short-run considerations would suggest abandonment. Put differently, core business skills need to be constantly exercised to maintain corporate fitness.

A firm's learning domain is defined in part by where it has been, and by the technological imperatives and opportunities thus encountered. Therefore, it is readily apparent that a firm has a limited, but by no means nonexistent, ability to change its business. The products it can produce and the technologies it employs are highly path-dependent, at least at the level of the individual business unit. More can be done at the level of the corporation, but this typically involves entering the corporate control market (that is, buying and selling businesses), not the market for factors of production. This is where transaction cost analysis is relevant.

The implications for strategy management should be obvious. Specifically, profit-seeking firms have limited abilities to change products and technologies, except by entering the market for corporate control. In addition, economies of scope appear to be constrained by the limited ability to apply routines across different product and technological environments/neighborhoods. "Related" diversification would appear to be feasible so long as it is consistent with the underlying path dependencies and/or imperatives, a matter which is to be discussed in more detail later.

The analysis has so far assumed relative stability with respect to technological regimes. Suppose, however, that the firm experiences a discontinuity in its technological environment that makes its skills obsolete and possibly renders its downstream assets valueless. In these circumstances, established firms will lack many of the research competencies needed in the new business environment. However, downstream competencies, particularly in sales and distribution, may remain relevant to the new technological regime. When the technology necessary for survival is well out of the neighborhood of the firm's traditional research inquiry, it may be extremely difficult to utilize existing in-house research competencies within the new paradigm. This is because of the path dependencies noted earlier. Accordingly, the relevant competencies may have to be purchased en masse, or collaborative technology transfer programs may have to be employed to educate existing personnel in the assumptions and logic of the new technology. Here, in-licensing and collaboration with the organizations responsible for pioneering the new paradigm (typically universities or new business firms) may be necessary. Organizational economics helps to establish when such collaboration is necessary, and the forms it should take.

Incumbent firms can thus be expected to change their boundaries when technological regimes shift, unless, of course, incumbents have been responsible for the shifts. However, if the know-how in question is not protected by intellectual property law, then the collaboration at issue is likely to be more in the form of imitation than of in-licensing. If the technology has a large tacit component, know-how licensing may still be necessary.

Technological change is often driven by certain imperatives in a trajectory that help define the firm's core business. However, the diversity of applications for a given technology is often quite broad, and there is the possibility of applying the firm's capabilities to different market opportunities, especially after growth opportunities in existing markets are exhausted. Suppose application areas outside of the core business do in fact open up. The question arises as to whether the potential scope economies are best captured through diversification or licensing. According to the organizational economics approach, whether the firm ought to integrate is likely to depend on four sets of factors: (1) whether the technology can be transferred to an unaffiliated entity at higher or lower resource cost than it can be transferred to an affiliated entity; (2) the degree of intellectual property protection afforded to the technology in question; (3) whether a contract can be crafted that will regulate the sale of technology with greater or lesser efficiency and effectiveness than department-to-department or division-to-division sales can be regulated by internal administrative procedures; and (4) whether the set of complementary competencies possessed by the potential licensee can be accessed by the licensor at a competitive price. If the licensee's competencies can be made available cheaper than the licensee's other alternatives, the available returns from the market will be higher, and the opportunity for a satisfactory royalty or profit-sharing arrangement will be correspondingly greater.

The above issues are explored in more detail elsewhere (Teece 1981, 1982, 1986). Suffice it to say that contractual mechanisms are often less satisfactory than the alternative. Proprietary considerations are more often than not served by integration, and technology transfer is difficult, both to unaffiliated and affiliated partners. The result is that integration (or multiproduct diversification) is the more attractive alternative, except where incumbents are already competitively established in downstream activities and are in a position to make de novo entry by the technology-based firms unattractive. Hence, multiproduct firms can be expected to appear as efficient responses to contractual, proprietary, and technology transfer problems in some circumstances. Mixed modes, such as joint ventures and complex forms of profit-sharing collaboration, will also be common, according to how the set of transactions in question stacks up against the criteria identified above.

To summarize, a firm's core business is usually tightly circumscribed by evolutionary considerations (learning, path dependencies, selection, and the like). However, at the corporate level there is considerable opportunity to adjust the firm's boundaries to either include or exclude certain businesses. The choice open to management depends very much on the selection environment, as well as on the specificity of the assets involved, issues discussed more fully elsewhere (Dosi, Teece, and Winter 1987). But even with the admittedly general discussion provided above, it seems that organizational economics does provide considerable promise for informing the field of strategic management.

TOWARD A SYNTHESIS

The above four economic literatures—neoclassical economics, industrial economics (structural and transaction cost), evolutionary economics, and organizational economics—provide varying, complementary, but sometimes contradictory, normative insights into strategy formulation and implementation. Table 3–1 illustrates and summarizes how these different literatures might inform various elements of strategic management. From these literatures, one can find help in understanding rent-generating opportunities and mechanisms for the isolation and capture of rents. Yet they do not help in matters of implementation. Economists know little about implementing change and must rely on other disciplines for insights into such matters.

Admittedly, to disaggregate the strategic process—whether in theory or in practice—into sensing, formulation, and implementation may be hazardous, especially for the practitioner. Recent comparisons of Japanese and Western models of management have shown two significant facts: (1) the strategic process tends to work more effectively in Japanese enterprises, and (2) the process used by the Japanese is not serial, but parallel. This is particularly so with respect to new product identification and development. (An appropriate metaphor, discussed by Takeuchi and Nonaka [1986], is relay versus rugby.) Elements of sensing, deciding, and executing are present throughout the strategic process, but in Japan there seems to be a

Table 3-1. Illustrative Concepts from Different Paradigms.

Elements of Strategy	Neoclassical Price and Production Economics	Industrial Economics		Evolutionary Economics	Organizational Economics
		Structural	Transactions Costs		
Size, market share	Economies of scale	Learning economies	Power structure of incentives, limits to control	Path dependency, learning, selection	Path dependency, learning, selection, organizational limits
Scope: vertical, lateral, conglomerate	Variable proportions theory	Foreclosure theory, leverage theories, economies of scope	Contractual theory, specialized assets	Path dependency, routines, cumulative learning	Cospecialized assets, core business, contractual theory
Product, price, and performance	Game theory	Cartel theory, oligopoly theory	Safeguards, hostages	Path-dependent learning, appropriability "lock in"	Cospecialized assets, path-dependent learning, appropriability regime
Internal organization	0	0	Multidivisional hypothesis	0	Multidivisional hypothesis
Financial structure	Modigliani-Miller irrelevance theory	0	Governance theory	0	Governance theory

greater recognition of constraints on change and of the importance of learning. As several eminent observers note, "U.S. companies actively develop and organize resources after relatively elaborate analysis and recognition of environmental opportunities and risks, while Japanese companies place more importance upon continuous in-house resource accumulation and development with a view towards survival under any type of environmental change" (Kagono, et al. 1985: 57).

In spite of the potential hazards, it seems appropriate to attempt to relate and synthesize the various aspects of strategic management, including the ones discussed above, to indicate where economic concepts may be useful. Such a synthesis is attempted in figure 3–5, which is highly stylized. It portrays a simultaneous system in which science, technology, and entrepreneurship shape revenues, costs, and ultimately, profits. Profits in turn shape entry, exit, asset accumulation, and next-period performance. The model assumes that the fundamental drivers of the business system are the rents available for distribution among what economists call the "factors of production"; others typically call them "stakeholders."

The logic of figure 3–5 can be best explained by example, Assume a change in (exogenous) science due, for instance, to breakthroughs in university research (point A in the figure). If these changes can provide the foundations for new products, opportunities for profit arise. Depending on the innovators' capabilities, skills, and assets, these opportunities can be sensed (point B), identified (point C), and converted into rent-yielding assets (point D). The point here is that not all opportunities are perceived correctly and acted upon; such activity is necessary before the possibility of capturing rents arises. Whether these rents are captured by the innovator or by imitators will depend on a variety of factors. On the revenue side, the key question is whether the rent stream can be shielded from the inroads of entrants, either incumbents or new entrants (points E_1, E_2, and E_3). The generation of rents will also depend on the availability of close substitutes. Needless to say, if incumbents and potential entrants can be effectively cartelized, an additional element of rent protection can be obtained and profits should be enhanced accordingly. So far, this is not too different from the structure-conduct-performance approach.

However, we also recognize the "lower loop" in figure 3–5, as well as feedback effects. The lower loop summarizes a set of factors typically dropped out of the picture in economic treatments of strategic management. We refer to internal operations, internal governance (such as appropriate organizational structure), and external governance (that is, the various structures the firm uses to couple with suppliers, customers, financial institutions, and the like). The lower loop corresponds more or less with efficiency concerns, while the upper loop corresponds with market control stemming from exclusionary behavior of one kind or another. Moreover, the lower loop is where transaction cost economics connects with corporate strategy; the upper loop is the domain of Porter's *Competitive Strategy* and its sequel. Feedback loops signal that there are steps in this process that must occur simultaneously, not sequentially, and that market structure and internal processes are as much a consequence of performance as they are a cause of it.

While the synthesis provided in figure 3–5 might seem appealing, it is at odds with much current practice, and with academic research and teaching. With respect to the latter, American business schools typically adopt one of two models for doing research and teaching in strategic management. First, because it has been a field with a weak paradigm, strategic management is not considered legitimate in some schools. Accordingly, these schools simply emphasize basic functions (for example, finance, accounting, marketing) and fail to give any attention to strategic or general management. Another approach is to separate the study of strategic management and treat it as a stand-alone field. Those taking this approach hope that the individuals assigned to teach and research in the area will grapple with the tough issues on the table and make some intellectual headway. However, both approaches are flawed, though the second less so.

As is apparent from figure 3–5, the subject matter and literature relevant to strategic management is extremely broad. Therefore, strategic management cannot be a specialist function, though it can be assisted by the specialist. As a result, it might make sense to organize strategic management in business schools not as a department but as an interdisciplinary program, with a focus on key issues such as those identified above. Once a central paradigm emerges and stands up to rigorous testing, the field of strategic management can more readily attain departmental status. Until then, an interdisciplinary program approach will prevent the gangplank from being drawn up too soon.

Figure 3-5.   Forces and Mechanisms Impacting Firm-Level Profits: Simplified View.

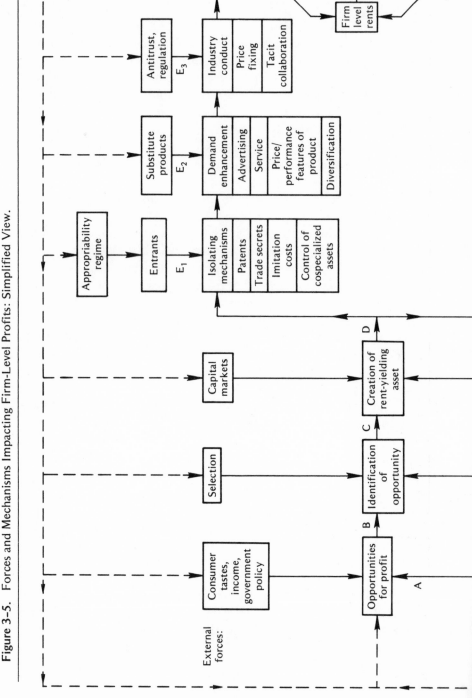

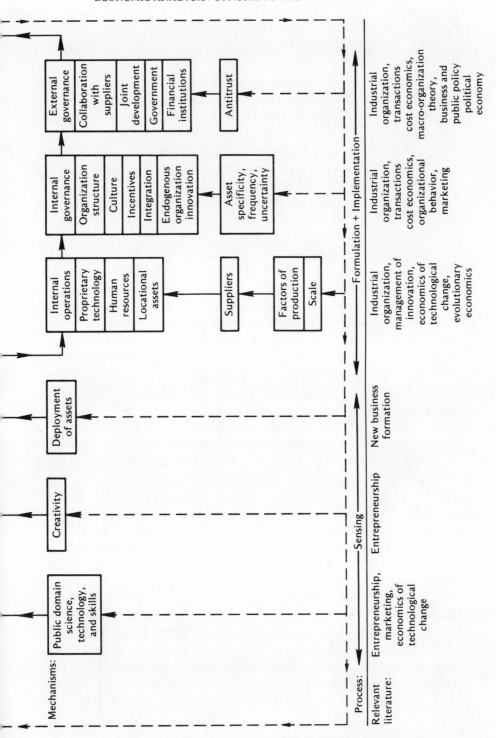

CONCLUSION

The field of strategic management is a new one with shallow intellectual roots. Yet the issues the field addresses are of central concern to both top management and students of the business enterprise. They are extremely challenging issues. Moreover, to admit weakness in the field of strategic management is to admit a more basic weakness in our understanding of the corporation, of competition, and of organizational growth and change.

In the last decade or so, the net contribution of economics to the study of strategic management has turned positive. While neoclassical economics provides both intellectual clutter and blinders, recent developments in industrial economics, in transaction cost economics, and in evolutionary and organizational economics have begun to provide the platform from which a powerful intellectual contribution can be made. Some of these concepts have been referenced here. Much more needs to be done in developing these concepts, testing them, and deriving their normative import. An organizing framework must also be developed to integrate these various contributions, as well as contributions from other fields, such as marketing and organizational behavior. One possible approach was sketched in the last section of this paper.

If strategic management can productively organize itself around such an approach, powerful linkages to other disciplines will be easier to forge. For instance, capital budgeting techniques for choosing among investments exist in corporate finance. However, these techniques cannot be intelligently employed as decision aids without a sense of the nature of the rent streams being evaluated. As a leading textbook in corporate finance (Brealy and Myers 1984: 786) laments, "Why do some companies earn economic rents while others in the same industry do not? Are the rents mere windfall gains, or can they be anticipated and planned for? What is their source and how long do they persist before competition destroys them? Very little is known about any of these important questions." A related question that Brealy and Myers seek answers to is, "Why are some real assets risky and others relatively safe?" (p. 786). Strategic management addresses just such questions. Once answers emerge, our understanding of basic issues in economics, finance, industrial development, and management will have advanced considerably. Only then can business school faculties feel confident that they are imparting to students an adequate understanding of the corporation and competition.

NOTES

1. Mintzberg (1987) suggests that strategic management cannot afford to rely on a single definition of strategy, and that multiple definitions can help practitioners and researchers alike. This position may well be valid. However, it is necessary to define terms in order for debate to proceed. The definition offered here is not the only one that could be offered, but it is one that helps frame the discussion that follows.

2. Carroll and Vogel (1987: 1) note that "for research to be legitimately labelled as being in the strategy area, it appears that only one of several sufficient criteria need be satisfied. These are:

    a concern with *performance* as the outcome variable of major interest;

    a *normative* orientation to research problems leading to discussion (if not investigation) of implications for managers; and

    an emphasis on the issues of interest to *top management*, including especially the decisions they face."

    As is apparent from what follows, the argument here is that it is the focus, explicitly or implicitly, on certain fundamental questions which is the key discriminating factor.

3. This treatment has benefited from many discussions with Richard Rumelt of UCLA who has helped shape my views on strategic management.

4. See Teece (1988) for a discussion of the concept of core business.

5. This history is documented by Mel Horwitch (1988).

6. Economic rents can be proxied at any point in time by Tobin's Q ratio, which is the firm's market value divided by the replacement cost of its invested capital.

7. This is consistent with Thomas (1986: 1).

8. This section is based partially on Teece and Winter (1984).

9. An excellent survey of empirical findings is contained in Thompson and Wright (1988: ch. 2).

10. For tentative steps in this direction, see Dosi, Teece, and Winter (1987).

11. For a clear statement of this position, see Hannan and Freeman (1984).

REFERENCES

Abernathy, W. J., and J. M. Utterback. 1978. "Patterns of Industrial Innovation." *Technology Review* 80, no. 7 (January/July): 40–47.

Alchian, A. 1959. "Costs and Outputs." In *The Allocation of Economic Resources: Essays in Honor of B. F. Haley*, edited by M. Abramovitz. Berkeley, Calif.: University of California Press.

Arthur, W. B. 1988. "Competing Technologies: An Overview." In *Technical Change and Economic Theory*, edited by G. Dosi, C. Freeman, R. Nelson, G. Silverberg, and L. Soete, ch. 26, pp. 590–607. London: Pinter.

Bain, J. S. 1956. *Barriers to New Competition*. Cambridge, Mass.: Harvard University Press.

Barney, J., and W. Ouchi. 1986. *Organizational Economics*. San Francisco: Jossey-Bass.

Bhide, A. 1986. "Hustle as Strategy." *Harvard Business Review* (September-October): 59–65.

Brealey, R., and S. Myers. 1984. *Principles of Corporate Finance*. New York: McGraw-Hill.

Carroll, G. 1988. *Ecological Models of Organizations*. Cambridge, Mass.: Ballinger.

Carroll, G., and D. Vogel. 1987. *Organizational Approaches to Strategy*. Cambridge, Mass.: Ballinger.

Casson, M. 1982. *The Entrepreneur: An Economic Theory*. Totowa, N. J.: Barnes and Noble.

Caves, R. E., and M. E. Porter. 1977. "From Entry Barriers to Mobility Barriers." *Quarterly Journal of Economics* 91 (May): 241–262.

Chandler, A. 1962. *Strategy and Structure*. Cambridge, Mass.: MIT Press.

Cournot, A. 1960. *Researches into the Mathematical Principles of the Theory of Wealth*. Translated by Nathaniel T. Bacon. Homewood, Ill.: Irwin Publishing. Originally published as *Recherches sur la Principes Mathematiques de la Theorie de Richesses* (Paris: L. Hachette, 1839).

Dosi, G., D. J. Teece, and S. G. Winter. 1987. "Towards a Theory of Corporate Coherence." Unpublished working paper (October).

Flaherty, M. T. 1983. "Market Share, Technology Leadership, and Competition in International Semiconductor Markets." In *Research on Technological Innovation, Management and Policy*, Vol. 1, edited by R. Rosenbloom, pp. 69–102. Greenwich, Conn.: JAI Press.

Hahn, F. H. 1973. *On the Notion of Equilibrium in Economics*. Cambridge, Eng.: Cambridge University Press.

Hannan, M., and J. Freeman. 1984. "Structural Inertia and Organizational Change." *American Sociological Review* 49 (April): 149–164.

Hartman, R., and D. J. Teece. 1988. "Product Emulation Strategies in the Presence of Reputation and Network Externalities." Working Paper EAP-27, Center for Research in Management, University of California at Berkeley (February). Forthcoming, *Economics of Innovation and New Technologies*.

Hax, A. C., and N. S. Majuf. 1984. *Strategic Management*. Englewood Cliffs, N. J.: Prentice-Hall.

Horwitch, M. 1988. "Post Modern Management." Unpublished book manuscript.

Kagono, T., K. Nonaka, K. Sakakibara, and A. Okumura. 1985. *Strategic Versus Evolutionary Management: A U.S.-Japan Comparison of Strategy and Organization.* Amsterdam: North Holland.

Kuhn, T. S. 1962. *The Structure of Scientific Revolution.* Chicago: University of Chicago Press.

Mintzberg, H. 1987. "The Strategy Concept: Five P's for Strategy." *California Management Review* 30, no. 1 (Fall): 25–32.

Monteverde, K., and D. J. Teece. 1982a. "Supplier Switching Costs and Vertical Integration in the U.S. Automobile Industry." *Bell Journal of Economics* 13, no. 1 (Spring): 206–213.

_____. 1982b. "Appropriable Rents and Quasi-Vertical Integration." *Journal of Law and Economics* (October): 321–328.

Nelson, R., and S. Winter. 1977. "In Search of a Useful Theory of Innovations." *Research Policy* 6, no. 1 (January): 36–77.

_____. 1982. *An Evolutionary Theory of Economic Change.* Cambridge, Mass.: Harvard University Press.

Pascale, R. T. 1984. "Perspectives on Strategy: The Real Story Behind Honda's Success." *California Management Review* 26, no. 3 (Spring): 47–72.

Phillips, A. 1971. *Technology and Market Structure.* Lexington, Mass.: Heath.

Porter, M. E. 1980. *Competitive Strategy: Techniques for Analyzing Industries and Competitors.* New York: Free Press.

_____. 1985. *Competitive Advantage.* New York: Free Press.

Richardson, G. B. 1960. *Information and Investment.* Oxford: Oxford University Press.

Rosenberg, N. 1976. *Perspectives on Technology.* Cambridge, Mass.: Harvard University Press.

Schumpeter, J. A. 1934. *The Theory of Economic Development.* Cambridge, Mass.: Harvard University Press.

Simon, H. 1978. "Rationality as Process and as Product of Thought." *American Economic Review* 68 (May): 1–16.

Stigler, G. 1964. "A Theory of Oligopoly." *Journal of Political Economy* 72 (February): 44–61.

Takeuchi, H., and I. Nonaka. 1986. "The New Product Development Game." *Harvard Business Review* (January-February): 137–146.

Teece, D. J. 1981. "The Market for Know-how and the Efficient International Transfer of Technology." *Annals of the Academy of Political and Social Science* 26 (November): 81–96.

_____. 1982. "Towards an Economic Theory of the Multiproduct Firm." *Journal of Economic Behavior and Organization* 3, no. 1 (March): 39–63.

_____. 1984. "Economic Analysis and Strategic Management." *California Management Review* 26, no. 3 (Spring): 87–110.

_____ . 1986. "Profiting from Technological Innovation." *Research Policy* 15, no. 6 (December): 286–305.

_____ . 1988. "Technological Change and the Nature of the Firm." In *Technical Change and Economic Theory*, edited by G. Dosi, C. Freeman, R. Nelson, G. Silverberg, and L. Soete. London: Pinter.

Teece, D. J., and S. G. Winter. 1984. "The Limits of Neoclassical Theory in Management Education." *American Economic Review* 74, no. 2 (May): 116–126.

Thompson, S., and M. Wright, eds. 1988. *Internal Organization, Efficiency and Profit.* Oxford: Philip Alan.

Weick, K. E. 1987. "Substitutes for Corporate Strategy." In *The Competitive Challenge: Strategies for Industrial Innovation and Renewal*, edited by D. J. Teece, ch. 10, pp. 221–233. Cambridge, Mass.: Ballinger.

Williamson, O. E. 1975. *Markets and Hierarchies: Analysis and Antitrust Implications.* New York: Free Press.

_____ . 1979. "Transaction-Cost Economics: The Governance of Contractual Relations." *Journal of Law and Economics* 22 (October): 3–61.

_____ . 1981. "The Modern Corporation: Origins, Evolution, Attributes." *Journal of Economic Literature* 19, no. 4 (December): 1537–1568.

_____ . 1985. *The Economic Institutions of Capitalism.* New York: Free Press.

Winter, S. G. 1988. "On Coase, Competence, and the Corporation." *Journal of Law, Economics, and Organizations* 4, no. 1 (Spring): 163–180.

4 HITCHING A RIDE ON A FAST TRAIN TO NOWHERE
The Past and Future of Strategic Management Research

Richard L. Daft
Victoria Buenger

In 1979, quoting extensively from Thomas S. Kuhn's (1962) remarkable extended essay, *The Structure of Scientific Revolution,* Dan Schendel and Charles Hofer urged scholars and practitioners in the policy field to accept a new paradigm. Converging on a single paradigm would end the continual and pointless redefinition of concepts and instead would lead to progress and efficiency in the further development of the field. They warned that the cherished status quo was never a true and long-term friend, for it stifled change and restricted progress. The new paradigm—strategic management—would offer a new set of questions and set an agenda so that specific research projects could be directed toward seeking answers to these questions.

THE STATE OF STRATEGIC MANAGEMENT

We do not imply that Schendel and Hofer invented strategic management, but they did herald, and in a sense sanctify, the ascension of this research paradigm. The effect on the field has been noticeable. The thin stream of articles investigating strategic management that

The authors claim joint responsibility for the theoretical arguments and analysis in this essay.

81

had trickled into the journals in the early 1970s has become a tide. Various journals have reoriented their content from nonstrategy to strategy topics to provide a forum for what has been a geometric increase in the volume of articles written. New journals have been born to accommodate the overflow. Strategy research has discovered a fast track, and all too willingly strategy scholars have boarded the train without realizing where it is headed.

Not that a fast train isn't just fine if you want to get from Point A to Point B rapidly, but what about another destination? If Point B is not where you want to arrive, a fast train is not so useful. But once the roadbed is built and the railings laid, the investment makes it difficult to change direction even if the tracks lead nowhere. The train steams forward, and passengers, such as strategic management scholars, perhaps not fully aware of the train's direction or of alternative destinations, may embrace the nowhere destination as somewhere. In some respects, we believe this has happened in strategic management research.

To explain this opinion, we will compare the evolution of strategic management with the evolution of two other disciplines, organization theory and behavioral accounting. Organization theory provides an interesting contrast with strategy because both view organizations through a macro lens, but their development has been strikingly dissimilar. Behavioral accounting has less content overlap with strategy, but it seems an appropriate comparison because of accounting's applied nature, which corresponds to the prescriptive aspirations of strategic management.

Our premise is that in the race to embrace its own paradigm, strategic management research has been ensnared by the rituals and paraphernalia of normal science. Along with agreed upon symbols and terms, preferred models, and exemplars that according to Kuhn allow clearer communication among scholars, strategic management has also made some limiting investments. It is these relics—a premature convergence onto a single assumption set; premature rationalization of research methods and procedures; and premature adoption of normative research approaches to achieve applied results—that have led us to conclude that strategy research is on a fast train headed nowhere. Our discussion of this belief will begin with a brief description of how a paradigm becomes a victim of its own existence. We will then expose the three points of comparison that restrain the development of new knowledge in strategy research. Finally, we will conclude with suggestions on how to deliver the field of strategic management from the fate of arriving nowhere fast.

NORMAL SCIENCE AND PARADIGM CONSTRUCTION

In every intellectual age, one style of reflection tends to become a common denominator for promoting understanding and clearer communication about the world people encounter. In the broadest sense, science has dominated Western civilization's intellectual universe for four centuries. The foundations laid by Descartes, Galileo, Huygens, and Newton have become an influence that has reached far beyond any special sphere of ideas or images. That science prevails does not mean that no other styles of thought or modes of sense-making exist. It does mean that more general intellectual interests tend to slide into the science arena, to be formulated there most sharply, and when so formulated to be thought somehow to have reached, if not a solution, at least a profitable way of being carried along. From that perspective science has acquired great prestige. Nonetheless, because science has been called to duty as a defining concept so often, its meaning has become muddled and imprecise.

If science is a common umbrella for organizing the world, then Kuhn's term "normal science" explains how individual disciplines arise within that tradition to organize the investigation of specific phenomena. The development of a normal science in a field of inquiry begins with the acquisition of a paradigm. Paradigms can assume various forms, but each provides model problems and solutions to a community of practitioners; each is sufficiently unprecedented to attract adherents; each is open-ended enough to leave much to resolve; and—especially—each is acknowledged as the foundation for further research. A community of scholars gradually emerges dedicated to a research program of articulating and specifying the paradigm. Key research issues are defined by the paradigm. A common language and preferred analogies emerge. Protocols develop concerning accepted modes and methods of investigation. Progress is measured by the number and precision of solved problems, the resolution of ambiguities in the paradigm, and increased accuracy in prediction. Compared with preparadigmatic research efforts, findings produced by normal science seem to emerge in efficient, systematic, and orderly fashion.

While the power of normal science is obvious and potentially enormous, hazards are evident. Fundamental agreement about assumptions driving the paradigm quickens travel down the research path, but also produces a shared mental set. Commitment to a way of thinking becomes a source of intellectual security that binds serious reflection and popular metaphysics to the tradition of the paradigm. At best, normal science becomes the false friend that Schendel and Hofer warned of when they discussed the status quo. In the worst-case scenario, according to C. Wright Mills (1959: 20), the discipline is marred by "a set of bureaucratic techniques which inhibit inquiry by methodological pretensions, which congest such work by obscurantist conceptions, or which trivialize it by concern with minor problems unconnected with relevant issues."

These hazards become particularly dangerous when a field embarks upon a tradition of convergent thinking before it has matured. By its nature, normal science forces the world into conceptual boxes. If this happens before a field is well defined, it is likely to stymie further intellectual growth, development, and differentiation. Where the preparadigmatic process is suited to producing a scholar without prejudice, alert to novel phenomena, and flexible in his approach to the field, the postparadigmatic scholar is trained to elucidate the tradition in which he was raised rather than to challenge it. The boundaries of the paradigm can shackle the field, and while research might be generated at a heady pace, its contribution will defend the extant point of view and may not be meaningful in terms of new knowledge.

Kuhn himself admitted that the pursuit of normal science was neither intended nor likely to produce fundamental discoveries or revolutionary changes in theory. The development of a normal science in a given field is a sign of maturity. Although Newton pointed the way with his discoveries in optics and his theory of light, the field of physics was not instantly conceived. Fundamental contributions to physical optics had been made for two millenia before Newton. The two prior centuries had narrowed possibilities considerably. Out of preparadigmatic confusion, Newton's articulation catapulted a receptive field toward a new understanding. The field coalesced around his ideas, crystallized by the paradigm, and normal science ensued.

The advantages to the field have been evident ever since policy scholars embraced a strategic management paradigm. The paradigm produces clarity about acceptable research ideas and methods, key issues can be agreed upon, and the number of research problems solved has increased geometrically. Perhaps the desire of policy scholars to be recognized as a mature and legitimate field of social science also motivated the rapid acceptance of the paradigm. However, commitment to a shared way of thinking can also inhibit intellectual growth, focus attention on relatively minor research problems, and lead to evaluation based on methodological pretensions. Thus, in terms of our imaginary train, the question is whether the strategic roadbed, tracks, and sidings were constructed before it was clear what direction the field wanted to go.

IS MORE RESEARCH YIELDING LESS KNOWLEDGE?

And now we are on our way: hurdling forward because we've adopted a paradigm that allows the field to develop cumulatively and quickly—but perhaps headed nowhere because we are entrapped by prematurely convergent thinking. This problem can be illustrated by comparing strategic management to other disciplines.

Basis of Comparison

The model in figure 4–1 shows the three areas we believe are most responsible for the current lack of progress in strategic management. The first circle, social science assumptions, represents strategic management's premature convergence onto a single set of assumptions. Circle two, theories and methods, stands for the field's early and firm attachment to a particular type of research method and its consequent deemphasis of theory. The third circle, labeled management applications, refers to the tendency of strategic management, from the beginning, to organize itself around normative research approaches to achieve applied results. As the arrows in figure 4–1 indicate, these ideas are distinct, but mutually influencing.

Figure 4-1.   Characteristics of Academic Disciplines.

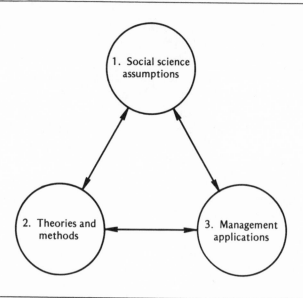

Social Science Assumptions.   Social science assumptions pertain to the basic philosophies that researchers adopt about what research means and how it should be performed. Often we take such assumptions for granted, much as we do the tenets of the religion we grew up with. Our training has ingrained certain research assumptions in us to the point that we rarely question them. This is part of the promise but also part of the difficulty of normal science. When we accept a set of research assumptions, we reduce what is arguable, but we also exclude possibilities.

Gibson Burrell and Gareth Morgan (1979) provided a framework for understanding social science assumptions. For example, one set of assumptions that characterize research is positivism versus anti-positivism. Positivists assume that the world works in systematic ways and that patterns can be observed and measured. Knowledge about the world can be gathered in a systematic and building way. Natural scientists adopt a positivist approach, as do many social scientists. Antipositivism argues, on the other hand, that the world, especially the social world, is not well patterned. To understand the world, we must experience it. Research must begin with the frame of reference of the actors and must treat events, happenings, and interpretations as unique. Furthermore, because the world is socially constructed, events, actions, and things have meaning only by virtue of shared interpretations.

For example, positivists in organization science assume that organizations have structures. Positivists measure and compare organizations' structures along quantifiable dimensions such as formalization, centralization, and complexity (for example, Hage and Aiken 1967; Blau 1970). Symbolic interactionists, on the other hand, could be considered antipositivist because they do not believe that organizations have permanent and tangible structures. Everything about an organization exists only in the cognitive processes of individuals. Thus, the organization is composed of an ever changing set of relationships defined by organizational members' perceptions (for example, Barley 1986; Ranson, Hinings, and Greenwood 1980).

Additional social science assumptions were also discussed by Burrell and Morgan. Most researchers make a number of implicit assumptions about human nature and the nature of the social world. These assumptions are crucial because they reflect a fundamental belief about the way the world works. They influence how problems are framed and how research is undertaken. Different assumption sets can lead to very different research outcomes. For instance, a scholar who believes in human free will is likely to ask different research questions, choose different variables, and investigate different situations than a scholar who believes that situational determinants control individual behavior.

Theories and Methods. Often tied to social science assumptions are notions concerning the acceptable way of building and testing theory. This topic, represented in figure 4–1 by the theories and methods circle, covers both the types and the range of research approaches tolerated within a discipline. The most common difference in type is "quantitative" versus "qualitative." These categories represent distinctly different ways of data-gathering and analysis. Quantitative or nomothetic approaches rely on systematic procedures and precise measurements to investigate the world, and their adoption typically is coincidental with positivist assumptions. Alternatively, qualitative research, also called ideographic research, focuses on concrete, individual, and unique situations. Qualitative researchers, commonly having adopted antipositivist assumptions, roll up their sleeves and go out to absorb the world personally.

Theory should dictate which research approach is best for addressing a research question, but preferred methods can dominate. When method counts, as often happens in normal science, unacceptable theories and methods are excluded from consideration. The preference for acceptable methods often will determine the research question and, ultimately, the answers obtained.

Management Applications.   The third element in figure 4–1, management applications, also tends to delineate what is acceptable for study within a field and what is not. The question is basically one of research focus. Should researchers aspire to translate research findings into specific management applications and to encourage practical reforms based on the findings? Or should researchers value knowledge itself without trying to solve organizational and management problems? This is essentially a question of basic research versus applied research. Does pure knowledge ultimately have the greatest impact on organizations, or should studies be designed to answer specific questions relevant to the problems strategic managers face? The value accepted within a discipline has implications for the types of research that will be accepted.

Comparison to Other Fields

The three issues described above—social science assumptions, theories and methods, management applications—provide the basis of our comparison of strategic management with organization theory and behavioral accounting. The summary of points that will guide our discussion are illustrated in table 4–1.

Organization Theory.   In the case of organization theory, we believe that social science assumptions are diverse and competing. During the first author's service as associate editor for *Administrative Science Quarterly,* reviewers with disparate assumptions commonly exhibited tolerance for one another when they reviewed manuscripts for the journal. People with a quantitative background did not automatically reject a qualitative approach, and vice versa. Both positivist and antipositivist views could be expressed. When assumptions about free will or determinism were made explicit within a paper, it was not automatically the kiss of death. The diversity of manuscripts published in a journal such as *ASQ* illustrates the breadth of assumptions that are accepted in organization theory.

The tolerance for diverse assumption sets in organization theory gives rise to different theories. For example, in table 4–1 we have listed three theoretical perspectives common in organization theory—Marxism, institutional, and resource dependence; each view is a competing yet acceptable way of explaining organizational phenomena. The Marxist view contends that organization structure is used to create and maintain the status quo—to keep certain people in power and others out of power. The hierarchy of organization keeps resources under the control of managers and out of the control of workers. The institutional view argues that organizations take action so that they will be perceived as legitimate in their environment. This means that organizations do things not because the actions maintain management's power or because the actions are rational and lead to higher performance. Rather, organizations take action because it looks good to others in the institutional environment. The third idea, resource dependence, explains organizational actions as attempts to reduce dependence on others for resources. This perspective explains why organizational boundaries are organized as they are, and why interlocking boards of directors and joint ventures occur among organizations. These three theoretical perspectives offer distinctly different points of view about the same phenomena, yet they and other perspectives exist together comfortably within organization theory.

Because so many theoretical perspectives find a home in organization theory, there tends to be room for diverse research methods as

Table 4–1. Comparison of Three Disciplines.

	Organization Theory	Behavioral Accounting	Strategic Management
Assumptions	Diverse and competing	Diverse and competing	Single and uniform (positivist)
Theory and method	Competing (e.g., Marxism, institutional, resource dependence)	Competing	Single (with normal science methods dominating)
Management applications	Only as outgrowth of new theory	Secondary (theory development is first)	Performance is top priority

well. Take, for instance, research exploring the concept of control. When control has been studied from a functionalist point of view, researchers have generally taken a quantitative approach. Tannenbaum (1968) asked respondents to report how much influence various levels of authority have in organizations, while Daft and Macintosh (1984) surveyed twenty corporations and found that department managers used four management subsystems—budgets, statistical reports, performance appraisals, and standard operating procedures—to monitor and control their departments. Gouldner (1954), on the other hand, viewed control as a relational phenomenon. To uncover the subtleties of control as a relationship, he adopted a case method that examined the employees and management of an operating gypsum plant. Gouldner argued that the wildcat strike he observed was caused by a growing divergence between management and labor over the appropriate level of control given compensation, job characteristics, and other factors. Methodology in each case is the researcher's tool. As long as the method fits the theory and addresses the research question, it seems to matter little whether the study relies on a single case, a complex, multivariate path analysis, or some other approach.

Finally, we turn to organization theory's attitude about management application. For the most part, organization theorists do not undertake research in a direct effort to solve problems for managers. The problem-solving capacity is there, but as an outgrowth of theory. The development of new theoretical knowledge for its own value is the primary criterion of research success. This assumes that if investigators understand organization phenomena well, they can develop a theory about those phenomena. And if investigators can develop a theory about organizational relationships that shows how organizations work, then this basic knowledge ultimately will have practical benefit for managers. Investigators do not start out trying to solve problems; they begin by trying to understand a phenomenon. But a successful theory typically will apply to managers.

Behavioral Accounting.   Behavioral accounting is the term for research into the organizational and social aspects of accounting, which is considered an applied discipline. One of the authors became involved in behavioral accounting through submission of manuscripts to a behavioral accounting journal and participation in professional association meetings. It was surprising to learn how diverse the social science assumptions were in behavioral accounting. Some people champion systematic data, and others challenge the use of systematic data. Moreover, competing theories are at work in behavioral accounting. One manuscript described a rather traditional approach in which budgets were used for resource allocation and management control. Another submission maintained a radical, almost Marxist perspective on budgeting, claiming that budgets give power to the already powerful and exclude the disenfranchised lower level workers. Even more unexpected in the field of behavioral accounting was the lack of concern for management applications. Researchers were focused on contributing to a theoretical body of knowledge rather than to the solution of management problems associated with accounting. Indeed, management applications were given low priority compared to making theoretical contributions and gathering appropriate data.

Strategic Management. Column three of table 4–1 contrasts strategic management with the other two disciplines. We have characterized the social science assumptions driving strategy research as singular and positivist. Our feeling is that most strategists adhere strongly to a belief in systematic, definable strategy procedures and structures that can be described, measured, analyzed, and compared. This assumption so dominates the discipline that it obscures any others that might compete with it. As this one set of assumptions drives others out, the clash of theoretical ideas is replaced by petty arguments about appropriate construct definition, sample size, operationalization of variables, and methodological validities. The search for understanding is restricted to a flat and narrow path and is reinforced by an audience of like-minded peers who are arbiters of professional achievement and the sole possessors of the game rules. There is no broader perspective about what strategic management is, or what scholars might do to enrich the research program.

Well-intended loyalty to the paradigm and to a single set of assumptions directly influences strategic management scholars' attitudes and practices concerning theory and method. Our impression from reading the journals is that positivist assumptions lead straightaway to dominance of research method over theory as the primary concern of investigation. The power of the paradigm adds to this tendency for, according to the implicit canons of normal science, if enough minute, careful, and methodologically valid studies are conducted, they will accumulate in a way that significant conclusions about strategic management can be drawn. This drives investigators to act as if to say, "We've got to get more data. We've got to analyze data statistically and be certain of our results." Theory is used for interpreting statistical findings, not as a guide to frame research questions in the first place. Empirical data are increasingly confined to those statistically determined facts and relations that are numerous, repeatable, and measurable. With both theory and data so restricted, their interplay dwindles. Rigid research procedures are not congruent with leaps of discovery.

Discovery of new knowledge is further dampened in strategic management by a fixation on performance. Many investigators not only insist on including performance in studies as a way to derive results that have management applications, but performance tends to be defined narrowly, depending to a large extent on accounting figures like return on investment (ROI). This masks the very complex nature of organizational performance and leads us to oversimplify not only what it is but how it is achieved. Taken together, dependence on precisely measured variables like ROI and the insistence that this measure has implications for improving firm performance severely restrict the range of problems that strategy researchers can concern themselves with.

IMPLICATIONS FOR STRATEGIC MANAGEMENT

Critical Problems

Each of the points of comparison in table 4–1 carries with it specific concerns about the fate of strategy research. Convergence on an assumption set leads to a single-voice consensus that cannot easily recognize or explain novel events. Furthermore, philosophical solidarity stands in the way of cultivating new theoretical perspectives like those seen in organization theory and behavioral accounting journals. Ultimately, with norms about methodology and a performance orientation dominating, strategic management will further entrench itself, making it increasingly difficult for scholars outside the accepted norms to be heard.

It would be overstatement to argue that the strategic management paradigm has encased and encrusted the policy field. Scholars outside the normal science tradition can still command attention and in many cases have been extremely influential. Research into strategy process by Henry Mintzberg, James Brian Quinn, and Robert Burgelman, for example, has not converged onto a single assumption set. But, while other strategy researchers acknowledge the value of these contributions, most continue to cling to the normal science view of the field, pursuing their own research programs and training their students to keep the faith.

Attachment to the strategic management assumption set has in real ways obscured theoretical possibilities and possible breakthroughs. For instance, if the assumption that strategies are adopted to improve firm performance was dropped, powerful alternative explanations might be forged. Consider the merger movement of the 1970s. Strategists have generally presumed that corporations bought other corporations as a logical way to improve bottom-line profits or to reduce risk. An alternative explanation from an institutional perspective might show that corporations merge to mimic other firms, or because it is a legitimating activity. Managers might be less concerned with corporate profits than with joining the corporate bandwagon and looking good. Such a perspective is plausible, perhaps even preferable, to a more rational, positivist explanation, but such interpretations are unlikely to appear in strategy-oriented journals because of the field's devotion to its paradigm.

Dominance of method and dominance of performance-orientation drive out theoretical understanding even more and make it hard for new knowledge to accumulate in strategic management. This process is illustrated in figure 4–2. In the top half of the figure, X_1 to X_4 represent variables in a study, and ROI is a performance variable with which the Xs are expected to be linked. A typical study would identify these variables, measure them, and run correlations or regressions to see which variables predict ROI. Implicit in this model of research is the idea that performance measured by ROI is the key dependent variable and that the independent variables are observable and measurable in large enough numbers that the statistical techniques applied will produce valid and reliable results. Theoretical interpretations of the discovered relationships can be developed to justify and explain what was found.

Figure 4-2. Normative Versus Theory-Building Research Approaches.

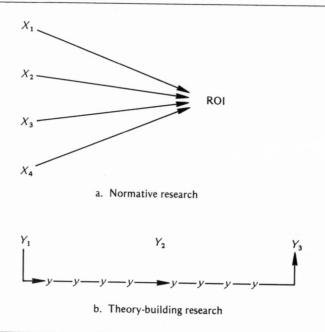

a. Normative research

b. Theory-building research

The lower part of figure 4–2 illustrates a study designed to facilitate theoretical understanding when the relationships among the variables are theory-based. The purpose is to unravel cause-effect explanations among variables. For example, Y_1 in figure 4–2 could be a personality characteristic, such as the desire to control others. Variable Y_2 might represent the strategy that is adopted by the organization, and Y_3 could be an outcome variable, such as return on investment. To fully understand the relationship between Y_1 and Y_2, there are a series of small intervening linkages that connect these two variables. For example, the personality of an individual might determine how he receives information, and perhaps the kind of people hired in other parts of the organization. These concepts link together to explain how the organization develops the strategy, which is Y_2, and provides the theoretical explanation for the relationship between Y_1 and Y_2. Then from Y_2 there is another set of linkages explaining how a specific strategy is implemented in the organization and how that process ultimately translates into performance, Y_3.

A theory-based study unravels these linkages. A theory-based study takes phenomena apart and tells the story about the intervening variables and processes that explain what is happening in the organization. For example, Paul Anderson's (1983) study of decision making is the kind of research that built new theory. Armed with the standard theoretical explanation of organizational decision making, Anderson reviewed and analyzed the archival documents from the Cuban Missile Crisis. Some of the theory adequately described the patterns he observed, but deviations cropped up that the theory did not predict. After unraveling the story, Anderson was able to develop an alternative characterization of the decision making task that emphasized sequential choice, goal discovery, and the avoidance of failure. Anderson's study, though it focused on only one organization, added to theoretical understanding because it illuminated the linkage between Y_1 and Y_2. We now have new insights about how the complexities of the task environment affect organizational decision making.

We do not mean to imply that all research should be done as in-depth studies of small samples. The key is the role of theory. As a practical matter, an investigator can never measure all intervening variables, so theory-building relies on conjecture and a willingness to speculate beyond the data. Indeed, scientific discovery is not the correlation between variables and ROI, but the support or rejection of the theoretical explanation of how and why variables are related to one another. Even more important, we could omit Y_3, the performance variable in figure 4–2, because there is no need to study performance to make a contribution to knowledge. If we just look at Y_1 and Y_2, the relationship between managerial control and the company strategy, and if we really understand the intervening linkages, these findings would have practical value and implications for managers. For example, we could explain why management style and strategy are linked. Although the purpose of the research is new knowledge rather than management application, fully understanding the phenomenon would have practical value for managers. Indeed, the theory-building approach often ends up having more practical value for managers because it yields a deeper explanation than does the research approach of gathering data and correlating variables with ROI performance.

Troubling Paradoxes

Strategic management's paradigm, with its convergence on a single set of assumptions, on methodological concerns, and on practical applications, leaves its adherents facing two paradoxes. First, *the attempt to provide useful information to managers and to use performance as an outcome variable actually prevents the field of strategic management from providing useful information to managers.* The heart of research is the development of models and frameworks that explain how organizations work. ROI and other performance variables do not have to be a part of that development. Yet this is not generally recognized and accepted in strategic management. We believe that scholars who ignore performance measures in favor of building new theory will continue to have a difficult time getting their work published in strategic management and will be little more than isolated voices in the field.

The second paradox is that *the attempt to be scientific in the field of strategic management actually leads to less new knowledge.* As suggested earlier, adoption of normal science produces inflexibility, bureaucratization of techniques, and methodological pretension. The desire to be scientific in strategic management has meant that most often only quantitative variables are measured. Those variables are analyzed with sophisticated statistical procedures, but the contribution is predictable. Lack of robust theory development leads to studies that fail to probe into deeper aspects of the phenomenon and thus fail to provide insight into how organizations work. The more the field embraces a single assumption set and the louder the insistence on rigid, quantitative procedures, the more likely it is that studies will fail to produce breakthroughs. Furthermore, the insistence that research be tied to organizational performance builds an even higher wall that blocks investigators from discovery or developing new theoretical understanding. The train moves faster and gets closer and closer to nowhere.

REDIRECTING STRATEGIC MANAGEMENT

Like doomsayers, we have taken the pessimistic position that strategic management is riding a fast train to nowhere. We base this judgment on a number of related observations that for the most part revolve around the premature adoption of the accoutrements of normal science. Rationalizing research procedures has sped the pace of strategy research much like rationalizing production processes can quicken the tempo of manufacturing. But new problems are created in the process. Restricting underlying assumptions leads to a single mind-set and reduces competition among ideas, while the emphasis on scientific procedures inhibits the drive for theoretical understanding. Moreover, the emphasis on issues of practical value to managers and on performance criteria restricts the range of phenomena that can be studied and the opportunity to find new theoretical solutions.

Why Is It So?

Though we have been critical of the strategic management paradigm and the effect it has had on the policy field, we cannot parcel out blame. A paradigm is attractive to scholars. It replaces seemingly haphazard research with a goal and a plan. Embracing a paradigm brings legitimacy and security. Colleagues can communicate with each other more clearly and with less likelihood of misunderstanding. Standards of achievement are more easily agreed upon, and thus are more recognizable and more easily rewarded. The desire to adopt quantitative measures and to develop management applications is equally attractive. What researcher can ignore a large and agreeable audience, especially when it is so easy to say, "Since resources are scarce, we must measure performance. We have to understand performance because that is what really counts in organizations."

Just because a research program is efficient and popular does not mean the field is advancing. We have pointed out how prematurely convergent thinking may stymie progress by restricting acceptable research topics and procedures. This is not easily correctable, however, because of another danger. Devotion to a normal science also creates an artificial self-conception. The focus on solving the puzzles of the paradigm directs attention away from external concerns. The discipline adopts an internal and necessarily conservative view, leading to a sense of self-absorption. This tendency deemphasizes understanding so as to concentrate on well-intended self-preservation, advancement, and propagation. As Kuhn (1962: 52) said, "Normal science does not aim at novelties of fact or theory and, when successful, finds none." As long as strategic management views its paradigm as unproblematic, it will probably continue down its current path. Meanwhile, journals, books, and curricula dedicated to strategic management are likely to become increasingly narrow, reinforcing the popular view.

Prospects for Change

Recognizing these tendencies in strategy research makes us uneasy, but hopeful. These feelings must be akin to those experienced by Mills (1959) over thirty years ago, when he wrote with candor and hope of the flaws and the promise of social science research. Like us, Mills saw a field being distorted by overenthusiastic devotion to the scientific trappings of the profession rather than to basic learning and understanding. He urged that scholars cultivate a sociological imagination to combat the morass. His explanation seems prophetic for strategic management:

> It is not only information that they need—in this Age of Fact, information often dominates their attention and overwhelms their capacity to assimilate it. It is not only the skills of reason that they need. . . . What they need is a quality of mind that will help them to use information and to develop reason to achieve lucid summation of what is going on in the world and of what may be happening within themselves. It is this quality . . . that may be called the sociological imagination (Mills 1959: 5).

For Mills, possessing a sociological imagination avoids the blindness of empirical data without theory and the emptiness of theory without data. More importantly, the sociological imagination gave rise to intellectual pivots: the capacity to shift from one perspective to another, and to see the relations between the two.

Can a sociological imagination have meaning for modern strategy research? And if so, does cultivating a strategy imagination mean abandoning the current paradigm? In answer to the first, we believe that the quality of mind that Mills suggests does have a place in strategic management. What he experienced as the Age of Fact has been technologically transformed into an Age of Information, creating an even greater flow of data to overwhelm our senses. Little training is required to write and mail out a questionnaire that may contain 100 or more variables. Computer hardware and software give even statistically untutored researchers the ability to generate reams of printouts analyzing any batch of data. Now more than ever we need the intellectual sensibility to grow beyond these data-based techniques to find the lessons from our research. This is especially true in strategic management, where convergent thinking has the potential to drive out theoretical understanding on many fronts.

But is imagination compatible with normal science? Kuhn himself wrestled with this question. His thesis in *The Structure of Scientific Revolution* implies a negative answer. Normal science cannot support the conflict that will produce new and pivotal intellectual positions. Researchers doing normal science would not willingly recognize competing schools of thought. For Kuhn, then, scientific revolution—and the ultimate crushing of the old paradigm—originated outside the field. Scholars outside the accepted tradition eventually produce enough anomalies that the old tradition shatters.

Kuhn attracted criticism for his pessimistic prediction about the fate of normal science and later tempered it. In a series of essays, collected under the title of *The Essential Tension*, Kuhn (1977) arrived at a conclusion much like the one Mills came to. First, citing Selye, he wrote that the basic scientist "must lack prejudice to a degree that he can look at the most self-evident facts or concepts without necessarily accepting them, and conversely, allow his imagination to play with the most unlikely possibilities" (p. 226). He then hailed the ability to support an occasionally almost unbearable tension between convergent and divergent thinking as the prime requisite for the very best sort of scientific research. Without it, he declared, science quickly turns to scientism. There must, he decided, be room in the professional group for both the traditionalist and the iconoclast, so that normal science's net of commitment does not turn to stone, but instead can be transformed or traded for another.

An Agenda for Change

The message to strategists, individually and as a professional group, is clear. Your responsibility is to take control of the runaway train. The future has not been sealed, but devotion to current practice must be tempered. Your grip on what is comforting, but potentially unproductive, can be loosened. Easy answers, though, are not available. Our remaining comments, based on remarks by Mills, by Kuhn, and from our own experiences and beliefs, offer suggestions about what is possible.

Encourage Diversity in Thinking and Research. The formulation and implementation of strategies across an almost infinite variety of organizations is too complicated a problem for any researcher to digest. Strategic management can mean many things, depending on what you want to find and the techniques used for investigation. A single assumption set or research method will inform us only of a narrow reality, and hence will provide an incomplete image of strategic management. Following a single paradigm means that many ideas will never be debated.

Strategic management is sufficiently complex to support several paths of inquiry. The challenge is to embrace diverse methods that will find several strategic management realities (Daft 1980). Imagine an opera in which the chorus, singing in unison, drowns out the soloist, the harmonic melodies, and the descant voices. The auditorium would be full of sound, even lovely sound, but the recital would not be as bold, as interesting, as enrapturing as when the contrast and blend of voices are heard. Avoiding the voice of a single paradigm means encouraging multiple theories, multiple methods, and multiple data sources. For strategic management researchers this means giving value to well-done LISREL analyses and qualitative case studies alike.

Seek Interesting Comparisons. By sharing and comparing ideas with those of colleagues outside the main paradigm, with scholars trained in other disciplines, and, yes, with practicing managers, strategic management can broaden its perspective. The boundary around the strategic management paradigm should not be a psychic prison. The boundary can be fluid, changing, and interpenetrating with other fields.

Another way to seek comparison is for scholars to consider the extremes of the topic of interest. If successful firms are the topic, also study failures. Contrasting objects and concepts helps one grasp the material and sort out key dimensions for comparison. Similarly, compare cross-sectional findings with the passage of time. People, ideas, and organizations are not isolated fragments. Any comparison that helps provide a context for interpretation will necessarily help build new and interesting theories about strategic management.

Focus on Theory Building.   As we said when we began, enthusiasm and interest in strategy research have increased enormously since the adoption of strategic management as a paradigm. The energy pouring into strategic management research can be harnessed by continuing to do empirical research with the powerful and elegant tools at hand. But these powerful tools do not substitute for theory. Indeed, theoretical storytelling is an essential overlay to give the data meaning (Daft 1983). Theories explain why. The "why" is most important, and researchers should be creative and ruthless in pursuit of it (Weick 1974). The why, not the data, is the contribution to knowledge. Theories broaden and deepen empirical studies to test and inform broader conceptions and assumptions. Focusing energy on theory building as well as empirical research has the potential to move the field ahead by significant leaps.

Cultivate an Active Mind.   This advice derives both from Mills's suggestion that imagination is essential and from Kuhn's concern with balancing the dual tension of convergent and divergent thinking. An active mind does not fear alternative perspectives but can move gracefully between them. Such a scholar is playful, curious, and perhaps enigmatic. This scholar has a fierce drive to make sense of the world.

To cultivate an active mind, individuals must read and study theoretical perspectives and be prepared to tell stories about the data. Scholars with active minds balance technical skills with storytelling, and skepticism with trust. They recognize simple observation and personal experience as important sources of original intellectual contributions. Such scholars shuttle between ideas and facts, and back to ideas, and again back to figures, and to frameworks, and back to ideas again. Above all, the scholar with an active mind never assumes that someone else, somewhere at some time, will place his or her work in the larger theoretical perspective. This the scholar with an active mind does himself.

Develop the Craft of Scholarship.   The strategic management discipline is not routine enough to prosper under a rigid set of procedures. Craftsmanship means avoiding fads of method and technique and expressing ideas clearly. The research craft means getting beyond written prescriptions for performing research. Method can be taught from a textbook, as can composition and public speaking. Crafts-manship, including the ability to build in room for error and sur-prise, storytelling, and making nonlinear, intuitive decisions, cannot (Daft 1983).

CONCLUSION

Perhaps the most important conclusion to be drawn from this chap-ter is an idea suggested by Boulding (1956) about scientific progress. Strategic management scholars can avoid accepting a level of re-search analysis too far below the complexity of the empirical world being investigated. The field must not shut the door on problems that do not fit easily into simple, mechanical approaches to research. For all the progress in developing a paradigm over the last few years, premature convergence onto a single assumption set, premature rationalization of research methods, and premature expectations for normative outcomes are restricting rather than enhancing theoretical insights. Although the field seems to be on a fast train, it still has a very long way to go.

REFERENCES

Anderson, P. A. 1983. "Decision Making by Objection and the Cuban Missile Crisis." *Administrative Science Quarterly* 28, no. 2 (June): 201–222.

Barley, S. R. 1986. "Technology as an Occasion for Structuring: Evidence from Observations of CT Scanners and the Social Order of Radiology Depart-ments." *Administrative Science Quarterly* 31, no. 1 (March): 78–108.

Blau, P. M. 1970. "A Formal Theory of Differentiation in Organizations." *American Sociological Review* 35, no. 2 (April): 201–218.

Boulding, K. E. 1956. "General Systems Theory: The Skeleton of a Science." *Management Science* 2, no. 3 (April): 197–207.

Burrell, G., and G. Morgan. 1979. *Sociological Paradigms and Organizational Analysis.* London: Heinemann.

Daft, R. L. 1980. "The Evolution of Organizational Analysis in *ASQ*, 1959–1979." *Administrative Science Quarterly* 25, no. 3 (December): 557–727.

_____. 1983. "Learning the Craft of Organizational Research." *Academy of Management Review* 8, no. 4 (October): 539–546.

_____, and Norman B. Macintosh. 1984. "The Nature and Use of Formal Con-trol Systems for Management Control and Strategy Implementation." *Journal of Management* 10, no. 1 (Spring): 43–66.

Gouldner, A. W. 1954. *Wildcat Strike: A Study in Worker-Management Relationships.* New York: Antioch Press.

Hage, J., and M. Aiken. 1967. "Relationship of Centralization to Other Structural Properties." *Administrative Science Quarterly* 12, no. 1 (March): 72–92.

Kuhn, T. S. 1962. *The Structure of Scientific Revolution.* Chicago: University of Chicago Press.

_____. 1977. *The Essential Tension: Selected Studies in Scientific Tradition and Change.* Chicago: University of Chicago Press.

Mills, C. W. 1959. *The Sociological Imagination.* New York: Oxford University Press.

Ranson, S., R. Hinings, and R. Greenwood. 1980. "The Structuring of Organizational Structures." *Administrative Science Quarterly* 25, no. 1 (March): 1–17.

Schendel, D. E., and C. W. Hofer, eds. 1979. *Strategic Management: A New View of Business Policy and Planning.* Boston: Little, Brown and Company.

Selye, H. 1964. *From Dream to Discovery: On Being a Scientist.* New York: McGraw-Hill Book Company.

Tannenbaum, A. S. 1968. *Control in Organizations.* New York: McGraw-Hill Book Company.

Weick, K. E. 1974. "Amendments to Organizational Theorizing." *Academy of Management Journal* 17, no. 3 (September): 487–502.

STRATEGY FORMATION
Schools of Thought

Henry Mintzberg

THE STRATEGY FORMATION BEAST

A fable to begin, often referred to, seldom known:

The Blind Men and the Elephant

It was six men of Indostan
To learning much inclined,
Who went to see the Elephant
(Though all of them were blind)
That each by observation
Might satisfy his mind.

The First approached the Elephant,
And happening to fall
Against his broad and sturdy side,
At once began to brawl:
"God bless me but the Elephant
Is very like a wall."

The Second, feeling of the tusk,
Cried, "Ho! What have we here
So very round and smooth and sharp?
To me 'tis mighty clear
This wonder of an Elephant
Is very like a spear!"

105

The Third approached the animal,
And happening to take
The squirming trunk within his hands,
Thus boldly up and spake:
"I see," quoth he, "The Elephant
Is very like a snake!"

The Fourth reached out an eager hand,
And felt around the knee,
"What most this wondrous beast is like
Is mighty plain," quoth he;
"'tis clear enough the Elephant
Is very like a tree!"

The Fifth who chanced to touch the ear,
Said: "E'en the blindest man
Can tell what this resembles most;
Deny the fact who can,
This marvel of an Elephant
Is very like a fan!"

The Sixth no sooner had begun
About the beast to grope,
Than, seizing on the swinging tail
That fell within his scope,
"I see," quoth he, "the Elephant
is very like a rope!"

And so these men of Indostan
Disputed loud and long,
Each of his own opinion
Exceeding stiff and strong,
Though each was partly in the right,
And all were in the wrong!

Moral

So oft in theologic wars,
The disputants, I ween,
Rail on in utter ignorance
Of what each other mean,
And prate about an Elephant
Not one of them has seen!

John Godfrey Saxe (1816–1887)

We are the blind men and strategy formation is our elephant. Since no one has had the vision to see the entire beast, everyone has grabbed hold of some part or other and "railed on in utter ignorance" about the rest. Robert Ornstein (1975: 10), in the *Psychology of Consciousness*, has concluded that we do not make an elephant simply by adding together all its parts. An elephant is more than that. Yet we also need to understand the parts to comprehend the whole.

This chapter describes the parts of the strategy formation beast—at least as they have been delineated in the literature—and thereby seeks to extract key dimensions and issues that underlie the process. The discussion is intended to provide a framework for considering how strategies actually form in specific situations.

In his colorful article, "The Magic Number Seven, Plus or Minus Two: Some Limits on Our Capacity for Processing Information," psychologist George Miller (1956) argues that categorization schemes tend to revolve around the number seven because of our cognitive makeup: Seven is about how many "chunks" of information we can comfortably retain in our short-term memories.[1] Three wonders of the world would fall a little flat, so to speak, while eighteen would be daunting. But those of us interested in strategy are, of course, no ordinary mortals—at least in terms of our cognitive capacity—and so should be able to comprehend, say, one more than the magic number seven plus two. Accordingly, this chapter outlines ten schools of thought on strategy formation.

Cognition aside, in reviewing a large body of literature, ten distinct points of view really did emerge. And each had a unique perspective that focused, like each of the blind men, on one major aspect of the strategy formation process. Each is in one sense narrow and overstated, yet in another interesting and helpful. An elephant may not *be* a trunk, but it certainly *has* a trunk, and it would be difficult to understand elephants without reference to trunks. In a sense, the handicap of blindness does have an advantage, imposing a certain concentration that can be insightful. Of course, none of these schools of thought captures all of strategy formation. In fact, each is presented here from its own limited perspective, as something of a caricature, and then critiqued, consistent with the theme of this volume, to extract both its limitations and its contributions. In conclusion, some integrating comments are offered on how these schools of thought developed over time, how they interrelate, where they seem to be taking the field of strategic management, and where they should take it. A fuller integration of these schools must await a more intensive consideration of the empirical research in its own terms, which is well beyond the scope of this chapter (which is long enough!).[2] The ten schools are listed below:

The *Design* School: strategy formation as a *conceptual* process
The *Planning* School: strategy formation as a *formal* process
The *Positioning* School: strategy formation as an *analytical* process
The *Entrepreneurial* School: strategy formation as a *visionary* process
The *Cognitive* School: strategy formation as a *mental* process
The *Learning* School: strategy formation as an *emergent* process
The *Political* School: strategy formation as a *power* process
The *Cultural* School: strategy formation as an *ideological* process
The *Environmental* School: strategy formation as a *passive* process
The *Configurational* School: strategy formation as an *episodic* process

These schools fall into three groupings. The first three are *prescriptive* in nature—more concerned with how strategies *should* be formulated than with how they necessarily *do* form. The first of these, which described in the 1960s the basic framework that underlies the other two, focuses on strategy formation as a process of informal *design*, essentially one of conception. The second school, which developed in parallel in the 1960s and peaked in a flurry of publications in the 1970s, formalized that perspective, describing strategy formation as a more detached and systematic process of formal *planning.* That school has been displaced more recently by the third prescriptive school, less concerned with the process of strategy formation per se than with the actual content of strategies. It is referred to as the *positioning* school because it focuses on the selection of strategic positions considered generically, in specific contexts also considered genetically.

The six schools that follow focus on specific aspects of the process of strategy formation and are concerned less with prescribing ideal strategic behavior than with describing how strategies do, in fact, get made. The first of these schools reflects a recurring theme in the literature, where strategy formation is viewed as an *entrepreneurial* process and strategy is associated with the vision of the leader. But if strategy can be personalized vision, then strategy formation also can be understood as the process of concept attainment in a single mind; accordingly, a small but important *cognitive* school has developed that seeks to enter the strategist's mind by extracting the messages of cognitive psychology.

Each of the four schools that follow seeks to open up the process of strategy formation beyond the individual and his or her cognition, to other forces and other actors. To writers of what is called here the *learning* school, the world is too complex to allow strategies to be developed all at once as clear plans or visions; hence strategies must emerge in small steps, as the organization adapts or "learns." Similar to this, but with a different twist, is the *political* school, which describes strategy formation as a process of exploiting power, whether by groups in a conflictive process within organizations or by organizations themselves with regard to their external environments. In contrast to this is another school of thought that considers the process to be rooted in the *culture* of the organization and thereby depicts it as one that is fundamentally collective and cooperative. And then there are the proponents of an *environmental* school, organization theorists who believe that strategy formation is a passive process and that power over it rests not in the organization but in its environment. Accordingly, they focus their attention on the power and the nature of environments that surround organizations.

The final group contains but one school, although it could be argued that this school really combines the others into a single perspective—that of *configuration*. Writers of this school, in efforts to be integrative, cluster the elements and behaviors of organizations—strategy-making processes, content of strategies, and structures and/or contexts—at distinct stages or episodes in their histories, sometimes sequenced over time in life cycle models.[3]

The schools identified here have appeared at different stages of the history of strategic management and business policy. Some have already peaked and declined, others are growing in prominence, and several have endured as thin (but nonetheless significant) trickles. We shall describe each in turn, and provide our interpretation and critique of its development and difficulties, before concluding with our final integrative comments.

Before proceeding, a word on the data base of this chapter is in order. It should be emphasized that what follows is largely a review of literature *in its own terms*, without effort to integrate the messages of its empirical content or of its conceptual insights. The literature reviewed is vast—a bibliography of the items already considered numbers 1,495, and it grows larger every day. Viewed narrowly, in terms of the field of strategic management itself, the literature is not all that large, although it is growing very rapidly. But taking strategy formation in its broadest sense—as systems of collective social action set direction and change it—opens up a huge array of literature.

Starbuck (1965: 468) has written that to discuss "all aspects of organization which are relevant to adaptation . . . means . . . that one could legitimately discuss everything that has been written about organizations." This comment in fact underestimates the problem because the last word in the quotation should not read "organizations" but "collective systems of all kinds." What biologists write about the adaptation of species (for example, "punctuated equilibrium") can have relevance for understanding the pace of strategic change, as well as for understanding strategy as position ("niche"); what historians conclude about periods in the development of societies (such as "revolution") can help explain different stages in the development of organizational strategies (for example, "turnaround" as a form of "cultural revolution"; see Firsirotu 1985); physicists' descriptions of quantum mechanics and mathematicians' theories of catastrophy may provide insights into how organizations change; and so on. Add to this the nonmanagement literature more commonly recognized as relevant to the study of organizations—psychologists who study human cognition and leader charisma, anthropologists who study societal cultures, economists who study industrial organization and entrepreneurship, urban planners who study formal planning processes, political scientists who study public policy-making, military historians who study strategies of conflict—and the result is an enormous body of literature capable of rendering fascinating insights. At the limit, strategy formation is not just about values and vision, PIMS and product life cycles, but also about the military and the Moonies, crisis and commitment, organizational learning and punctuated equilibrium, industrial organization and social revolution.[4]

THE DESIGN SCHOOL:
STRATEGY FORMATION AS
A CONCEPTUAL PROCESS

The most deeply rooted view of the strategy formation process—because of its popularity as the base of the traditional MBA policy course as well as a good deal of conventional writing and consulting—is as a process of information conception, the use of a few essential concepts by a leader to design "grand strategy." The basic model need not be dwelt on here—SWOT (strengths, weaknesses, opportunities, trends) is well known; our rendition of it, similar to others, is presented in figure 5–1. The most essential concept of the model is that of congruence or fit. In the words of this school's best-known proponents, "Economic strategy will be seen as the match between qualifications and opportunity that positions a firm in its environment" (Christensen, Andrews, Bower, Hamermesh, and Porter 1982: 164). "Capture success" seems to be the motto of the design school.

The design school has generally been associated with the general management group at the Harvard Business School, especially in Christensen et al. (1982), whose text material, first published in 1965, has generally been attributed to Kenneth Andrews (see also Andrews 1971, 1980, 1987). But claims that this school of thought, or even that the concept of business strategy itself, originated with this group at Harvard (Bower 1986: vii), do not hold up to scrutiny.[5]

In fact, some of the most important concepts of this school seem to have appeared in print for the first time in Philip Selznick's book, *Leadership in Administration* in 1957. There he introduced the notion of "distinctive competence" (1957: 42–56), discussed the need to bring together the organization's "internal state" with its "external expectations" (1957: 67–74), and discussed building "policy into the organization's social structure" (1957: 91–107), which later came to be called implementation. Selznick also wrote of "what the organization can do and to some extent what it must do" (1957: 62), reminiscent of Andrews' later words of "what a company might do . . . [and] can do," "want to do," and "should do" (Learned et al. 1965: 20, 21). Selznick did not use the word *strategy*, but Alfred Chandler, while at MIT, popularized it in the business literature in his 1962 book *Strategy and Structure*.

Figure 5-1. Basic Design School Model.

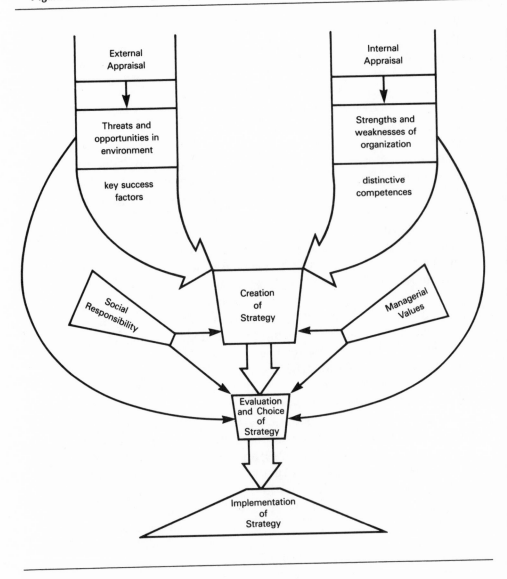

It was probably William Newman of the Columbia University Business School who first used the word strategy in the management literature in the contemporary sense, in the 1951 edition of his textbook (1951: iii, 110–118). Newman's subsequent textbooks with his various coauthors (Newman, Summer, and Warren 1967; Newman, Warren, and Schnee 1982) belong to this school (with elements of the planning school), as does the Tregoe and Zimmerman book *Top Management Strategy* (1980) and Ohmae's *The Mind of the Strategist* (1982). The recent troubles of the planning school (to be discussed later) have driven a number of practitioners back to the design school view of the process (for example, Gluck et al. 1980), although they have tended to present it as some new discovery rather than a fallback to the ideas of the 1960s.

Premises of the Design School

A number of basic premises underlie the design school, some fully evident, others only implicitly recognized (sometimes to this school's detriment). Seven are listed below (together with supporting references to the Andrews text):

1. *Strategy formation should be a controlled, conscious process of thought* (Christensen et al. 1982: 94, 543). Strategies should be developed neither intuitively nor in emergent fashion, but through a conscious, deliberate process based on formal training (1982: 6, 185).
2. *Responsibility for that control and consciousness must rest with the chief executive officer: that person is THE strategist* (1982: 3, 19, 545). "Architect" of strategy is a favorite expression in this school (1982: 361); see this characterization of the design school by Zand (1981: 125).
3. *The model of strategy formation must be kept simple and informal; elaboration will kill it* (1982: 12, 14). Andrews in fact prefers the label "imposing idea" to "model" (1982: 12); Rumelt calls it "a set of constructs" (1984: 558).
4. *Strategies should be unique; the best ones result from a process of creative design* (1982: 107, 186, 187). Hofer and Schendel refer to this as the "situational philosophy" (1978: 203), Evered

to strategy "more as a fluid to be worked than a theory to be actualized" (1981: 11).

5. *Strategies emerge from this design process full-blown.* Andrews frequently refers to "choice" of strategy or to "decision" (e.g., 1982: xiv). The view is, in a sense, biblical—of grand strategy. Hence our characterization of the process as one of conception!

6. *These strategies should be made explicit and, if possible, articulated, which means they have to be kept simple* (1982: 105–106, 554, 835).

7. *Finally, only after these unique, full-blown, explicit, and simple strategies are fully formulated can they then be implemented* (1982: 543, 551).[6]

Critique of the Design School

The design school may be critiqued on a number of grounds. For example, one could argue that it has not adapted to new findings on incremental aspects of the strategy-making process (Quinn 1980) or on the roles of other actors (Burgelman 1983a, 1983b, 1983c). Indeed, Andrews virtually dismissed all other theory or research as of no or little use (in Learned et al. 1965: 6; Christensen et al. 1982: 6, 554).[7]

But a criticism more to the point concerns the relevance of the model itself: not that it has gone out of *date* but that it could go out of *context.* Clearly, there are times when organizations need to use something akin to the design school approach: to assess centrally their strengths and weaknesses and match them to external threats and opportunities in order to design full-blown strategies that can be implemented. More broadly, even as Andrews would argue, this "informing idea" could well underlie a good deal more of strategic thinking. The question remains, however, whether the model or its underlying concepts are in some situations inappropriate or indeed dysfunctional. We proceed to answer this in the affirmative, particularly when organizations must engage in a learning process to develop their strategies.

Consider the step of assessing strengths and weaknesses. The assumption of the design school is that an organization can know its distinctive competences by conscious thought. One gets the image of a group of executives sitting in a room and talking, much as do students in a case study classroom. It is assumed that strengths and weaknesses can somehow be known *in general*. Yet there is a good deal of evidence, especially with respect to diversification activities (e.g., Miles 1982; Quinn 1980: 26; Mintzberg and Waters 1982: 489), that coming to know this must often constitute a learning process, that an organization can really know its capabilities only by testing them, which suggests also that these capabilities *may be distinctive to time, even to specific application* (see Lenz 1980 and Radosevich 1974: 360). A survey by Stevenson has indicated that managers do not generally agree on what are strengths and weaknesses; indeed one manager dismissed such an appraisal as an "academic exercise" whose "only real value . . . comes in the light of a specific deal" (1976: 65).

Likewise, consider the dichotomy of formulation and implementation, which by separating thinking from acting impedes the development of strategy as a learning process. The implication that thinking stops when the strategy is decided on—at least the broad thinking of the senior management, once an articulated strategy has been handed over to others for implementation—discourages adaptation *of* the strategy (as opposed to *within* the strategy). The high failure rate of deliberate strategies has generally been attributed to problems of implementation (e.g., Kiechel 1984: 8). This has resulted in a growing literature on the subject, both in business (Hrebiniak and Joyce 1984) and in the public sector (Majone and Wildavsky 1978: 105; Kress et al. 1980; Lipsky 1978), where labels such as "policy slippage" and "drift" have been coined. But this may only block recognition that the blame more typically belongs not in implementation, not even back in formulation itself, but in the very fact of having separated the two, and so impeding the natural processes of learning in an organization. Like strengths and weaknesses, environments, when they are diverse, complex, and undergoing unexpected changes, cannot easily be known in advance, especially not at central places atop organizational hierarchies.

Similarly, contrary to what Chandler argued in 1962, structure must no more follow strategy than the left foot must follow the right in walking. In other words, structure always follows and responds to the existing strategy no more than strategy always follows and responds to the existing structure (as Chandler himself showed). Indeed, what is the assessment of strengths and weaknesses in the design school model but the consideration of the impact of existing structure on the proposed strategy?

Finally, having to make strategy explicit promotes inflexibility, since the more clearly a direction is articulated, the more difficult it is to change. This has even been demonstrated in the psychologists' laboratory with regard to the thinking of a single individual (Kieser 1971).

To conclude this critique, we wish to draw attention to the relationship between the design school model and the case study method. Surely the convenient fit between the two is not coincidental, given that the model has been most vigorously promoted by case study teachers. The assumption that a central strategist can be fully informed is reminiscent of the twenty-page case as the data base for class discussion; the assumption that the world stands still during implementation corresponds to the case as a static document; the assumption of the separation between formulation and implementation reflects the fact that one is convenient in a classroom of conscious thought while the other is not possible.

But what are the consequences of training managers in this way? What does it do to expect people to become instant experts on complex organizations by reading short documents twice a week? What is the effect of having to decide in eighty minutes of classroom discussion the nature of a complex industry, the distinctive competences of a complicated organization, and the strategy it should pursue? If the case study method, based on the design school model,[8] encourages future leaders to oversimplify strategy, it gives them the impression that "if you give me a synopsis, I'll give you strategy." If it denies that strategy formation is a long, subtle, and difficult process based on deep understanding, if it encourages managers to detach thinking from acting, remaining in their offices waiting for pithy reports instead of getting outside where the real information for strategy making usually has to be dug out, then it may have done a major disservice to organizations and to society.

Context and Contribution of the Design School

Our conclusion about the design school is not that the model is wrong but only that it has limited applicability. The proponents of this school should have heeded their own prescription about fit. To use this model, an organization must be simple enough to be understood fully in one central place, and it must exist in a situation stable or predictable enough to enable it to settle on a clear strategy that will be viable well beyond the period of implementation. We believe this best describes structures we have called machine bureaucracy (Mintzberg 1979), which can best use the model during periods we call *reconception*—coming out of a time of contextual change into one of new stability.

This school is not, however, only a model; it is also a set of concepts. And a number of these, such as distinctive competence and fit, have done well to infuse strategic management. In other words, the major contribution of the design school may well turn out to be not a model that has limited applicability but a vocabulary that has helped to inform a good deal of strategic thinking.

THE PLANNING SCHOOL: STRATEGY FORMATION AS A FORMAL PROCESS

The planning school developed in parallel with the design school—its most influential early book, *Corporate Strategy* by Igor Ansoff, was also published in 1965—but its fortunes followed a rather different course. It grew to dominate the field in the 1970s before major setbacks seriously undermined it. Today, while hardly absent, it is barely a shadow of its former influence. Its problem was that quantitatively the "strategic planning" literature developed extensively but qualitatively it developed hardly at all. One basic set of ideas, almost trivial in concept and rooted in the design school model, was repeated in this literature in endless variety.

When not propagating these ideas, planning theorists wrote endlessly about organizations having to engage in planning, as some kind of imperative, or about the "pitfalls" that impeded them from doing so—above all, that senior managers were not giving strategic planning the attention it deserved. Seldom was the possibility entertained that these managers might have been giving it more than it deserved. To many writers, planning became not just an approach to strategy formation but a virtual religion to be promulgated with the fervor of missionaries. Correspondingly, hardly any empirical research was undertaken in this school—few of its proponents bothered to find out how planning really worked in practice. Lorange, who attempted "to survey the empirically based research literature on long range formal planning processes for corporate strategy" (1979: 226), cites less than thirty empirical studies, almost all questionnaire surveys from a distance, many of which set out to prove that planning paid, although collectively they never did. The few in-depth studies of planning, almost never conducted by people associated with this school of thought, uncovered major failings of the model and its underlying premises, as we shall soon see.

Premises of the Planning School

The planning school accepted most of the premises of the design school, save one and a half. But these made all the difference. First, the model was the same, but its execution was prescribed to be highly formal, at the limit almost mechanical. Thus, the simple, informal model of the design school became an elaborated sequence of steps, each comprising all kinds of checklists and techniques. The summary figure of the Ansoff model (1965: 202–203) contains fifty-seven boxes. Thus, decomposition based on rationality in the narrow sense drove a generation of writers. Underlying the whole exercise was the machine assumption: Produce each of the components as specified, assemble them according to the blueprint, and the desired end product (in this case strategy) will result. In other words, analysis will provide synthesis, or as Jelinek (1979) put it in her study of planning at Texas Instruments, "innovation" can be "institutionalized."

As for the *half* premise, the CEO was to remain the architect of strategy, in principle. But in the planning school this architect did not design the plans so much as approve them. For along with planning came the planners, no more than staff advisors, mind you, but in much of the prescribed practice *the* major players in the process. See for example, Pennington's guidelines to planners, including "involve top management at key points, only at key points," such as four days per year in one steel company (1972: 3).

The emphasis of this school on decomposition meant that the most operational steps received the attention. Thus, while almost nothing was written about where strategies actually come from (some models literally presented boxes with labels such as "add insights," for example, Malmlow 1972), a great deal was included on scheduling, programming, and budgeting techniques. Indeed, there was often so much of this that *strategic* planning often reduced to a "numbers game" that had little to do with strategy. But not only the process was decomposed; so too were the strategies themselves—into corporate, business, and functional of various kinds. And the resulting plans were then decomposed into budgets at various levels, hierarchies of objectives and programs, and all kinds of action plans and performance controls.

If we think of planning in terms of four parallel hierarchies, one each for budgets, objectives, strategies, and programs, the assumption of the planning school was that all these were knitted together in a single process. It began with objectives, flowed across to the strategy hierarchy, down that and across to the program hierarchy, and down that; the results were then integrated into the hierarchies of budgets and objectives. The reality of the formal technique, as well as informal practice, was that a "great divide" existed between routine budgets and objectives on one side (for purposes of performance control) and ad hoc strategies and programs on the other (for purposes of action planning). As a result, in the real world of "strategic planning" we tend to find the numbers game on one side, informal strategy making (free of the planning school) on the other.

To summarize the premises of the planning school:

1. *Strategy formation should be a controlled, conscious, and formal process, decomposed into distinct steps, each delineated by checklists and supported by techniques.*
2. *Responsibility for the overall process rests with the chief executive in principle; responsibility for its execution rests with the staff planners in practice.*
3. *Strategies emerge from the process full blown, to be explicated so that they can then be implemented through detailed attention to objectives, budgets, programs, and operating plans of various kinds.*

Critique of the Planning School

The failures of planning to perform as promised have been well documented in the popular press (*Business Week*, September 17, 1984; Hayes 1985) and the few intensive empirical studies that have probed into its functioning (Sarrazin 1975, 1977–1978; Gomer 1973, 1974, 1976; Quinn 1980; Mintzberg, Brunet, and Waters 1986; Dube 1973; Koch 1976). Even the survey research could never prove in any consistent way that planning paid—their overall result being "inconclusive," to quote the Bresser and Bishop review (1983: 588) (see also the reviews by Shrader, Taylor, and Dalton 1984 and Lorange 1979: 230). In the equivalent PPBS (planning, programming, budgeting system) experience in government, Wildavsky has concluded that "PPBS has failed everywhere at all times" (1974: 205). Thus we might do well to ask whether the phrase "strategic planning" is, like progressive conservative or civil engineer, an oxymoron. In other words, can strategy be planned? Can it, as proposed in this school, be made in a formal process?

Planners' responses to the failures of planning have ranged from pure faith—in the words of this school's most prolific writer, "Plans are sometimes useless but the planning process is always indispensable" (Steiner 1983: 15)—to demands for ever more elaboration (more sophisticated forecasting techniques, contingency planning, stakeholder analysis, and so on; see especially the development of Ansoff's work in this regard) (Ansoff 1975, 1979, 1984). Yet all of this might simply be viewed as an effort to plug the holes while upping the ante.

But the most popular planner response to failure has been to fall back on excuses labeled the "pitfalls" of planning, notably that planning has lacked the proper managerial support or a climate congenial to its practice (Steiner 1979; Ringbakk 1971). In a sense, however, pitfalls are to planning what sins are to religion—cosmetic blemishes to be removed so that the more noble work of serving the Almighty can proceed. But there is one big difference: While sins are attributed to "us," planning pitfalls are usually attributed to "them." The fault inevitably lies with distracted managers, politicized organizations, and so on, not with planners or their planning systems.

The unasked question was why the pitfalls persisted. Surely no technique has ever had more managerial attention than strategic planning. Why then should the problem of top management support have persisted? Do senior managers perhaps know something that planners don't? Witness General Electric's FIFO experience—first into planning in a major way, first out. America's supposedly most sophisticated planning corporation pulled back dramatically in the early 1980s (*Business Week*, September 17, 1984; see also Hamermesh 1986 for a fuller accounting of the story). Likewise, we may ask whether a climate hostile to planning may be right for some organizations, while one congenial to planning might sometimes impede effective strategy formation.

Under some circumstances planning can impede the commitment necessary for effective strategic management. This can be obviously true for the managers lower down the hierarchy, who are subjected to the imposed controls of centralized planning. But it may be equally so for those at the top, who may be largely bypassed in the process (as discussed earlier) and whose intuition tends to be derided in the planning school, by even so main line a writer as George Sterner (1979: 93). A General Electric division manager told *Business Week* about "grabbing hold" of his business from an "isolated bureaucracy" of planners (1984: 62).[9]

Thus, planning may be thought to displace an approach potentially rooted in commitment with one rooted in calculation. As Brunsson characterizes this distinction, there is a "commitment building type behavior," which is more an act of will than a cognitive process, and a "critically scrutinizing type behavior," which disregards "emotional involvement" and is "more apt to reject than to accept," while even "acceptances are not very commiting" (1976: 12). The implication of this, in sharp contrast to an implicit assumption of the planning school (and more so the positioning school), is that there is no such thing as an optimal strategy. Rather, a good strategy is one that committed people infuse with energy. Therefore, every problem of implementation becomes also a problem of formulation.

While planning is promoted as dealing with change and especially with "turbulent" environments, the fact is that organizations plan in order to set direction, not to encourage change. In other words, planning by its very nature is designed to be *inflexible*. Newman recognized this (1951: 63) long before planning underwent its great wave of popularity. Even Steiner recognized this, noting that "Plans . . . limit choice . . . reduce initiative in the range of alternatives beyond the plans," although he dismisses this as "not a serious limitation" (1979: 46), itself hardly serious. In fact, it can be argued (based on the evidence cited earlier) that not just plans but the planning process itself encourages incremental change at the expense of quantum change, generic thinking at the expense of creative thinking, and a short-term orientation at the expense of a long-term perspective. This seems to stem from the decomposed nature of the process, particularly the fact that planning procedures tend to overlay on existing categories in the organization. Specifically, planning is usually carried out with regard to the forms of strategy that already exist (for example, corporate, business, functional) and the components of structure already in place (as in doing budgeting in terms of the existing hierarchy of subunits). Thus planning tends to preserve the existing categories while serious strategic change generally requires that such categories be reconstituted.

As for the pitfall of politicized climates, it could be argued that planning can in fact promote these. Just consider the disparaging comments made in the planning literature about managerial intuition and about organizations that fail to embrace planning. As someone once remarked, all too often being objective means treating people as objects. And political climates that arise through other means may actually promote major strategic change, through challenge, while planning may support the status quo (see Mintzberg 1983: 229–230 for an elaboration of this point).

An expert has been defined as someone who avoids all the many pitfalls on his or her way to the grand fallacy. Accordingly we should like to go beyond the pitfalls to suggest what we believe to be the fallacies of "strategic planning." We shall discuss three, which in fact fold into a single "grand" fallacy.

First is the fallacy of *predetermination.* Ansoff's (1984) claims notwithstanding, in the words of one of the leading students of forecasting, the formal prediction of discontinuities is "practically impossible" (Makridakis 1990). This means that formal planning typically reduces to the extrapolation of known trends and favors periods of relative stability (or else ones of favorable growth, when errors that exceed the forecasts can be forgiven, as was the case often in the 1960s, the golden years of planning).

Second is the fallacy of *detachment,* the separation of strategic management from operating management, with the former to be informed by an MIS of hard data. Because hard data typically lacks the rich detail needed for strategy making, often proving too thin, too aggregated, and too late (as discussed in Mintzberg 1975; see also Devons 1950), a management that relies on it instead of being in close touch with operating details can prove superficial in its strategy making.

Third is the fallacy of *formalization.* It assumes that decomposing a process into formal steps, each supported by hard data and technique, can produce novel strategies. As already noted, the process proved to be no more than a series of black boxes on paper that, instead of showing how to create strategies merely implored managers to do so. What the formal process really did was provide a means to *program* the strategies created by other means (Mintzberg and Waters 1982). Thus, in the final analysis, "strategic planning" really did turn out to be an oxymoron.

All three fallacies reduce to one grand fallacy, that analysis can provide synthesis. Strategy is an integrating concept, and strategy formation, undertaken to set new courses of action for an organization, requires synthesis. Neither decomposition nor formalization could provide it; all they ever did was support synthesis by defining some of its possible components at the outset and by elaborating some of its consequences afterward. No amount of rearranging the boxes, and no amount of technique loaded into those boxes, could solve the problem of the boxes themselves. That is because the process of strategy formation has to transcend boxes. Ironically, then, what finally undermined the planning school was its violation of the design school's original premise to keep the process simple. In a word, innovation could never be institutionalized.

Context and Contribution of the Planning School

In spite of the problems noted, there is no need to throw out the planner baby with the planning bathwater. Planners do have roles to play around the black box of strategy formation, if not within it. They can act as analysts, by providing data inputs at the front end, particularly the type of analyses managers are prone to overlook, and later by scrutinizing the strategies that come out the back end. They can also act as catalysts, not in the traditional sense of promoting formal planning as some kind of imperative, but rather in encouraging whatever form of strategic thinking and strategy-making process seems appropriate for a particular organization at a particular time. When necessary, but only then, planners can carry out formal planning too, as the means to program the strategies that come out of the black box—first to codify them, then to elaborate them and to translate them into ad hoc programs and routine plans and budgets, and finally to use these for purposes of communication and control. Of course, creative planners can sometimes be strategists too (for example, enter the black box), but that has nothing to do with planning technique per se.

Some of the above roles are formally analytical, others less so. This means that organizations might do well to distinguish two types of planners, which can be labeled left-handed and right-handed. The latter, concerned particularly with periods of *strategic programming*, suit contexts that tend to be relatively simple and stable, or at least predictable, again the case of machine bureaucracy (Mintzberg 1979). But when change must be dramatic, even in machine bureaucracy, or if the organization must function with a different form of structure (for example, the simple structure of the entrepreneur or the adhocracy of intrapreneurs), then the organization is likely to fare better by relying on the looser forms of strategy making first, the left-handed planners second, and the precepts of the planning school last.

THE POSITIONING SCHOOL: STRATEGY FORMATION AS AN ANALYTIC PROCESS

In the early 1980s, a wind from economics blew through the strategic management field, blowing away, or at least into a corner, much of its traditional prescriptive literature. Although the positioning school accepted most of the premises that underlay the planning and design schools, as well as their fundamental model, it added content in two ways: It added literal content, emphasizing strategies themselves more than the process by which they were to be formulated; and it added substance—after all those years of empty pronouncements from the planning school and the endless repetition of the design school model, the positioning school, by focusing on the content of strategies, opened the prescriptive side of the field to substantial research. Scholars now had something to sink their teeth into: They could study the specific strategies available to organizations and the contexts in which each seemed to work best.

The watershed year was 1980, when Michael Porter published *Competitive Strategy*. While one book can hardly make a school, that one acted as a stimulant to draw together a good deal of the disenchantment with the design and planning schools, as well as the felt need to focus on substance. Much as a simple disturbance can freeze a supersaturated liquid, *Competitive Strategy* gelled the interests of a generation of scholars. The book pointed the way, and a huge wave of research quickly followed and has continued to the present time, becoming the dominant effort in the literature of strategic management.

Of course Porter's book was not the first on strategy content. (Nor was it only on content, since much of it also addressed process in the form of techniques to do competitive and industry analysis.) Earlier content work had been done in the field, especially at the Purdue University Krannert School, led by Dan Schendel and Arnold Cooper and their doctoral students (including Hatten, Woo, Montgomery, Galbraith, and Cool).[10] And Porter took his lead from the economics field of industrial organization, which had long addressed related issues. However, that work concentrated more on context (what they call "structure," meaning the structure of an industry) than on "conduct" (meaning strategy), and more on the implications of aggregated behavior for public policy than of strategic behavior for business policy (B. Chamberlain 1933; Bain 1956; Caves 1974; Caves et al. 1980; Sherer 1980; Hay and Morris 1979; see also Porter 1974, 1979, and Caves 1980).[11]

Three Waves of the Positioning School

If the positioning school focuses on the selection of specific strategies, as tangible positions in particular contexts, then it is a good deal older than might be assumed. Indeed, it is by far the oldest school of strategy formation: The first recorded writings on strategy, which go back over two millenia, dealt with the selection of optimal strategy of specific position in a given context—namely, in military warfare. As a consequence, we refer to the military writings—of Sun Tzu (1971), which date back to about 400 B.C., Clausewitz (1968) of the last century, and Liddell-Hart (1967) of this one, among others—as constituting the first wave of the positioning school, and we label it that of "military maxims." In a way, these writers did what today's writers of this school do: They delineated categories of strategy and matched them to the contexts that seemed most suitable. But their work was not systematic, at least not in the contemporary sense of empirical research, and thus their conclusions tended to be expressed in imperative terms (hence the label "maxims"). A similar orientation can sometimes be found in the business literature, mostly prior to the 1970s, in the writings of authors who proposed like maxims to deal with business situations (Katz 1970: 349, 350, 353, 358, 362–363; Newman 1951: 111–118; see also Quinn 1980: 155–168 who sought to extract the messages of military strategy for business).

A second wave of the positioning school developed in the 1960s and 1970s, which can be labeled "consulting imperatives." Associated especially with the Boston Consulting Group (BCG 1972), particularly in its growth-share matrix, as well as the PIMS work (Schoeffler et al. 1974; Schoeffler 1980; Buzzell et al. 1975), this wave was composed of efforts by consultants to prescribe strategic behavior. Although the data bases were often empirical, the prescriptions themselves were no less imperative, and indeed sometimes far more so (one need only compare the nuances of Sun Tzu with the pronouncements of BCG, see Henderson 1979). For example, market share was considered beneficial per se, as was the rapid cumulation of production experience, no matter what the context.

The third wave, stimulated by Porter's book in 1980, in which more systematic study was used to uncover "research contingencies"—essentially which strategies worked best where—finally gave the prescriptive side of the strategic management field the viability it so badly needed. The discussion that follows concerns itself largely with this third wave.

Premises of the Positioning School

The positioning school tended to displace the planning school and attracted its proponents with the opportunity to make substantive contributions of a prescriptive nature. But it did not depart radically from the premises of that school, or those of the design school. The differences were subtle, but they did serve to reorient the literature.

As in the other two schools, strategy formation in the positioning school remained a controlled, conscious process of thought that produced full-blown strategies. They, in turn, were to be made explicit before being formally implemented. But here the process focused more narrowly on calculation—to be more specific, on the choice of tangible strategic positions rather than the development of integrated strategic perspectives (as in the design school) or of coordinated sets of plans (as in the planning school). The notion of strategy preceding structure was also accepted in this school, but another form of structure, that of the industry, was added before strategy. As in the planning school, the formulation process was formal and elaborate, specified in terms of well-defined steps. (Porter 1980 was especially detailed in the steps of competitor and industry analysis, as part of the external appraisal.) Again, the chief executive was the strategist in principle, with the planner the power behind the throne, except that the positioning school elevated the planner's importance another notch. Now that person became an analyst, a numbers-oriented technical person who amassed and studied reams of hard data to recommend optimal strategies. And most notably, the old design school premise of strategies being unique was discarded. To the positioning school, strategies became *generic*; in other words, they were clearly delineated categories—well-defined positions in the economic marketplace. In effect, the analyst did not design strategies (indeed, did not even formulate them) so much as *select* them.

To summarize, in the positioning school

1. *Strategies are generic, specifically common, tangible positions in the marketplace.*
2. *That marketplace (the context) is economic and competitive.*
3. *The strategy formation process is therefore one of analytical selection based on calculation.* The object is to analyze formal data (preferably quantitative) on the industry and the competition in order to select the optimal generic strategy.
4. *Strategies as positions lead other types of strategies (e.g., functional ones), sometimes within clusters that define generic type "strategic groups" of firms within industries.*
5. *Analysts play a major role in this process, feeding the results of their calculations to managers, who officially control the choices.*
6. *Strategies thus emerge from this process full blown and are then articulated and implemented; thus, market structure dictates positional strategies that dictate other strategies that dictate organizational structures (including systems and plans) that determine performance.*

A Matrix of Positioning School Research

Porter did not provide a framework so much as a foundation for content research. That is, his 1980 book provided a set of concepts that could be worked with—generic strategies, generic industries, strategic groups, and so on—but it did not weave them into an integrated theory. (This is suggested by the virtual absence of reference to either strategic groups or generic industries in his follow-up book in 1985.) Perhaps this reflects this school's orientation to analysis rather than synthesis, so that even its own concepts are treated as decomposed parts.

One possible framework by which to consider the interrelationships among the various research activities of this school—in effect, a way to position the efforts of the positioning school—is shown in the matrix in figure 5-2. Research is divided into that concerned with single variables as opposed to clusters of variables and that concerned with static conditions as opposed to dynamic ones. Research activity in this school can be found in all four of the resulting cells, as noted, although the tendency has been to favor the simpler forms of research.

The greater part of the empirical research to date probably fits into the single-static cell. Some of this focuses on the equilibrium conditions under which a particular generic strategy is pursued most effectively, while other work, more in the spirit of the second wave of this school, concerns whether that strategy is profitable (for example, on diversification, Rumelt 1982, Montgomery 1982; on vertical integration, Harrigan 1984, 1985; on niche, Cooper et al. 1984). Still other studies reverse this, by focusing on a particular condition and investigating the strategies most viably pursued there (for example, on low market share see Woo and Cooper 1981; on commodity products, Gram and Crawford 1985).[12]

The strategist's job involves not just selecting individual positions but weaving various positions into integrated strategies. Accordingly, research in the second cell focuses on clusters of dimensions, but still in a static context. Clusters of strategies have generally been considered in terms of "strategic groups," meaning organizations within an industry that pursue similar strategies (Hatten and Schendel 1977; Brunet 1986). And clusters of conditions, again following the lead of Porter, have generally been considered in terms of generic-type industries—for example, fragmented (Kobrin 1984) or mature (Collomb and Ponsard 1984).

Research on dynamic change is more difficult to do and so has been less common. Work in the third cell considers the effect of a

Figure 5-2. Progress of Research in the Positioning School.

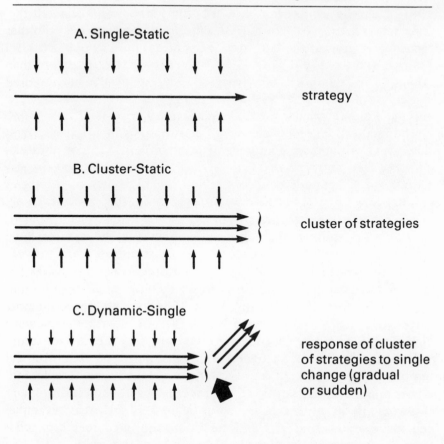

A. Single-Static

strategy

B. Cluster-Static

cluster of strategies

C. Dynamic-Single

response of cluster
of strategies to single
change (gradual
or sudden)

D. Dynamic-Cluster

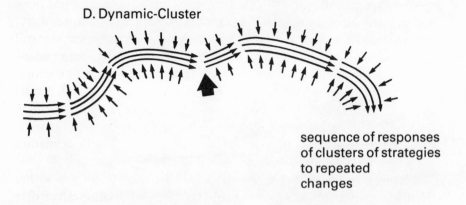

sequence of responses
of clusters of strategies
to repeated
changes

single change (for example, in technology, Cooper and Soukup 1983 or in seller concentration, Caves and Porter 1980) on strategy. Researchers here have considered substantive responses as well as signalling responses, the later treating strategy more as ploy than as position (Porter 1980: chs. 4, 5). Studies of strategic turnaround (Hofer 1980; Hambrick and Schecter 1983) are also typical of this single-dynamic research cell, as are studies of mover advantage in entry and exit (Schmalansee 1978; Schnaars 1986).

The final cell considers clusters of relationships in a dynamic setting, which is the most comprehensive and difficult form of research and therefore the type that has received the least attention. Issues that might be considered here include the dynamics of strategic groups (how they rise and develop over time, for example, Cool and Schendel 1986), the patterns of change and disturbance in industry evolution, and the rise and fall of competition and its effects on strategic positions. What has received more attention are a variety of strategy-related life cycles, dealing with sequences of clusters of strategies or conditions over time, especially with regard to products (Warnerfelt 1985; Thietart and Vivas 1984) and to technological forces (Utterback and Abernathy 1975). Of course, Chandler's (1962) work on life cycles of strategy and structure is best known.[13]

It should be evident that these four cells, in the order presented, represent a progression of research activity as much as they represent a portfolio of research options. Each succeeding one can incorporate the work of the others, as shown in figure 5-2, such that the final cell incorporates strategies and conditions clustered together, subjected to patterned or idiosyncratic changes that over time dictate an industry's evolution.

This brief survey suggests that there is no shortage of interesting research possibilities in the positioning school, but there is a need to impose some structure on them. Synthesis of overriding frameworks should be added to this school's impressive analytical capabilities.

Critique of the Positioning School

The positioning school can be critiqued on the same grounds as the design and planning schools because it extends some of their tendencies. As was stressed about the former, the separation of thinking from acting—formulation to be done at the top, through conscious thought (and here formal analysis), implementation then to take place lower down, through action—places undue emphasis on strategy making as a deliberate process and thereby slights the importance of strategic learning. And as was stressed about planning, the process can be undermined by the fallacies of predetermination (that discontinuities can be forecast), of detachment (that hard data can sufficiently inform the strategist), and of formalization (that the process can be based on decomposition and ultimately that analysis can produce synthesis). At a conference this author organized in the south of France in 1976, the poem "The Blind Men and the Elephant" was used to introduce the various perspectives of strategy formation presented. A number of the presentors answered with their own verses. Derek Channon (1977: 41) provided one in his paper on the "analytical" perspective:

> They built a model of the beast
> Precise in every plane
> But its Behavior just would not conform
> For they could not simulate its brain.

Like the other prescriptive (and nonprescriptive) schools, the approach here has not been wrong so much as narrow. First, the *focus* is narrow. It is oriented to the economic and especially the quantifiable, as opposed to the social or political or even nonquantifiable economic. Thus, for example, there can be bias in the selection of strategies because cost leadership strategies may have more hard data to back them up than, say, those of quality differentiation. This can be seen clearly in the second wave of this school, notably the BCG emphasis on experience curves, and in some other consulting firms' virtual obsession with perceiving strategy in terms of managing costs.

This school's bias toward the economic over the political is noteworthy. For example, the words *political* and *politics* do not appear in Porter's *Competitive Strategy*, at least not in the table of contents or index. Yet the book can easily be taken as a primer for political action. If profit really does lie in market power, then there are clearly more than competitive economic ways to gain and sustain that power. It does not take a great deal of imagination to read between the lines of sentences such as "the threat of entry into an industry depends on the *barriers to entry* that are present, coupled with the *reaction* from existing competitors that the entrant can expect" (1980: 7, italics in original); or "government can limit or even foreclose entry into industries with such controls as licensing requirements and limits on access to raw materials" (1980: 13); or "strategy can be viewed as building defences against competitive forces" (1980: 30). Occasionally, in fact, Porter clearly steps across that fine line between competitive economics and political maneuvering:

> For large firms suing smaller firms, private antitrust suits can be thinly veiled devices to inflict penalties. Suits force the weaker firms to bear extremely high legal costs over a long period of time and also divert its attention from competing in the market. Or . . . a suit can be a low-risk way of telling the weaker firm that it is attempting to bite off too much of the market. The outstanding suit can be left effectively dormant through legal maneuvering and selectively activated (inflicting costs on the weaker firm) if the weaker firm shows signs of misreading the signal. (1980: 86)

It must be concluded that although each school helps to clarify certain concepts, it is only when the different schools begin to inform each other that a rich understanding of the strategy formation process will develop.

A second concern is that the *context* of the positioning school is narrow. For one thing, there is a bias toward traditional big business (which, not so incidentally, is where market power is greatest, competition least effective, and the potential for political manipulation most pronounced). There have been studies of niche strategies and fragmented industries, but these are far outnumbered by studies involving mainline strategies and mature industries. That, of course, is where the hard data is, and the positioning school—in practice as well as in research—depends on large quantities of such data. Consider, for example, the enormous favorable attention given to market share in the second wave of this school, by both BCG and PIMS; also consider BCG's 1970s obsession with the scale benefits of experience. And in his chapter on fragmented industries in *Competitive Strategy*, Porter discusses at some length strategies to consolidate fragmented industries, but nowhere does he balance this with discussion of strategies to fragment consolidated industries (which is, of course, a favorite behavior of small firms). Porter also discusses in one section "industries that are 'stuck'" in a fragmented situation, but nowhere does he discuss ones that are stuck in a consolidated situation.

This big firm bias may be most evident in the PIMS data base. PIMS aggregates statistics from its member companies, which buy into its system by providing detailed data on many aspects of their various businesses. In return, they get reports on the aggregated results. To participate in PIMS certainly requires considerable hard data, which likely requires having an established planning department that has the time and the energy to produce such data (and use the results). In other words, it is the planning department (or equivalent) that likely connects with PIMS. But which firms have the most established planning departments? Clearly the largest and most mature, in terms of industry structure. Thus, there could well be a systematic bias in the PIMS data base, which might, for example, explain why PIMS finds that capital intensity has a negative effect on profitability.

There is a difference between "getting there" and "being there," and PIMS people may be studying the effects of being there (i.e., functioning as the large established player in a mature industry) while extrapolating back to getting there (in other words, what caused a firm to become the major player in the first place). Indeed, this may be a bias in the contemporary positioning school research in general. By giving undue attention to the cross-sectional studies of large organizations, it may falsely attribute the carryovers of earlier aggressive growth, which established market positions, to later strategies designed to hold on to those positions.

The bias in this school is not just toward big established business but toward *conventional*, big established business. One count of the industries referred to in Porter's *Competitive Strategy* found only 11 out of 177 that considered capital goods producers. Generic strategic thinking applies most readily to commodity, mass production, and mass service industries, not, for example, to producers of customized products, which turn out to be far more common than is suggested in this literature (Lampel and Mintzberg 1987).

The bias toward the big, the established, the conventional, and the mature also reflects itself in a bias toward conditions of stability, as in the design and planning schools. Instability encourages fragmentation and is common in customizing industries; it also breaks down barriers of various kinds (entry, mobility, exit). Fragmentation makes it difficult to find or develop hard data and makes such data, when it does exist, less reliable—the world must hold still for data to harden in a reliable way. All of this, of course, renders more difficult the conducting of the historical competitor and industry analyses on which this school depends.

There is another interesting paradox here. Although the central thrust of the positioning school is toward conducting formal analyses under conditions of relative stability, another side of this school focuses attention on the dynamic aspects of strategic positioning. These include signaling, posturing, and first and later mover advantages. Yet this side requires a very different orientation from the other, both in practice (quick maneuvering based on relatively little information, and much of that soft, as compared with the time consuming study of large quantities of hard data) and in research (the need for softer concepts and more imagination in trying to understand how firms use surprise to do the unexpected, as compared with how they slot generic strategies into given conditions). The result is a conceptual schism in this school. It tells the practitioner to study carefully and move generically, and then it offers advice on moving quickly and unexpectedly. One approach contradicts the other.

As already implied, the third aspect of narrowness of approach in the positioning school relates to *process.* Its message is not to get out there and learn but to stay home and calculate. "Massaging the numbers" is what is expected in the planning offices no less than the MBA classrooms. The positioning school strategist is expected to deal in abstractions on paper, detached from the tangible world of making products and closing sales. Fully in the spirit of today's positioning school, Clausewitz argued in the last century that "calculation" is "the most essential thing to . . . the end" of attaining superiority. Yet he also acknowledged that "an infinity of petty circumstances" produce "unexpected incidents upon which it [is] impossible to calculate" (1968: 164, 165). But there is nothing petty about the world unfolding in ways that happen to be inconvenient to strategic analysis.

Calculation, as already suggested in our critique of the planning school, can impede not only learning and creativity but also personal commitment. With planners sequestered in central offices feeding reports to top managers, everyone else gets slighted as a mere implementator. Each is required to pursue the strategies dictated not by the nuanced appreciation of a complex business rooted in experience but by some fairly pat calculations carried out by numerate analysts.

Finally, *strategy* itself tends to have a narrow focus in the positioning school. It is seen as generic position, not unique perspective. At the limit, the process reduces to a formula, or a recipe—the selection of a position, itself pat, from a restricted list, or in the case of strategic groups, joining one club or another, which itself dictates the portfolio of strategies to be pursued. At least the design school promoted strategy as perspective and encouraged its creative design. By focusing on strategies as generic, the effect of the positioning school can be exactly the opposite. Although it is true that selecting a strategy of, say, differentiation hardly restricts what is done under that label, it also seems true that the emphasis on calculation tends to draw organizations toward results that are generic in their detail as well as in their orientation. (The same effect seems to occur in research, which favors boxing strategies into particular categories, rather than studying their nuanced differences.)

Some of the most famous battles of business and war have been won not by doing things correctly but by breaking the rules, by *creating* the categories. Burger King might join the "fast food hamburger group," but it was McDonald's that wrote the rules in the first place and created the initial vision that gave rise to the group. Kodak might study the market for instant cameras, but Polaroid created that market. Some firms do competitor analyses, while others succeed by developing new niches that avoid existing competitors. The positioning school focuses its attention on strategies that have already become generic, on industries that are already established, on groups that have already been formed, and on competitors that have already positioned themselves. If you make ballpoint pens and you are not BIC, chances are BCG will call your business a dog. You have a small share of a slow-growth industry and should exit. But if you fill that pen with erasable ink and put an eraser on the end, through just this tiny bit of creativity you may have turned your dog into a star: You may now have 100 percent of a new growth industry. Again, on its dynamic side the positioning school may have a category called "first mover advantage." But its own orientation to the strategic analysis of hard data in existing categories discourages taking that advantage. By the time a firm is through analyzing, the first movers might be out of sight.

It is another interesting irony that the positioning school, so pro-active in its tone, so encouraging of free will, is in fact among the most deterministic of all the schools of strategy formation. While proclaiming managerial choice, it has spent its time trying to design boxes into which organizations must fit if they are to survive. This school's first wave tended to promote maxims; its second wave, imperatives. Market share was good, as was mass production experi-ence; capital intensity was bad. Its third wave offers options and con-tingencies, but these are not full choices. They are presented in the belief that there is a best generic strategy for a given set of condi-tions, whereas strategic success may have more to do with commit-ment than with calculation.

Contribution and Context of the Positioning School

The process of strategy formation is messy and dynamic; strategic analysis, in contrast, is orderly and static. Thus, its job is to *support* that process, not to *be* it. Reducing its role to conducting studies that feed into strategy making has therefore proved appropriate for the positioning school. Of course, the planners lost influence when they became analysts, but only in principle; in practice they gained influence. Instead of promoting strategy-making systems that never worked, they instead provided tangible advice to strategists.

Such strategy analyses would appear to be appropriate inputs to strategy formation where conditions are sufficiently simple and stable so that the appropriate data can be collected and analyzed at a single center. This corresponds, as in the previous two schools, to the structure we call machine bureaucracy (Mintzberg 1979), oriented to mass products and services in more mature industries, also to periods of *recalculation*, when changes of position can take place within given perspectives. Such analyses can never, however, be allowed to dominate the process of strategy making, even in these contexts. A host of soft factors must always be considered alongside the hard ones. In other words, no Gresham-like law of strategy analysis can be allowed to operate, in practice or research, whereby the hard inputs drive out the soft, and whereby a portfolio of positions drives out thinking about an integrated perspective. If analyzing the numbers or even reading the results keeps strategists, or researchers, from getting out into the tangible world of products and customers, then the posi-tioning school will have done strategic management a great disservice.

Assuming this can be avoided, the positioning school, in its first significant decade, must be counted as having made a major contribution to strategic management. And it shows the potential for making an even greater one in the next decade. This school has opened up tremendous avenues for research and has provided the foundation of a major set of concepts. But it must build from these, with a synthesis that encompasses a broader perspective: The positioning school must use its powerful foundation not to restrict strategic vision but to enlarge it.

THE ENTREPRENEURIAL SCHOOL: STRATEGY FORMATION AS A VISIONARY PROCESS

From the schools of *prescription*, we now move to those of *description*, which seek to understand the process of strategy formation as it unfolds. First is the entrepreneurial school which takes a view not altogether different from that of the design school.

The design school, if not the planning and positioning schools that followed it, took formal leadership seriously, rooting the strategy formation process in the mental processes of the chief executive. That person was the "architect" of strategy. But the design school stopped short of building a cult around that leadership. Indeed, by stressing the need for a conceptual framework, and by dismissing intuition, it specifically sought to avoid the softer, more personalized elements of leadership. What we are calling the entrepreneurial school does exactly the opposite.

Not only does this school focus the strategy formation process exclusively on the single leader, but it also stresses the most innate of mental states and processes—intuition, judgment, wisdom, experience, insight. This promotes a view of strategy as perspective, associated with image, sense of direction, and above all, vision. Note, however, that here the strategic perspective is not collective or cultural, as in other schools to be discussed. Rather it is the personal, flexible construct of one individual. Consequently, the organization becomes subservient in this school, responsive to the dictates of the leader. And the environment, if not exactly subservient, becomes terrain on which the leader maneuvers with some ease, at least in terms of directing the organization into a protective niche (see Meindl et al. 1985, on "The Romance of Leadership").

In one sense, the entrepreneurial school, like the positioning, grew out of economics. The entrepreneur was the central actor in its classical theory. This was, however, an actor who could make no choices. He played obediently the role that economists assigned to him: maximizing profit in response to the dictates of a competitive market. Classical economics never put any flesh on this skeleton of the leader, let alone allowing for the spirit of free will. But the entrepreneurial school in fact received its initial impetus from several not-so-classical economists who did—for example, Schumpeter (1934), Cole (1959), and Strauss (1944)—who argued that the key to economic success, indeed overall economic growth, lay in the initiative of the visionary leader. Thus this person was given not only choice and free will but sometimes grand choice and almost mystical will.

Mainstream economics always held back on the role of the leader. It preferred the abstraction of the competitive market and the predictability of the skeletal leader to the vagaries of strategic vision and the innovative market niche. Thus, it was really in the field of management that the entrepreneurial school developed, although it has never represented more than a trickle of writing and research, with occasional waves of interest. Proponents of this school saw personalized leadership, based on strategic vision, as the key to organizational success. They saw this especially in business but also in other sectors, and not only in starting up and building new organizations but also in turning around faltering established ones. Therefore, although the label "entrepreneurship" was originally associated with the creators of their own businesses, the word was gradually extended to describe various other forms of personalized, proactive, single-minded, leadership in organizations. For reasons to be discussed shortly, this chapter uses the word broadly to describe leadership that is personalized and visionary but specifically centralized (that is, at the helm of an identifiable organization).

Premises of the Entrepreneurial School

The following premises underlie this view of strategy formation:

1. *Strategy exists in the mind of the single leader as perspective, specifically, as a sense of long-term direction, a vision of the organization's future.*

2. *The process of strategy formation is semiconscious at best, rooted in the experience and intuition of the leader.*
3. *The leader maintains close personal control of the implementation as well as the formulation of the vision, tying the two together tightly through personalized feedback on actions.*
4. *The strategic vision is thus malleable, as is the leaders's organization, a simple structure responsive to his or her directives.*
5. *The entrepreneurial strategy tends to take the form of niche, one or more pockets of market positions protected from the forces of outright competition.*

The Literature of the Entrepreneurial School

Of all the writings on entrepreneurship, only a small proportion has been theoretical, and little has been systematically empirical. A great deal has been popular—sometimes referred to as the "great man school" of management—and can be found in the business press or in biographies and autobiographies of the great tycoons of industry and other famous leaders of organizations. Entrepreneurship can, for example, be followed biweekly in *Fortune*, a magazine that tends to attribute business success to the vision of the chief executive and business failure to the absence of such vision.

A stream of early writing in economics provided theoretical materials, often to define entrepreneurship and to delineate its components. Schumpeter stressed the innovative function—"new combinations" (1934), in particular "the doing of new things or the doing of things that are already being done in a new way" (1947)—and assumed the risk was borne by the capitalist. Knight (1967) saw entrepreneurship as synonomous with handling uncertainty. And Papandreou (1952) discussed the "organizer-manager," in contrast to Schumpeter, who argued that while the entrepreneur may remain at the helm of the organization he or she founded, that person ceased to perform an entrepreneurial function as soon as he or she stopped innovating. Cole (1959), who popularized the phrase "bold stroke" to capture entrepreneurship, mentioned four types of entrepreneurs—the calculating inventor, the inspirational innovator, the overoptimistic promoter, and the builder of a strong enterprise.

Cole's adjectives suggest a second body of literature on entrepreneurship, which is probably the largest in empirical content. It consists of descriptions of the entrepreneurial personality, often negative—for example, in terms of an obsession with hoarding power (Collins and Moore 1970; Kets de Vries 1985). Among the various characteristics attributed to the entrepreneurial personality have been strong needs for control, for independence, and for achievement, a resentment of authority, and a tendency to accept moderate risks. As Baumol summarizes McClelland's (1961) study, the entrepreneur is not a "gambler" or a "speculator," "not essentially a man who chooses to bear risks," but a "calculator" (1968: 70; see also Mintzberg and Waters 1982).

There has been some attention to entrepreneurship in the (strategic) management literature, with a recent resurgence (for example, Drucker 1970, 1985; Murray 1984; Carland et al. 1984; Van de Ven et al. 1984; Cooper and Dunkelberg 1986; Kaplan 1987; Peterson 1981). Three themes would seem to be most consequential for strategic management. One is on strategic vision (Normann 1977; Noel 1989; Westley and Mintzberg 1988, 1989), a subject that has attracted interest in recent years, likely due to the failures of the planning school. The other themes concern two phases of the organizational life cycle—startup and turnaround—when visionary, entrepreneurial leadership would seem to be most necessary (see, for example, the tracking strategy studies of Mintzberg and Waters 1982, 1984 on the former and Mintzberg 1978 on the latter).

In an economy of large organizations, there has been increasing interest in the subject of revitalization through strategic initiatives. They often take the form of corporate venturing, product championing, "fellows" programs, and the like. Some writers have chosen to view this as internal entrepreneurship—hence the label "intrapreneurship." But given the problems of institutionalizing the entrepreneurial function, and given the resistance to such initiatives in large organizations (as we shall discuss in the cultural school), this concept belongs not in a school that focuses on the power of leadership, but in one that describes how organizations learn from the bottom up.

Contribution, Critique, and Context of the Entrepreneurial School

The entrepreneurial school has identified important dimensions of strategy formation, most notably concerning its proactive side and the role of personalized leadership and strategic vision. Most great organizations probably owe their initial impetus to such factors; indeed they figure importantly in many strategies that are novel and tightly integrated. These strategies stand in sharp contrast to the all-too-common "me too" strategies that seem to result from literal adherance to the dictates of the planning or positioning schools. But the entrepreneurial school exhibits some serious deficiencies, as well.

On one hand, the entrepreneurial school has viewed strategy formation as wrapped up in the vision of a single individual. On the other hand, it could never really say much about what that process was. It remained a black box, buried in human cognition. Thus, for the organization that ran into difficulty, this school's central prescription was all too obvious, and facile: Find a new visionary leader. Moreover, this school never really came to grips with the fact that the behaviors that were glorious and energizing to some of its writers became pathological and deadening to others. Was it a slight excess that drove the leader over the edge? Did conditions change so that what functioned well suddenly became dysfunctional? Or did these differences merely reflect the differences among the writers, pessimists writing alongside optimists, some seeing the glass of entrepreneurship as half-empty, others as half-full? Clearly we can say yes to all these questions.

Once again necessary but largely missing is research on context: surveys of where various forms of entrepreneurship seem to function most effectively as well as intensive investigations into how those forms work in practice. The few intensive studies of entrepreneurship suggest that it is less glorious than typically described but also more functional, as in the earlier conclusion about the avoidance of undue risk.

In spite of the paucity of research, we do have some indication of the appropriate contexts of the entrepreneurial school. Clearly, as already noted, *startup* is one situation in need of forceful leadership and rich vision, since direction must be set and niches secured. Likewise, in *turnaround* situations, even large organizations often have to defer to visionary leaders. In both cases, the context is dynamic, yet it must be simple enough to come under the control of a single brain. Moreover, many organizations of *sustained small size* lend themselves to the personalize control of leaders who do not care to defer to other managers, let alone staff planners. Clearly, there are important pockets of organized society that have great need for the kind of strategy formation promoted by the entrepreneurial school.

THE COGNITIVE SCHOOL: STRATEGY
FORMATION AS A MENTAL PROCESS

If we are really serious in our efforts to understand strategic vision, then we may have to probe into the mind of the strategist. That is the role of the cognitive school: to get at what strategy formation means in the sphere of human cognition. In any complex organization, the process is, as we shall see in the later schools, a fundamentally collective one. But that collectivity is composed of individual brains, so that even there, how those brains handle information to develop strategies is an important question in this field.

Four Aspects of the Cognitive School

Perhaps the "cognitive school" is not so much a school of thought on strategy formation as work that could eventually grow into such a school. We include it here, however, because of the importance of understanding cognition. A few publications have sought to draw out lessons of cognitive psychology for strategy making, including in management Nystrom (1979: ch. 7), who presents such a model of strategy formation, Duhaime and Schwenk (1983), Schwenk (1984), Stubbart (1987), Kiesler and Sproull (1982), Hogarth and Makridakis (1981), and in the public sector Steinbruner (1974), Jervis (1969), and Holsti (1978).

At least four aspects of cognitive psychology can be identified as relevant to strategy formation: (1) perception, how the strategist gets informed; (2) concept attainment, how the strategy itself forms; (3) reconception, how the strategy changes or why it does not; and (4) strategic style, how strategists differ in their cognitive orientations.

Perception. Studies of perception are numerous, but they seem to focus mostly on pathology—distortions and limitations in the way people get their information. Herbert Simon (1957; March and Simon 1958) popularized the notion of bounded reationality some time ago: The world is large and complex, human brains are small and their information processing capacities limited by comparison. Thus, strange things can happen when people try to deal with complex issues (Tverskey and Kahneman 1974). In a paper written for purposes of managerial forecasting and planning, Hogarth and Makridakis (1981) offer a three-page list of "information processing biases" uncovered in psychology.

Still, it would be useful to know not just how the mind distorts but also how it is sometimes able to handle and to integrate such diversities of complex inputs—how some people manage to make remarkable leaps of cognition. Given the claim in cognitive psychology that human beings can process only about seven chunks of information in their short- or intermediate-term memories (as Miller 1956 was cited in the opening of this chapter), how is it that strategists are sometimes able to synthesize vast ranges of soft information into new perspectives? Might the tendency of this research to focus on chunks—namely, discreet categories based on analytical decomposition—preclude necessary attention to images, which somehow synthesize all kinds of vague knowledge? Have the cognitive psychologists been looking for clues to mental behavior in the lightness of verbal protocols while the answers are lost in the darkness of the processes we label intuition and insight? Perhaps the real limitations and distortions lie not in the behavior of strategists themselves as much as in the methods of cognitive psychology.

Concept Attainment. As vision or perception, a strategy seems to be, in some fundamental sense, a concept in the mind of the actor. Accordingly, the study of what is sometimes called "concept attainment" should be key to understanding the cognitive processes of strategy formation. Early work by Jerome Bruner and his colleagues (1956)—in which they distinguished simultaneous scanning, selective scanning, consecutive focusing, and focus gambling—is of some interest here, but again it is difficult to find much later work that is useful in this regard.

There exists, in fact, a set of labels related to concept—such as map (Axelrod 1976), frame (Misky 1975), schema (Neisser 1976)—but not a great deal of insight into how such things develop in the minds of actors. Again, these may be hidden in the dark recesses we call intuition and so are inaccessible to the more formal methods of cognitive psychology. For example, Polyani's (1983) point about "tacit knowledge"—in simple terms, that we know far more than we can tell—seems to hold an important message for strategic management, yet such knowledge is obviously beyond research that relies on verbal protocols. Likewise, there is interesting work on creativity, including some early studies of sudden insight (Hadamard 1945; Köhler 1925), but not in mainline cognitive psychology. Ironically, one of the most important findings for strategic management—on the role of the mute right hemisphere of the human brain in processes of visual perception as it relates to synthesis—comes not from psychology, but physiology, in the work of people such as Sperry (see 1974). And overall, to date we have probably gained our greatest understanding of "strategic thinking" from writers in general management (such as Vickers 1965; Ohmae 1982; Quinn 1980; and Weick 1979, 1983) rather than from researchers who claim to be experts on thinking itself!

Reconception. Reconception (sometimes called "reframing") refers to the changing of strategies (or visions, concepts, maps) that have already formed in a mind (see Pondy and Huff 1985 for a management study of this). Here there is considerable activity, but again with more emphasis on pathology—notably resistance to change—than on healthy behavior. Terms like "mental set" and "functional fixedness" (Duncker 1945) convey the notion that once the mind has set itself on a concept, it tends to block out contrary or undermining evidence. In fact, experiments that show this to be even stronger when the concept has been publicly articulated (Kiesler 1971) have important implications for the premise of the prescriptive schools that all strategies must be made explicit. What this research seems less inclined to do, however, is recognize that side of human nature prone to testing and experimentation, to trying new things just for the sake of variety.

Cognitive Style. Strategists, of course, vary in their cognitive orientations. Psychologists who study attributes of human behavior, such as cognitive complexity (Schroder, Driver, and Streufert 1967), openness (Rokeach and Restle 1960), and field dependence (Witkin et al. 1974), offer concepts relevant to "strategic style." This may be especially true if their findings can be coupled with more applied work in strategic management (for example, on opportunistic, incremental, and political approaches to strategy making). Holsti (1976) has proposed "some 'cognitive process' approaches to decision making," and Wissema et al. (1980) have delineated various "types of managers" based on "strategic directions." An understanding of strategic styles will likely prove an important component in helping us to understand the strategy formation process.

Premises of the Cognitive School

The cognitive school is, at best, an evolving school of thought on strategy formation, hence its premises are presented here to conclude this brief review of the literature.

1. *Strategy formation is a cognitive process that takes place in the mind of the strategist.*
2. *Hence, strategies are perspectives, or concepts, that form in that mind.*
3. *The strategist's environment is complex, his or her cognitive capabilities limited by comparison; consequently, the receipt of information is restricted and biased and the process of strategy formation thereby distorted.*
4. *Specifically, strategies are difficult to attain in the first place, considerably less than nonoptimal when attained and subsequently difficult to change when no longer viable.*
5. *As a result of their individual cognitive makeups, strategists vary significantly in their styles of strategy formation.*

We do not personally subscribe to these premises—at least not to their one-sided tone, but they do reflect the current literature here.

Critique, Contribution, and Context of the Cognitive School

As noted at the outset, this school is characterized more by its potential than by its contribution. The central idea is valid—that the strategy formation process is also fundamentally a cognitive one, particularly in the attainment of concepts. But strategic management has yet to draw sufficiently on the lessons of cognitive psychology, or perhaps more accurately, cognitive psychology has yet to adequately address the questions of prime interest to strategic management, especially how concepts actually form in the mind of a strategist. Although it is interesting and informative to learn about distortions in the process, our understanding itself risks becoming distorted when phenomena such as experiental wisdom, creative insight, and intuitive synthesis are ignored. Careful study of strategy formation behavior in organizations repeatedly bears witness to phenomena of this nature—at the very heart of the process. We might conclude that the entrepreneurial school has raised important questions that the cognitive school has failed to answer.

In spite of its shortcomings, however, the cognitive school reminds us that strategy formation is also a mental process, and that funny things can happen on the way to a strategy. It further reminds us that strategists vary in their cognitive orientations, with important consequences for the strategies pursued. In this sense, the cognitive school is less deterministic than the positioning school, and more personalized than the planning school. It is also the first of the five schools so far discussed to recognize that there is an interesting environment out there—that strategists don't just design their world at will or hide in convenient niches or slot passively into set conditions. Rather, they get buffeted around by a nasty world that, in the view of this school at least, is too complicated to be fully understood.

As for context, the cognitive school seems to apply best to strategy formation as an individual rather than a collective process. (Not that cognition is not relevant to the collective context, just that the interaction of different cognitions has to be orders of magnitude more complex, and so hardly amenable to comprehension by a research community that has had its hands full with the problems of individual cognition.) This school also draws attention to particular stages in the strategy formation process, notably a period of *original conception* of strategy, a period of *reconception*, and especially a period of *clinging* to existing strategies due to cognitive fixation (as has been shown, for example, in our studies of the strategies of Volkswagenwerk and of the U.S. experience in Vietnam) (Mintzberg 1978). Above all, the cognitive school tells us that we had better understand cognition if we are to understand strategy formation. But this has more important implications for cognitive psychology as a supplier of theory than strategic management as a consumer of it.

THE LEARNING SCHOOL: STRATEGY FORMATION AS AN EMERGENT PROCESS

If the world of strategy is as complex as implied by the cognitive school, particularly when compared with the cognitive capacities of the strategist, then it must be concluded that the design school, the planning school, and the positioning school dangerously simplify the process and thereby mislead practitioners who take their pre-scriptions seriously. Of course, this was the basis of this chapter's critique of these three schools—that the static processes they pre-scribe are not compatible with the dynamic and difficult world of strategy making.

If strategists cannot rely on procedure and technique, and *when* they cannot design strategic perspectives in some analytically sequen-tial or personally visionary process, then how are they to proceed? Our sixth school of strategy formation suggests an answer: They learn over time. This is simple enough in concept, but putting it into practice is another matter. According to this school, strategies emerge as strategists, sometimes individually but more often collec-tively, come to know a context and their organization's capability of dealing with it; eventually the organization converges on patterns of behavior that work. Lapierre has put it well: Strategic management becomes "no longer just the management of change but management by change" (1980: 9).

It was the publication of Charles Lindblom's (1959) provocative article, "The Science of 'Muddling Through,'" that initiated this school. Lindblom suggested that policy-making in government is not a neat, orderly, controlled process, but a messy one of trying to cope with a world the policymaker knows is too complicated for him or her. Lindblom's notions violated virtually every premise of "rational" management. It struck a chord because it described be-havior with which everyone was familiar, sometimes seemingly as prevalent in business as in government (for example, Wrapp 1967).

Some related publications followed, but it was James Brian Quinn's book of 1980, *Strategies for Change: Logical Incremental-ism*, that signaled the growth of what we are here calling the learning school. A fairly steady flow of literature has followed and subse-quently entered the mainstream (or at least formed a major current) of strategic management.

Evolution of the Learning School

We can trace the evolution of the learning school—how it itself learned, if you like—through several phases, that really represent fairly distinct bodies of literature that now seem to be converging.

Disjointed Incrementalism. In his early 1960s book with a colleague (Braybrooke and Lindblom 1963), Lindblom elaborated his theory at greatest length, under the label "disjointed incrementalism." He described policy-making as a "serial," "remedial," and "fragmented" process in which decisions are made at the margin. These are made to solve problems rather than to exploit opportunities, and with little regard for ultimate goals or even for connections between different decisions. Lindblom suggested that many actors get involved in the process, with little coordination achieved by any central authority through plan or vision: "various aspects of public policy and even various aspects of any one problem or problem area are analyzed at various points in time with no apparent coordination" (1963: 105). At best, the different actors engaged in informal "mutual adjustment."

In a later book, Lindblom (1968) well summarized his theory with the statement that "policy making is typically a never-ending process of successive steps in which continual nibbling is a substitute for a good bite" (1968: 25–26). He argued further that "the piecemealing remedial incrementalist or satisficer may not look like an heroic figure. He is, nevertheless, a shrewd, resourceful problem-solver who is wrestling bravely with a universe that he is wise enough to know is too big for him" (1968: 27).

But the question remained: Was this incrementalist a strategist? Did anything come out of the process Lindblom described that can be called strategy? Was there deliberate direction or even emergent convergence that defined common positions or collective perspective? Because the answer was no (Bower and Doz 1979: 155), Lindblom's theory stopped short of being one of strategy formation. True he sought to describe public policy-making, especially in the U.S. congressional system of government. But even there, strategies can be discerned (consider, for example, the overall consistency in U.S. foreign policy with regard to the Soviet Union through the 1950s, 1960s, and 1970s). But Lindblom did, nonetheless, point the way toward a new school of thought on strategy formation.

Logical Incrementalism. James Brian Quinn (1980) picked up some years later where Lindblom (and Wrapp) left off. Quinn agreed with Lindblom on the incremental nature of the process but not on its disjointedness. That is because he believed in a central actor, at least in the context of the business corporation, and in that actor's ability to direct the process toward a final strategy.

Quinn started with the belief that organizations are able to arrive at strategies as integrated conceptions. To find out how, he interviewed the chief executives of several large, successful corporations and concluded that while planning did not describe how they formulated their strategies, incrementalism did. But his incrementalism had an underlying logic that knitted the pieces together. Hence, Quinn called this process "logical incrementalism," where "the real strategy tends to evolve as internal decisions and external events flow together to create a new, widely shared consensus for action among key members of the top management team. In well-run organizations, managers proactively guide these streams of actions and events incrementally toward conscious strategies" (1980: 15). The organization, for Quinn, consisted of a series of "subsystems"—for example, related to diversification, reorganization, external relations. And strategic management meant trying "to develop or maintain in [top executives'] minds a consistent pattern among the decisions made in each subsystem" (1980: 52). One gets the impression reading Quinn of strategy management being done on the run.

But there was an interesting ambiguity in Quinn's theory. Incrementalism can be applied in two ways: on one hand to develop the strategic vision itself, and on the other to implement a vision already in the strategist's mind. In the first case, the central strategist learns incrementally; in the second, he or she maneuvers tactically, almost politically, in incremental fashion through a complex organization. Quinn's strategist does not face the responsive organization of our first four schools; it has a mind of its own, so to speak, although that is not a strategic mind. The central strategist—in Quinn's view, the team of top executives, led by the chief executive officer—remains the architect of strategy. Thus Quinn writes about top executives "selectively moving people toward a broadly conceived organizational goal" (1980: 32), and he devotes a large part of his book (1980: 97–152) to what might be called "political implementation"; the subjects covered here include "building credibility," "broadening support," "systematic waiting," and "managing coalitions."

Perhaps Quinn's ambiguity on this point reflects an ambiguity in practice: Strategists may sometimes have to carry out formulation and implementation concurrently. In effect, they have to promote politically a strategic vision that itself is undergoing change and improvement. That seems to be Quinn's stand. He refers to the process as "a continuous, pulsing dynamic" and concludes (1980: 145) that

> successful managers who operate with logical incrementalism build the seeds of understanding, identity, and commitment into the very processes that create their strategies. By the time the strategy begins to crystalize in focus, pieces of it are already being implemented. Through their strategic formulation processes, they have built a momentum and psychological commitment to the strategy, which causes it to flow toward flexible implementation. Constantly integrating the simultaneous incremental processes of strategy formulation and implementation is the central art of effective strategic management.

Although the above process may have been common in the organizations Quinn studied, broader theory may have to be developed by representing the relationship between formulation and implementation along a continuum. On one side the two are thoroughly intertwined, with strategy formation as primarily a learning process. On the other is the implementation of a more or less well-formulated vision, through the political-type factors Quinn describes. The latter corresponds more closely to the design school, with shades of the political school, while the former comes out clearly in the learning school. Thus Quinn, who positions himself toward the middle of this continuum, cannot be considered to stand squarely in the learning school as much as to straddle this and the design school (with a toe or two in the political school).[14] This is especially evident in the dominant role he gives the top management team in strategy formation, relegating other people to bit parts. But the foot Quinn did place in the learning school proved important in its development, giving incrementalism a prominent place in the literature of strategic management. It also shifted its role from just plain adapting to one of conscious learning.

Strategic Initiatives. Meanwhile, on another front the collectivity was being heard from. Starting perhaps with Bower's (1970) description of the resource allocation process (especially in the context of capital budgeting) and advanced by a number of his doctoral students at Harvard and then especially by Burgelman's (1980) thesis at Columbia on corporate venturing (see also Burgelman 1983a, 1983b, 1986), the notion was advanced that strategic initiatives often develop lower down in the hierarchy and are then championed or given impetus by middle-level managers who seek the approval of senior executives.

This introduced to strategy formation the notion of multiple strategic actors, much as in Lindblom's theory, except that here they functioned in organizations with hierarchies of authority. But again, as in Lindblom's earlier work, it was not at all clear how all these initiatives welded themselves into comprehensive strategy, let alone how they connected to the strategies already in place. For a full flowering of the learning school, therefore, two main themes had to be connected: multiple initiatives by a variety of actors, and the integration of these into strategies through a process of learning.

Emergent Strategy and Retrospection. Two concepts, one that we have been working on for some years now (emergent strategy), the other that Karl Weick has been promoting for even longer (retrospection), may supply the link needed to combine multiple actors with strategic learning.

Our own research (Mintzberg 1972, 1978; Mintzberg and McHugh 1985; Mintzberg and Waters 1982, 1983, 1984), by defining strategy as pattern in action, has been able to distinguish deliberate strategies from emergent ones. Only the former are recognized in the three prescriptive schools, which emphasize control almost to the exclusion of learning: In those schools, organizational attention is riveted on the realization of explicit intentions (meaning implementation), not on adapting such intentions to new inputs. It is the concept of emergent strategy that opens the door to learning, because it acknowledges the organization's capacity to experiment. A single action can be taken, feedback can be perceived, and the process can continue until the organization converges on the pattern that becomes its strategy. In other words (to make use of Lindblom's metaphor), organizations need not nibble haphazardly. Each taste can influence the next, leading eventually to a focused orientation, so that all the nibbling may end up looking like a big bite (or, alternately, may allow the organization finally to take one big bite!).[15]

Emergent strategy can result from the efforts of an individual chief or a small executive team, as Quinn has suggested. But the concept allows itself to be interpreted more broadly. The prime actor may be an alter ego, or even a clandestine player who conceives a strategic vision and then conveys it to the chief as if the latter invented it, or simply foists it upon an unsuspecting organization. (In that case, the strategy is deliberate for the actor but emergent for the organization.) But the "strategist" can just as well be collectivity as well. Various people can interact and so develop a pattern that becomes a strategy. This process can be rather simple: For example, all the salesmen get together, discuss among themselves, and decide they will all refuse to sell to one type of customer in favor of another. Thus the firm's market strategy changes. But the process can also be complex. Consider the one Burgelman describes, with initiatives down below, champions in the middle, and authorizers at the top. Then superimpose on this the idea of convergence, that somehow the consequences of these initiatives lead to some kind of integration, pattern, or strategy. This means that strategies can develop in all kinds of unusual ways, as people interact, mutually adjust, learn from each other, conflict, and develop consensus. At the limit is a kind of "grass roots" model of strategy making: Strategies grow initially like weeds in a garden, taking root in all kinds of strange places; some proliferate to become broadly organizational, sometimes without even being recognized as such, let alone being consciously managed to do so (Mintzberg and McHugh 1985).

Emergent strategy means, literally, unintended order. So in its most extreme form there is technically no learning. The patterns just form, driven by external forces or needs rather than the conscious thoughts of any actors. But real learning surely takes place at the interface of thought and action, as actors reflect on what they have done. In other words, strategic learning must combine intention with realization. We need another element in the model. And here is where the ideas of Karl Weick come in.

In a book (1979) and several articles (for example, 1983), Weick has long described a concept that proves to be key to the learning school (even though, until very recently, the concept of organizational strategy never appeared in his writings). Using the ecological model of enactment (or variation), selection, and retention, Weick describes the organization as acting first ("do something!"), finding out what works, making sense of that in retrospect, and then retaining the behaviors that seem desirable. This may sound logical enough, but it should be recognized that it reverses the central thrust of the three prescriptive schools. They assume that strategies should be thoroughly thought through before being implemented—in other words, that learning stops before acting begins. In Weick's description, learning is not possible without acting. Of course, either approach may be viable, depending on the situation. The strategist who can figure out the environment—not just as it is but as it will be—can proceed in the deliberate fashion of the prescriptive schools, while the one who cannot had better act and react, so that the organization can learn over time. When Weick writes that "all understanding originates in reflection and looking backward" (1979: 194), he is in fact describing both cases.

Combining these notions of emergence and "sense making" raises all kinds of fascinating issues. For example, organizations may learn by recognizing patterns in their own behaviors, thereby making their emergent strategies of the past deliberate for the future. In other words, learning informs planning. Of course, the opposite can happen too. For example, learning can take place within a broad vision or perspective—what we have referred to as "umbrella strategy" (Mintzberg and Waters 1985)—so that the strategy is deliberate in its orientation but emergent in its details. Similarly, the organization can use a "process strategy" (Mintzberg and Waters 1985), where the central leadership manages the process (who gets to make strategy and in what structure) while leaving the specific content (that is, what these strategies are to be) to others. For this leadership, process becomes content!

The interplay between thought and action can also be fascinating for the learning school. Issues that can be addressed include the diffusion of strategic intentions, not just down a hierarchy, but up and across it (Demers 1987); organizational revitalization through steady learning (as opposed to of having to revert to dramatic turnaround); and that wonderfully elusive concept of the "organization's mind." If an organization can be defined as collective action in the pursuit of common mission, then the concept of the organization's mind (i.e., collective cognition) becomes not just viable but useful. It can help to explain the limitations of the first four schools as well as the Quinn and Lindblom notions of incrementalism. Many people can act with one mind, so to speak, most obviously when there is a strong ideology (as shall be discussed in the cultural school; see also Brunsson 1976, 1982), but also when other forces drive them to behave in common ways.

This discussion suggests that a learning model of strategy formation is now evolving. There has, of course, been a long and somewhat active literature on organizations as learning systems, dating back at least to Cyert and March's *A Behavioral Theory of the Firm* (1963), and including the work of Richard Normann (1977), Chris Argyris (1976), and Donald Shon (1974, 1978); see Shrivastava (1983) for a review of this literature as well as Hedberg's handbook review article (1981). But much of this was not written from the perspective of strategy formation (see Fiol and Lyles 1985). There have been, however, a few in-depth studies of how particular organizations really did learn in a strategic sense. Notable are Miles's (1982) account of diversification as learning in the tobacco industry and Pascale's (1984) fascinating presentation of the story told by Honda middle managers about of how they learned their way into dominance in the American motorcycle business.[16]

Emerging Premises of the Learning School

This discussion can now be concluded by inferring the following premises from the evolving collection of writings we call the learning school:

1. *The complex and dynamic nature of the organization's environment, often coupled with the diffusion in the organization of its knowledge base for strategy making, precludes deliberate control; strategy making must above all take the form of a process of learning over time, in which, at the limit, formulation and implementation become indistinguishable.*
2. *While the leader must learn too and sometimes can be the sole learner, more commonly it is the collective system that learns: There are many potential strategists in most organizations.*
3. *That learning proceeds in emergent fashion through behavior that stimulates thinking retrospectively, so that sense is made of action.* Strategic initiatives are taken by whoever has the capacity to learn and the resources to support that capacity. This means that strategies can take root in all kinds of strange ways and places, often in response to external pressures and events. These initiatives may be left on their own to develop or flounder, or else they may be championed by managers higher up in the organization, who integrate them with other strategic initiatives or with elements of the existing strategy and then promote them to

senior management for approval. Either way, the initiatives create streams of experience that are sometimes reinforced, converging into patterns that become emergent strategies. This may happen naturally, even spontaneously, as an initiative proliferates to pervade the behavior of the system at large. Or the process of proliferation may be consciously managed, as emergent patterns are recognized and made formally deliberate.

4. *The role of leadership then becomes not to preconceive deliberate strategies, but to manage the process of strategic learning.* Senior managers give particular attention to the people involved and the structures used to facilitate learning, and are prepared to recognize, shape, and direct the strategies that do emerge. Ultimately, then strategic management involves crafting the subtle relationships between thought and action, control and learning, stability and change.

5. *Accordingly, strategies appear first as patterns out of the past, and only later perhaps as deliberate plans for the future, ultimately perhaps as broader perspectives.*

Critique of the Learning School

One should not expect harsh condemnation of the learning school from one of its adherents. This author favors it because it offers a counterbalancing force to the "rational" but artificial deliberateness so long promoted in the conventional literature and practice of strategic management. But this school faces the same dangers of excess. For example, Andrews (1980b) refers to Lindblom's organization as "purposeless" and to Wrapp's article as "anti-strategic." Although this criticism cannot apply to the more recent work in this school, it appears true that an organization that proceeds through incrementalization of any kind—that prefers constant nibbling to a good bite—runs the risk of not being able to converge on a clear strategy. Of course, this is not always a bad thing, as was argued in the critique of the design school. But disjointed activities can sometimes reduce the effectiveness of an organization, as its people work at cross purposes.

For example, if the signals coming in from the outside vary widely, an organization, to achieve a sense of direction and focus efforts, may have to choose some and ignore others. But with many actors free to choose, independent of strong central direction, the organization may continually bounce back and forth between competing perspectives promoted by different groups. Of course, the opposite danger can be present too—that one perspective may win not because it is better but because its proponents are better politicians or champions.

Collective learning can also be a cumbersome way to deal with certain types of strategic change, notably when major commitments are required (Makridakis et al. 1982: 18). To quote Connolly (1982: 45): "Nuclear wars and childbearing decisions are poor settings for a strategy of 'try a little one and see how it goes.'"! Through incrementalism, organizations can also be lured into positions they never intended via a process Staw (1976) has labeled "escalating commitment": the negative consequences of the previous incremental action encourage further investment to recoup losses. The organization learns in the negative sense; the U.S. experience in Vietnam is perhaps a prime example (Mintzberg 1978).[17] In fact, the label "foot in the door" technique refers to the practice, common in government, where proponents of a program use incrementalism to achieve its full realization: They attain support for one small initiative and gradually enlarge that until the whole program has been adopted. In effect, emergentness is used as a ploy to realize a strategy that is deliberate for its proponents.

Similarly, an organization in crisis may not have the time to learn in a decentralized, incremental way. Therefore, it may be better off with a forceful leader who already has a strategic vision to save it or at least can develop one quickly. Even when not in crisis, some organizations need strategic visions that are novel and tightly integrated— what we have called "gestalt strategies" (Mintzberg 1978)—and these are more likely to come through a centralized entrepreneurial approach than one of decentralized learning.

Finally, organizational learning can be expensive. It takes time; resources must be invested in false starts; people must be convinced of the benefits of one strategy or another; and the organization may have to bounce around repeatedly and pay the price of not settling down quickly and concentrating its resources. It is much more convenient to have a visionary at the helm pronouncing a clear vision for all to follow or, even better, to be handed an optimal strategy from the computers of the positioning school analysts.

Contribution and Context of the Learning School

This previous sentence, of course, also suggests the contribution of the learning school. Visionaries are not always available, and even when they are, the situation in which they can "envision" is not always present. Likewise, the positioning school computers often come up short, offering banal solutions to complex problems. Then the organization that wishes to develop effective strategy may have no choice but to learn collectively.

Such learning seems particularly necessary in organizations that operate in rather complex environments, where the knowledge needed to create strategy is widely diffused in the organization and cannot be brought to one center. Of course, organizations decentralize for other reasons too—for example, because power rests legally in the hands of many people (as in the U.S. Congress, about which Lindblom wrote, or hospitals whose physicians retain powerful legal perogatives). Here, strategy formation may have to be a process of collective learning simply because no central authority has the power to impose it on the whole organization. The various actors must work it out by mutual adjustment, if they can. Quinn's (1980) corporations are like this to a partial degree: The central managers may be able to formulate strategy, but the political realities dictate that implementation must be a process of collective agreement, if not collective learning.

Also, any organization that faces a novel situation usually has to engage in a process of learning (whether individual or collective, depending on its ability to bring the relevant information to a central place) in order to figure out what is taking place. Even the organization's own strengths and weaknesses may have to be discovered empirically, through a process of gradual learning.

For example, when a mature industry is subjected to an unprecedented discontinuity—say, a technological breakthrough that upsets its established recipes (Grinyer and Spender 1979)—organizations in it have to engage in a process of learning in order to develop new viable strategies. Of course, if the environment does not settle down but instead remains dynamic and unpredictable, then these organizations may not be able to converge on a clear strategy, even as pattern in action. But even in this case, the approach of the learning school may have to be favored because (in the spirit of Weick's concepts) it allows the organization to do *something*—to respond to an evolving reality in individual steps instead of having to wait for a full-blown strategy.

Thus, the learning school approach might be most common in those organizations we have referred to as adhocracies and professional bureaucracies (Mintzberg 1979), and also in organizations of any type during periods of *dramatic* or *unprecedented change* in the environment or simply ones of *evolving strategic change* due to the need for political maneuvering.

To conclude, the learning school has brought a reality to the study of strategy formation that has been lacking in the other schools so far discussed in this chapter. Based largely on descriptive research, it has told us not so much what organizations are supposed to do as what they actually do do when faced with a complex external or internal situation. But good description can be prescriptive too—indeed, sometimes better than prescriptive theory because it can reveal exemplary behavior under particular circumstances.

A similar conclusion can be offered about the notion of free will. While the prescriptive schools, especially that of positioning, are more deterministic than they would have their readers believe, the learning school is less so. Within what appears to be passive, reactive responses to outside forces, the organization actually learns and creates—it comes up with novel and interesting strategies. Nowhere is this better recorded than in Pascale's (1984) story of how Honda did everything wrong to emerge as the market leader in the American motorcycle industry. Grabbing initiative, no matter how serendipitously, no matter how messy the process, no matter how initially confused the actors, is ultimately voluntaristic. In contrast, slotting oneself into a supposedly optimal strategy, as dictated by the formal analysis of one's context, is deterministic. Much as setting out to maximize profit may prove ineffective (because it is so compulsive), setting out to be in total control may in fact forfeit control (for the same reason).

The entrepreneurial school too offered little in the way of formal prescription. Strategy formation was considered a black box, closed to the comprehension of the conscious mind. Short of advising organizations to find visionary leaders, the entrepreneurial school has been of little help in explaining or improving strategy formation practice. Of course, the cognitive school was supposed to fill that gap—to tell us how visionary leaders conceived their strategies—but it has yet to do so. Our own belief is that the learning school, in contrast, has provided us with greater understanding. Its research is based on simple methods that seem better suited to explaining the complexities of strategy making than the sophisticated techniques of so much social science. In any event, it is critically important that we come to understand strategic thinking, both individual and collective. The learning school, whose literature base is small compared with those of the planning and positioning schools, has nonetheless made a major contribution in this regard. And it will likely continue to do so.

THE POLITICAL SCHOOL: STRATEGY FORMATION AS A POWER PROCESS

The learning school, especially in the writings of Quinn and Lindblom, has already introduced power and politics into this discussion, in contrast to the first four schools, which ignore it entirely. What is here labeled the political school takes off the gloves altogether and characterizes strategy formation as an overtly political process.

We assume a rather broad definition of politics here and, ironically, in so doing take our lead from the positioning school. If the purpose of a commercial organization is to compete legitimately in an economic marketplace, then we might use the label "political" for what does not fit this—alegitimate as well as illegitimate behaviors (Mintzberg 1983: 172). In effect, politics becomes synonymous with the exploitation of power in other than purely economic ways. This would obviously include clandestine arrangements to subvert competition (such as establishing cartels), but it might also include cooperative arrangements that have the same effect (such as joint ventures).

Indeed, as noted earlier, strategies that are generic for the positioning school can, with a slight twist of orientation (by the observer or the actors in question), become political. Likewise, we could talk of political strategic groups and political generic industries. Justification for doing this comes, we believe, from the fact that the line between economic and political intent is both fine and subtle. With the positioning school having so carefully situated itself on one side, the political school has to be on the other. But such a distinction must be considered artificial; real behavior spans the continuum of the two, with distinctions impossible to make at the margins.

Politics can surround an organization; it can also infuse it. Therefore, we shall distinguish between two branches of the political school. What we shall call *micro* politics deals with the play of illegitimate or alegitimate power *inside* an organization, in its processes of strategic management. *Macro* politics will concern the use of power *by* the organization in illegitimate or alegitimate ways—in other words, where the organization acts as a political vehicle. As an example of the former, we might consider the internal intrigue and bargaining over the issue of divesting a major division. An example of the latter might be the organization on the verge of bankruptcy that pressures a government for loan guarantees. One focuses on actors conflicting with their colleagues, usually out of self-interest; the other considers the organization acting out of its own self-interest, in conflict, or cooperation, with other organizations.

The literature of the political school that has come out of strategic management must be considered small—hardly more than a trickle since the early 1970s, although it has grown somewhat in recent years. But when we add the associated literature from political science, on government policy-making as a political process, it becomes quite large and long-established.

Of the political science literature on policy-making, much is not of use to strategic management, either because it is concerned with specific policies (for example, foreign affairs or police reform) devoid of general conceptual insight, or because it gets into tedious debates about abstract nuances of the process (such as those concerning incrementalism). Moreover, a good deal of the rest falls into our other schools, especially the planning school (a large literature on the PPBS experience in government) and to a lesser extent the positioning school (some of the "policy science" writings). But there is a good deal in the spirit of the political school too, some quite insightful and potentially helpful, although little of it widely recognized in the literature of strategic management.

Of this work, probably best known in management is Graham Allison's (1971) model of "governmental politics," perhaps the most comprehensive description available of strategy formation as a process of internal politics. Other interesting, though less known, works include Schoettle (1968), Bauer and Gergen (1968), Wildavsky

(1965, 1974, 1979), a number of the papers in the Rosenau (1969) volume on *International Politics and Foreign Policy*, including Jervis (1969) and Hilsman (1969), and a literature on "policy slippage" and "policy drift" (Majone and Wildavsky 1978: 105; Kress et al. 1980; Lipsky 1978) that considers, in ways unlike the literature of strategic management, distortions in the implementation of strategies.

Premises of the Political School

The premises of the political school are as follows:

1. *The strategy formation process is fundamentally a political one—that is, based on illegitimate or alegitimate means and usually parochial ends that often generate conflict, whether focused within the organization (micro politics) or reflecting actions by the organization (macro politics).*
2. *Political strategies, whether realized via deliberate plans or emergent patterns, tend to take the formed positions and especially ploys rather than perspectives.*
3. *In micro politics, there is no dominant actor, but rather a number who vie with each other to control organizational outcomes, or else who challenge vulnerable central actors.*
4. *In macro politics, the organization promotes its own welfare through aggressive deliberate strategies of a political nature.*
5. *Micro politics tends to take place in times of major change, either imposed on the organization externally or else arising internally as a result of the realignment of the organization's power system (the rise of a previously weak source of influence or the breakdown of an established one).*
6. *Macro politics reflects the closed system nature of an organization, namely its power relative to the external influencers around it.*

Micro Politics: Political Strategy Making within Organizations

If strategy making can be a process of planning and analysis, cognition and learning, then it can also be one of politics. Different actors, or coalitions of them, with power, use political means (meaning outside the ordinarily acceptable ones of authority, expertise, and ideology) to vie with each other over outcomes. Strategy formation thus becomes a process of bargaining and negotiation.

Our interest here is in outcomes that become strategies, or forces that impede their formation. But the very fact that the process is political means that the organization is likely driven more by parochial interest than common interest, which makes it difficult to arrive at strategies—whether deliberate or emergent. Deliberate strategies are discouraged by the fact that strategic intentions are disputed rather than shared, and emergent strategies—namely, the convergence of actions into patterns—are discouraged by the fact that the bargaining process is haphazard, rewarding different actors at different times. (We noted a similar result of Lindblom's theory, for the same reason: As he originally stated it, it was significantly one of politics.) Yet strategies can emerge from political processes. Sometimes a single commitment arrived at politically (such as a "strategic candidate" successfully promoted) may be important enough to set a precedent and thereby impose a pattern on a stream of subsequent actions. Or when political battles erupt over major changes in strategy, typically when a group of "young Turks" promoting the change engages an "old guard" resisting it, whoever wins sets strategy.

The management literature of the political school was rather thin until about 1975. Everyone knew politics happened, but researchers rarely studied it. An exception was the work of Cyert and March (1963), who described organizations as political entities, coalitions of influencers who engaged in continual processes of bargaining to produce series of outcomes. Cyert and March did not discuss strategy per se, and their notion of "sequential attention to goals," in which different centers of influence each took their turn collecting benefits, was one thing that discouraged strategies from forming. Yet they did recognize the existence of relatively stable streams of commitments, though more of an operating nature, in the form of budgets, standard operating procedures, and the like (which presumably reflected strategies).

Then in the later 1970s there was a sudden interest in the subject, though hardly not an explosion. MacMillan (1978) produced a text entitled *Strategy Formation: Political Concepts* (see also the second edition, MacMillan and Jones 1986); Sarrazin wrote a thesis (1975) and subsequently an article (1977–1978) on the political side of planning; Pettigrew (1977) and Bower and Doz (1979) also published on strategy formulation as a political process. That literature continued into the 1980s with, for example, MacMillan and Guth (1985) on "Strategy Implementation and Middle Management Coalitions," Narayanan and Fahey (1982) on "The Micro-Politics of Strategy Formulation," Hardy (1983) asking "Is Strategy Making a Political Process?" and our book *Power in and around Organizations* (Mintzberg 1983), which included discussions on such political games as "young Turks" and "strategic candidates" as well as sections on the role of politics in promoting and resisting strategic change (see also Gray and Ariss 1985 for a related but more elaborate discussion of the role of politics in strategic change at different points of the organizational life cycle).

Organizations may be mildly or occasionally political. In fact, only the smallest and most autocratically run organization is likely able to avoid politics completely during periods of major change. On the other hand, organizations can become entirely captured by pervasive politics so that every issue is disputed (see Mintzberg 1983: ch. 23 on the "political arena"). In these organizations, the literature of public policy-making (for example, Allison's governmental politics model) becomes directly applicable to understanding strategic behavior.

Macro Politics: The Pursuit of Political Strategies

Organizations may also be considered instruments of external power groups, functioning as directed from the outside (Rhenman 1973; Mintzberg 1983: ch. 18) or else as systems closed to external influence and so able to act as political entities themselves (Mintzberg 1983: ch. 19). There has long been a literature on the latter, in the context of the large business corporation (Berle and Means 1968, first published in 1932; the various writings of Charles Perrow, see, for example, 1970, 1972; and Galbraith 1967). But perhaps the first major contemporary work on strategy formation in the closed system organization was Pfeffer and Salanik's (1978) book *The External Control of Organizations* (where the *of* should have been *by*). They described how powerful organizations are able to pursue clear, deliberate strategies of a political nature. In fact, the strategies they described were no less generic than those of the positioning school; indeed in some cases they were the same ones! For example, where vertical integration or merger was an economic strategy to that school, this school considered it a political means pursued for political ends.

Subsequent work on political strategies (or conventional strategies pursued politically) include, for example, Birnbaum (1985), Gram and Crawford (1985), Galbraith and Stiles (1984), Keim et al. (1984), and Moulton and Thomas (1987), the latter on "Bankruptcy as a Deliberate Strategy." Attention should also be drawn here to work on "collective strategies"—namely, those of cooperation between organizations (Astley and Formbrun 1983; Astley 1984).[18] Other works of a macro political nature describe how organizations are able to maneuver politically in their environments to establish strategies (Hirsch 1975, on how particular industry conditions facilitate this, a kind of political industry analysis; Murray 1978, on the strategic behavior of a utility; and Hafsi and Thomas 1985, on the use of planning as a device for communicating with, and garnering the support of, external constituencies).

We should add that in our opinion the writings on "stakeholder analysis" (Freeman 1984) do not belong in this school. That corporations can sit back and analyze who has power over them and how it should be dealt with seems naive (and reflecting an unquestioning acceptance of the closed system nature of the corporation). We believe such efforts should be dismissed as futile attempts to bring processes that are intrinsically political under the control of the planning school models (and, correspondingly, of the organization's administration).

Of some interest, yet hardly broached in this literature, is the relationship between micro and macro politics. For example, what effect does the internal politicization of an organization have on it as a political actor externally, and vice versa? There may also be a number of interesting relationships between the political and the other schools—for example, as organizations grow larger and more powerful in mature industries perhaps a tendency to favor first the positioning school and later the political school. (Of course, consideration of all kinds of interrelationships among the various schools would be of interest.)

Critique, Context, and Contribution
of the Political School

By now, our critiques of the different schools are forming their own pattern, at least in one respect. Strategy formation is political, but it is not *only* political. Clearly, this school, like each of the others, overstates to make its points. The role of integrating forces such as leadership and ideology tends to get slighted here, as does the notion of strategy itself. By concentrating attention on devisiveness and fractioning, the political school may miss patterns that do form, even in rather conflictive situations. Moreover, while it is true that politics can play a positive role in organizations (especially in promoting needed change blocked by the more established and legitimate forms of influence; see Mintzberg 1983: 224–231, 446–452), many who write about it tend to view it, if not favorably, then at least with a certain perverse affection. But this may cloud issues that need to be addressed. For example, in our opinion what we have called macro politics creates severe problems of power and collusion in a society of large organizations, yet that aspect is hardly addressed in the literatures of resource dependency and collective strategy.

These concerns aside, it hardly makes sense to describe strategy formation as a process devoid of political activity. This is especially evident during periods of *major change*, when power shifts and conflicts arise, especially in large, mature organizations (closed system machine bureaucracies and divisionalized forms) as well as in complex organizations of experts (professional bureaucracies and adhocracies) (see Mintzberg 1979, 1983). Political activity also tends to be more evident during periods of *blockage*, when strategic change cannot take place, often because of political intransigence, and periods of *flux*, when an organization is unable to establish any clear direction and so decision making tends to take the form of a free-for-all.

The political school has contributed its share of vocabulary to the field of strategic management—for example, "coalition," "political games," and "collective strategies." It has also highlighted the importance of politics in generating strategic change, where forces promoting it must often overcome established powers seeking to maintain the status quo. Of course, politics is also used to resist strategic change, but perhaps not so effectively as the force represented by the next school of thought on strategy formation.

THE CULTURAL SCHOOL:
STRATEGY FORMATION AS
AN IDEOLOGICAL PROCESS

Hold politics up to a mirror and the reverse image you see is culture. Politics takes the entity called organization and fragments it; culture knits a collection of individuals into an integrated entity. In effect, one focuses primarily on self-interest, the other on common interest. So too, the literature of what we are calling the cultural school—strategy formation as a process rooted in the integrating force of culture—mirrors the political school. One tends to focus on the influence of politics in promoting strategic change; the other concerns itself largely with the influence of culture in maintaining strategy, indeed, in actively resisting strategic change.

Culture became a big issue in the management literature in the 1980s, apparently in response to the enormous success the Japanese had in competing with U.S. business. Their way of organizing—especially around organizational culture and ideology—seemed to explain much of that success. But for the most part, that new literature had nothing to do with strategy per se; almost all of it dealt with how organizational cultures were created and maintained, not with the effect they had on strategy. Indeed, the most successful practitioner book on the subject—Peters and Waterman's *In Search of Excellence* (1982)—had little to say about strategy per se. (The word appears only twice in the index, both times with regard to the titles of books—by Chandler and Rumelt.) Rather, it described organizations with remarkably stable strategic perspectives, suggesting that organizational culture had more to do with strategic continuity than change. But there was a literature on the relationship between culture and strategy, a rich and insightful one that developed in the 1970s but has not been well known outside of its native Sweden.

Culture and Ideology

Every field of study seems to have its one central concept—market in economics, politics in political science, and strategy in strategic management. Likewise, culture appears to be the central concept in anthropology. Accordingly, anthropologists debate its definition endlessly. We shall ignore all that and define culture simply as the established patterns of beliefs shared by the members of a collectivity, in our case, a formal organization. Culture, then, is collective cognition; it represents the "organization's mind" with regard to shared beliefs, typically reflected in traditions and habits as well as more tangible manifestations such as stories, symbols, credos, and the like. All of these create or at least reflect norms that, in turn, establish expectations and so shape behavior. At the conference in the South of France, John Edwards (1977: 13) introduced the cultural perspective by adding his verse:

> A Seventh, a pace behind the rest,
> A Step or so away,
> Did strive to sense what was the beast?
> What rules did he obey?
> By smell, by trace, by atmosphere,
> To him the Elephant did appear.

Ideology, in the organizational sense, shall be taken here to mean *rich* culture—a strong set of beliefs shared passionately by the members of a particular organization that distinguish it from all other organizations. Thus, while the *culture* of, say, Howard Johnson's may be associated with fried clams and orange roofs, the *ideology* of McDonald's is associated with an almost fetish belief in efficient service and cleanliness. Note that we are here distinguishing *organizational* ideology from ideology of a broader political nature (even though one can occasionally serve as the basis for the other, as in an Amway's embracing of the ideology of capitalism).

Premises of the Cultural School

The following are the premises of cultural school:

1. *Strategy formation is fundamentally a process of collective behavior, based on the beliefs shared by the members of an organization.*
2. *As a result, strategy takes the form of perspective above all, not position or ploy, and is rooted in intentions (though not necessarily explicit), and reflected in patterns, which makes it deliberate.*
3. *Coordination and control in the organization are largely normative, based on the influence of the shared beliefs.*

4. *Given the importance of the internal belief system, the organization tends to be proactive in comparison with an environment that appears to be passive and diffuse in its influence.*

5. *Culture and especially ideology do not encourage strategic change so much as perpetuate existing strategy; at best they allow for shifts in position within the organization's overall strategic perspective* (Dunbar et al. 1982).

The Swedish School

In 1965, the Swedish organization SIAR—Scandinavian Institutes for Administrative Research—was formed as kind of a consulting firm-cum-research establishment. Its intellectual leaders were Eric Rhenman and Richard Normann. Rhenman's book *Organizational Theory for Long-Range Planning* appeared in English in 1973, but the Swedish edition was published in 1969. Normann published various papers (for example, 1971); his main book, *Management for Growth*, was finally published in English in 1977.[19] These two men laid out a conceptual framework (rooted largely in organizational culture), a style of theorizing (open-ended to say the least, with few constraints on the choice of vocabulary), and a methodological approach (ambitious inferences from few, intensive studies) that created a school of its own. Through the 1970s, a generation of researchers at Swedish universities wove intricate theories from intensive field studies, using colorful vocabulary to label some rather woolly concepts. After reading the likes of Michael Porter and the Boston Consulting Group, not to mention George Steiner and others of the planning school, to come across concepts such as "ghost myth," "misfits," and "organizational drama" is itself a form of culture shock, though perhaps not unwelcome in the often drab literature of strategic management.

The most active center for this school was the University of Gothenburg, in the work of Sten Jonsson (n.d.), Bo Hedberg (1973, 1974, also with Targama 1973, with Jonsson 1977, with Starbuck [not strictly Swedish] 1977, and with Starbuck and Greve, a Norwegian, 1978), and Rolf Lundin (with Jonsson 1977 and with Jonsson and Sjoberg 1977-1978). At the French conference, in their paper "Strategy Formulation as a Discontinuous Process," Hedberg and Jonsson (1977: 88) too added a verse:

The Eighth, he knew that Elephants,
Cannot be seen at all,
These creatures live in human brains,
As myths which rise and fall.
Thought: Let these blokes watch Elephants,
Then I'll give each a call!

By the late 1970s, as the Gothenburg group scattered and SIAR lost its missionary zeal (founder Rhenman having moved to Boston to work on its behalf there, Normann to Paris to work on his own), the Swedish school, such as it was, petered out, although research in the same spirit has continued in Sweden, in English at least as a scattered trickle (Berg 1979; Kylen 1982; Brunsson 1976, 1982; Melin 1982, 1983, 1985).

The Swedish school addressed far more than culture. It interwove a rich network of concepts, some from the other schools we have been discussing, including fit or consonance (in the spirit of our design and configuration schools), values, images or myths, politics, cognition, and organizational learning, around themes of organizational stagnation, decline, crisis, and turnaround. In ambitious efforts rarely reflected elsewhere in the field (Pettigrew 1985 and Grinyer and Spender 1979 in the United Kingdom, and Miles 1982 and Quinn 1980 in the United States among the few exceptions), it sought to integrate this wide array of factors into explanations of strategic change in organizations. (It should be noted that the word *strategy* itself did not figure prominently in its vocabulary.) In this respect, slotting this exclusively into any one school of thought is not correct. But because we believe that this literature does have one overriding theme—namely, the problems of adaptation in a collective context (above all the need for collective "reframing" as a prerequisite to strategic change), we do not consider it an injustice to discuss it here, within our cultural school.

Culture and Strategy in the Anglo-Saxon World

As noted earlier, outside of Scandinavia culture was not a big issue in the management literature prior to 1980. There was the paper by Edwards, an Englishman, in 1977, a significant U.S. study in organizational sociology on the "distinctive college" (Clark 1970, 1972), and of course, Selznick's book *Leadership in Administration* (1957), among others. Each had important things to say about organizational ideologies. But it was the success of Japanese business—discussed initially in two American best-selling books (Ouchi 1981 and Pascale and Athos 1981), followed by Peters and Waterman's best-seller *In Search of Excellence* (1982), about similarly inclined American corporations—that stimulated a rapid growth in this literature, especially in the United States, but also to some extent in Britain and Canada. Most of this literature, as already noted, had little to do with strategy per se; it was concerned with the study, the delineation, and the construction of organizational cultures and ideologies (Schein 1985; the September 1983 issue of *Administrative Science Quarterly*, Jelinek et al. 1983).

In the mid-1980s, however, a small literature did begin to develop that focused on the relationship between strategy and culture. We have already noted the Pettigrew (1985) study in England; in the United States Feldman (1986) considered the relationship of culture to strategic change, and Barney (1986) asked whether culture can be a source of sustained competitive advantage; in Canada, Firsirotu (1985) wrote one award-winning thesis on "strategic turnaround as cultural revolution" (see also Allaire and Firsirotu 1985), and Rieger (1987) wrote another, also at McGill, that considered the influence of national culture, acting through organizational culture, on strategy and structure in airlines around the world; Kets de Vries and Miller (1986) addressed the role of culture in mediating between executive personality and strategy; and Westley (1983) associated strategy making with image making.

Of course, there has long been a literature on resistance to change (for example, Staw 1976, 1981) that has indirect links to the culture-strategy relationship. Much like the stakeholder approach to power, there is also a pseudo-cultural school literature on techniques to design culture. But this too really belongs in the planning school— "To match your corporate culture and business strategy, something like the procedures outlined above [four steps] should become a part of the corporation's strategic planning process" (Schwartz and Davis 1981: 4). See also Uttal's (1983) critique of "the corporate culture vultures" in *Fortune* and Weick's subsequent comment, reported in Kiechel (1984: 11), that "A corporation doesn't have a culture. A corporation is a culture. That's why they're so horribly difficult to change."

Critique, Contribution, and Context of the Cultural School

If the positioning school could be faulted for artificial precision, then the cultural school can be faulted for conceptual vagueness. Especially, but not only in its Swedish version, the concepts come and go with remarkable speed, although they are not really much different from one another. As Richard Rumelt once quipped, "If two academics have the same idea, one of them is redundant!" (Strategic Management Society conference talk in Montreal 1982). On the other hand, the "hard" methods of social science are bound to miss the point about a phenomenon as ethereal as culture, much as they did in the study of leadership (Mintzberg 1982). And so we should really applaud the imagination of the Swedish researchers, as long as someone stands ready to sort through all the labels and synthesize all the concepts.

One danger of this literature is that, taken prescriptively, it can promote stagnation. It favors the management of consistency, of staying on strategic track, so to speak. By emphasizing tradition and consensus and by characterizing change as complex and difficult, it discourages strategic revolution. Ironically, however, while culture itself may be difficult to build in the first place and even more difficult to reconstruct later, it is not difficult to destroy. Any good old-fashioned strategy type, given enough authority, can do so easily enough. Indeed, the steps are spelled out (however inadvertently) in the standard approaches of the planning and the positioning schools. Concentrate on strategies as separate positions rather than integrated perspective, so that everything becomes a portfolio; be objective, which means to treat people as objects; calculate rather than commit, so that formulation looks optimal even if implementation doesn't work; and so on. This is often done inappropriately, so that rich cultures are needlessly destroyed. But when a culture has outlived its usefulness, when strategy as perspective must be changed, then perhaps the cultural school is not the literature to read.

Of course, this is not to argue that the contribution of the cultural school has been unimportant. In comparison with the disjointed conflict of politics, it offers the integrated consensus of ideology; against the individualized thinking and personalized style of the design and entrepreneurial schools, it introduces collective cognition and organizational style; in contrast to the ahistorical tendencies of the planning and positioning schools, it roots strategy in the rich tapestry of an organization's history. In this school, strategy formation becomes the management of collective cognition—an important element of the process though hardly an easy one to manage.

The cultural's school's implications are obviously particularly applicable to "missionary" type organizations, which have powerful ideologies (Mintzberg 1983: ch. 21), also to large, established machine bureaucracies whose stagnant cultures reinforce set procedures. They also seem to apply to particular periods in the lives of organizations, especially ones of *reinforcement*, in which rich strategic perspectives are pursued vigorously or, failing that, periods of *resistance to change*, in which necessary strategic adaptation is blocked by the inertia of a given strategic perspective. And perhaps this school can also help us to understand periods of *reframing*, during which new collective perspectives develop and even periods of *cultural revolution* that sometimes accompany strategic turnarounds.

THE ENVIRONMENTAL SCHOOL: STRATEGY FORMATION AS A PASSIVE PROCESS

Among the actors put at the center of the schools so far discussed—the chief, the brain, the planner, the organization, and so on—one has been conspicuously absent—namely, forces outside the organization, what organization theorists loosely label the "environment." Writers who favor these forces tend to describe the organization as passive and tend to reduce strategy formation to a kind of exogenous event rather than an internal process (much as did industrial organization economists by skipping strategy and trying to connect industry structure directly to performance). This may seem to put their approach outside the boundaries of strategic management (a conclusion we in fact favor), but there are good reasons to include it as our ninth school.

For one thing, this approach has helped bring our view of strategy formation into balance, by positioning environment alongside leadership and organization as one of three central actors in the process. Although the debates that this school evoked over the very existence of "strategic choice" were, at the limit, silly—to deny it entirely, any more than to attribute omniscient powers to the strategist, surely tells us more about the myopia of the protagonists than anything else[20]—in more moderate form they forced people in strategic management to consider the range of the decisional powers available in different contexts. Moreover, this school has helped to delineate certain attributes of the environment and to suggest their possible role in strategy formation.

Of course, the environment has not been absent in the other schools we have discussed. For example, in concluding that the positioning school represents determinism in the clothing of voluntarism, we drew attention to the role it implicitly accords the environment (specifically the economic environment of industry and the competition). Likewise, the cognitive school's emphasis on bias and distortion in cognition reflects the influence of an environment too complex to be easily understood. The learning school likewise emphasizes the complexity of the environment, but in this case, rather than mangling its messages, the strategists instead learn in a positive way. In our other schools, however, the environment has tended to be absent or incidental or at least passive.

In the environmental school, it is organization and leadership that become passive. Indeed, as we have moved through the various schools, the power of the central strategist has gradually diminished. In the design, and later the entrepreneurial school, the chief dominated. The planning and positioning schools tempered this slightly, by introducing the planner and analyst as clandestine strategists, while the cognitive and learning schools drew attention to the limitations of strategic thinking in a complex world. Additional strategists were introduced by the learning and then the political schools, and these became the collectivity in the cultural school. But through all this, the notion of strategists continued to reign supreme, whoever they were—individuals or the collectivity, whether cooperative or conflictive.

Now the environment becomes the central actor. But it is not an environment like the others. In this school, environment consists of a set of vague forces, kind of an atmosphere "out there"—in effect, everything that is not organization. Sometimes it is no more than a vague general force that drives the organization into some sort of ecological-type niche. Other times, it is delineated into a set of abstract dimensions. To the proponents of this school, the environment is not an angry customer banging at the company's door but "malevolent"; not an unexpected series of technological breakthroughs but "dynamic"; not the intricacies of transplanting hearts but "complex." Of course, we have already used some of these labels ourselves to distinguish the appropriate contexts for the different schools, as we did in a book on structure (Mintzberg 1979).

The environmental school first grew out of so-called contingency theory, which postulated that given environmental dimensions dictated specific attributes of the organization—for example, that stability of context requires formalization of structure. Eventually these dimensions came to be described as influencing the strategy-making process as well. Then certain organization theorists, under the label "population ecology," took a big step and postulated that conditions forced organizations into strategies—namely, market niches: Organizations did as the environment told them or else were "selected out." What was certainly selected out in this description was strategic choice, as power passed to that vague concept called environment.

Premises of the Environmental School

The premises of the environmental school are as follows:

1. *The environment, in general or manifested as a set of abstract forces, dictates strategy by forcing organizations or their attributes into ecological-type niches; those that refuse to so adapt must eventually die.*
2. *Thus there is no real internal strategist nor any internal strategy-making process, and leadership, as it has long been depicted in the strategic management as well as its own literature, is a myth.*
3. *Strategies are positions, niches where organizations are sustained until whatever nourishes them there runs out.*

The Population Ecology View

The environmental school finds its strongest expression in the works of people who label their approach "population ecology" or "natural selection." Using the well-known variation-selection-retention model, but with a different focus and result than Weick, they perceive organizations the way biologists perceive fruit flies—from a distance, in terms of collective behavior. Organizations, as members of populations, are born, find ecological niches, and eventually die. Aldrich and Pfeffer (1976: 82) emphasize the passive nature of this model, especially with regard to variation, where independent choice might be argued to exist:

> As a model of organizational change, the natural selection perspective is indifferent regarding the source of variation or change in the first place. Selection of social structures is accomplished by differential survival of structural forms, rather than by the adaptation of a single organizational unit. . . .
>
> Since selection is made by the environment according to some dimension of fitness, a theorist using this model could, in explaining only long-run changes, safely neglect intraorganizational managerial processes. In the long run only those organizations that fit the environment will survive and, consequently, one need not be as concerned with the processes by which such an organization-environment match is achieved. Stated in this form, the ecological perspective can be seen to be virtually isomorphic with the economic theory of perfect competition . . . and similar to elements of what has been called structural contingency theory.

Hannan and Freeman (1977) published what is probably the most widely cited article in this regard; among other things, it expressed their "doubt that the major features of the world of organizations arise through learning or adaptation" (1977: 957) (see also Hannan and Freeman 1984). Other well-known publications in this spirit include Aldrich (1979) and McKelvey and Aldrich (1983). In addition, some literature has appeared recently that seeks to tie the population ecology approach directly to the concerns of strategic management (Aldrich and Auster 1986; Aldrich et al. 1984; Freeman and Boeker 1984; Hrebiniak and Joyce 1985; Wholey and Brittain 1983–1984; Singh et al. 1986).

Critiques of the population ecology approach have been numerous and revolve around a number of obvious issues. "Where did these variations in the population come from?," asks Van de Ven in his review of Aldrich's book. He answers, "probably . . . in the many individual choices made by entrepreneurs and inventors" (1979: 324). Astley adds that environments are often "quite open and receptive to whatever variations are imposed on them" (1985: 41).

From a distance, behavior may look as it is described in this view. The question is, How great is that distance and how relevant that view for those practicing and studying strategic management? Hannan and Freeman (1977: 960), in seeking to justify the argument that "even the largest and most powerful organizations fail to survive over long periods," find it necessary to go back to the American Revolution to show that only twenty of the firms that existed then survive today (seven as divisions of other firms). They comment: "Presumably one needs a longer time perspective to study the population ecology of the largest and most dominant organizations" (1977: 960). But surely their argument is weakened rather than supported by their need to go back 200 years.

Indeed, even in true population ecology, debates abound over the capacity of species to adapt, not by natural selection, but by internally induced change. A good deal of this has been stimulated by Steven Jay Gould's model of "punctuated equilibrium," which argues that change has been fast, in ecological terms at least, and by his point that Darwin's claims that the intermediate stages in the fossil record would one day be filled-in have not yet been realized. Instead "the geologic record seems to provide as much evidence for cataclysmic as for gradual change," in other words, for "sudden appearance . . . 'fully formed'" (Gould 1980: 180). In pointing out that "extinction is no shame," Gould concludes that life "is a story of intricate branching and wandering, with momentary survivors adapting to change local environments" (1982: 12).[21] Thus, in the management literature, Astley has been able to distinguish individual and communal adaptation, the former possibly genetic but also possibly somatic: "an individual organism [can meet] local variations in its environment," sometimes even temporarily (1984: 530), much as do organizations when they make strategy.

Delineating the Environment

Contingency theorists did not go as far as the population ecologists in their pronouncements, although as already noted, they did not leave much more room for free choice either. But they did add two contributions to the literature of strategy formation. One is a delineation of the dimensions of the environment—as complex, dynamic, hostile, diverse, and so on. Contingency theory also focused on dimensions such as the age and size of the organization, the technical system it uses, and the power relationships that surround it. (For reviews of such dimensions of the environment, see Khandwalla 1977, Mintzberg 1979, and Starbuck 1976, whose thorough review also includes many tangible dimensions.)

The second contribution of contingency theory was a postulated set of relationships between these environmental dimensions and attributes of strategic management (beyond those of structure and power in more conventional organization theory). Some of the work of Miller (1979, 1983, 1987) and Miller and Friesen (1983) has been notable in this regard. Other publications related to strategy formation in the spirit of contingency theory include Cook (1975), Prescott (1986), and Jauch and Kraft (1986) (see also Dutton and Freedman 1985 and Smircich and Stubbart 1985 for other work on the relationship between environment and strategy).

One drawback of this work for strategic management is that the dimensions are too often abstract and aggregated. Strategy has to do with the selection of precise niches. Strategists are people who sometimes find places to stand in deep lakes (or, alternately, who sometimes drown in lakes that are on average shallow). That is why differentiation is such an important concept in this field. In reality, no organization faces an environment that is munificent or complex or hostile or dynamic (let alone turbulent). There may be periodic pockets of such things—in one market or another, with regard to some particular technology, sometimes even on several fronts but then usually temporary—but not permanent aggregates. It is, therefore, risky to manage strategy at such aggregate levels. What strategists need are "fine grained" probes that provide "thick" descriptions, nuanced as to time and area of application and context. As we shall argue in the configuration school, strategic management may be better served by a rich typology of environmental types, each of which describes in detail what organizations experience at particular points in their histories—in other words, episodes more than dimensions.

Critique, Contribution, and Context of the Environmental School

We have already presented most of our critique of this school in the discussion of its two major components. One issue is examined here: the debate over strategic choice.

Debating whether organizations make choices is about as useful as debating whether people are happy. There is a wide range of each, and prophesies here tend to be self-fulfilling; besides, engaging in such debates makes people unhappy and takes time away from making choices. In any event, the answers depend partially on one's perspective. Viewed from afar, fruit flies may respect the laws of natural selection; viewed close up, they are continuously making choices—"a story of intricate branching and wandering," much like the experiences of the writers of population ecology who chose their own niche. Perhaps the point is best made by Hannan and Freeman (1977: 961) themselves, in commenting on the effect of "large dominant organizations [that] can create linkages with other large and powerful ones so as to reduce selection pressures." In their view, "the selection pressure is bumped up to a higher level. So instead of individual systems failing, entire networks fail." True enough, except that the ultimate network is society itself. As we all go down together, realizing that (carrying this argument to its own "natural" conclusion) we are all pawns in a larger order, we may ask why anything matters at all (including Hannan and Freeman's article, itself no doubt dictated by some superior force).

The fact is that to serve its own niche, strategic management must view organizations close up, ideally in the shoes of the strategist. And there it should consider not the *existence* of choice, but the *conditions* that enlarge or restrict its breadth. Hage (1976) has argued, for example, that organizations choose constraints and thereby constrain choices.

We have found several interesting occurrences in this regard in our own research on patterns in strategy making. For example, Air Canada, in the latter years of our study period, was a large, powerful organization, the major player in secure and regulated markets. Yet its size restricted choice. As we asked in our report (Mintzberg et al. 1986), could any such "world class" airline possibly not have ordered jumbo jets when they came out? Alternately, in the 1930s, Steinberg's was a tiny supermarket chain functioning in a severe depression. Yet because of its strengths (perhaps more "Peterian" than "Porterian"—that is, based on excellence of operations more than on the selection of an advantageous strategic position) it made choices that the big chains could not—in fact, moving into the stores that they vacated (Mintzberg and Waters 1982). And Taylor (1982) studied the responses of four small organizations to what seemed like a hostile environment (anglophone institutions in a francophone region of an increasingly nationalistic Quebec). He found that their internal culture—what he labeled "the will or desire of the organization to change strategy" (1982: 343)—was the major factor in adaptation. For example, by all indications the hospital that Taylor studied should have been the most constrained. But in fact it adapted quite well. As Taylor concluded (1982: 342),

> A great deal of strategic discretion exists with respect to the speed of organization adaptation, and with respect to the direction that adaptation will follow. If anything, the external constraints on strategic adaptation found in this research were extremely broad, allowing a great deal of room for organizational maneuver.

This is perhaps the central message of strategic management!

What makes strategic management such an exciting field is that practitioners and researchers alike are constantly confronted with a rich and nuanced world, full of surprises, that favors imagination and action combined with thought. In our opinion, strategists who are successful get in close and understand the details—and so do successful researchers.[22] What distinguishes this field from others in management is its very focus on strategic choice—how to find it, where to find it, how to create it when it can't be found, and then how to exploit it. Thus, strategic management has no more need for debates over the existence of choice than do population ecologists for ones over the existence of populations.

Let us therefore learn about populations of organizations from the environment school, about the environments of organizations and especially about the different forms these can take. And let us take account of the contexts in which the ideas of this school seem most applicable, asking ourselves what types of organizations seem most constrained and when does strategic change seem most limited—for example, during certain stages of an organization's life cycle (for example, maturity). But let us not get sidetracked by excessive abstraction, overstatement, and unresolvable debate.

THE CONFIGURATIONAL SCHOOL: STRATEGY FORMATION AS AN EPISODIC PROCESS

All of the above: That is the message of the configurational school but with a particular angle. Each at its own time, in its own place, as an integrated phenomenon. In other words, the configurational school focuses on typologies and episodes of various kinds—types of organizations, kinds of environments in which they operate, distinct periods in their histories—ideally all integrated into stages which are sequenced over time, in life cycles (thus Lenz and Engledow 1983 refer to these as "era models"). Writers who favor words such as "mode," "archetype," "configuration," "period," "stage," and "life-cycle" tend to belong to this school of thought. They have not been terribly prolific—this is not one of the larger schools—but (for reasons to be discussed later) what has been published tends to get more than its expected share of attention.

Darwin (1887: 105) once distinguished "splitters" from "lumpers." Environment school people, in fact organization theorists in general, tend to be intemperate splitters; they like to isolate "variables," lay them out along continuous scales, and then study the relationships between their pairs. Configurational school people (present company included) are unabashed lumpers; they see the world in terms of integrated categories. Nuanced variability is assumed away to the benefit of overall clustering; outliers are ignored in favor of central tendencies. This, of course, also simplifies. In fact, the best critique of the configurational school may be the profundity of the work of the very few sophisticated splitters in strategic management, such as Quinn and members of the Swedish school, who (as noted earlier) have managed to weave together a wide array of factors into intricate, nuanced theories. The theories of the configuration school lumpers, in contrast, are rather more simple—perhaps categorical is a better word—although we like to believe they are equally revealing of reality, and certainly easier to comprehend.

The configurational approach can be found in all of the social sciences, although seldom in their mainstreams. What likely keeps it out is their obsession with being scientific (in the narrow sense), particularly with regard to quantification for purposes of validation and replication and the use of mathematics for its presumed intellectual rigor. These tendencies pervade the social sciences, although they are probably most pronounced in psychology and economics. One notable exception is history,[23] in which lumping is common, although theorizing is not: Historians like to isolate distinct periods in history and then study them intensively, if differentially. An historian who investigates one revolution, for example, will not typically claim expertise on revolutions in general.

Some historians do, however, conceptualize, for example, focusing on the concept of revolution (Crane Brinton 1938). And occasionally a Toynbee (1946–1957) or a Rostow (1971) comes along to present comprehensive periods of history. With a small leap of imagination, from behaviors in societies to strategies in organizations (for example, political revolution as equivalent to business turnaround), this work can, in fact, help to inform strategic management, especially about patterns of social change and collective responses to it. There are even historians who have written conceptually about "periodization"—the bases on which periods in the history of a social collectivity can be isolated (Gerhard 1956, Pokora 1966, Popescu 1965)—whose work could prove of direct use to the configuration school of strategic management.

While there has long been an active literature of business history, the literature that links this to strategic management is not large and has not generally been influential, although there have been recent papers calling for more of this or explaining how it should be done (see, for example, Ebert and Wehrall 1984; Alpert 1984). There has, however, been one notable exception.

If Alfred Chandler is not a chartered member of the configuration school of management, he is certainly among its most important ones. His best-known book in management, *Strategy and Structure* (1962), in the tradition of history concerned itself largely with specifics—namely, how strategies and structures developed in four influential U.S. corporations. But its last chapter, itself on "chapters in the history of the great industrial enterprise," laid out a theory of strategy and structure in a sequence of four distinct stages, which Chandler labeled "accumulating resources," "rationalizing the use of resources," "continued growth," and "rationalizing the use of expanded resources." In lumper labels, these were the strategies of expansion and vertical integration, the structure of functional for machine bureaucracy, the strategy of diversification, and the structure of divisionalization. (Chandler also drew a widely cited conclusion that structure follows strategy, which we commented on in our critique of the design school, but it should be noted here that a small literature also grew up to debate and dispute that point—for example, Burgelman 1983b and Hall and Saias 1980.)

We outline the premises of the configuration school below before proceeding with our discussion, which shall first consider the work of ourselves and our colleagues at McGill University and then other configuration work in the field.

Premises of the Configuration School

The premises of the configuration school are the premises of all of the schools brought together in well-defined contexts:

1. *The behaviors of organizations are best described in terms of configurations—distinct, integrated clusters of dimensions concerning state and time.*
2. *In particular, strategy formation is an episodic process in which a particular type and form of organization, matched to a particular type of environment, engages in a particular form of the process for a distinguishable period of time.*
3. *Accordingly, the process can be one of conceptual design or formal planning, systematic analysis or intuitive vision; it can be one of individual cognition and/or collective learning or politics; it can be driven by personalized leadership, organizational culture, or the external environment; and the resulting strategies can take the form of plans or patterns, ploys, positions, or perspectives; but each must be found at its own time and in its own context.*
4. *These periods of the clustered dimensions tend to sequence themselves over time in patterned ways that define common life cycles of strategy formation.*

Configurational Work at McGill

It probably would not be considered immodest to claim that the most concentrated effort to use a configurational approach in strategic management has taken place in McGill University's Faculty of Management. This can be traced to the arrival at McGill of Pradip Khandwalla in the early 1970s. In his doctoral dissertation at Carnegie-Mellon, Khandwalla (1970) uncovered what amounted to an empirical justification for configuration, although he neither used that label nor pursued that concept. Effectiveness in the organizations he studied related not to the use of any particular attribute but to the intercorrelations among several attributes. In other words, organizations appeared to function effectively because they put attributes together in synergistic ways.

This finding stimulated our own interest in configuration, reflected especially in two books that delineated types of organizations, one in terms of structure and context (Mintzberg 1979), the other in terms of power systems (Mintzberg 1983). These were not about strategy per se, although they did consider a number of issues related to strategic management. But a major research project, which began in 1971, did link the concepts of configuration and strategy formation (Mintzberg 1972, 1978; Mintzberg and McHugh 1985; Mintzberg and Waters 1982, 1984, 1985; Mintzberg et al. 1984, 1986, 1987). Designed to track strategies of different organizations over long periods of time, the approach was essentially historical although the intentions were not: The study sought to draw conclusions about the strategy formation process. For example, our interest was not in the history of Air Canada or even the airline industry in general, but in how large, secure machine bureaucracies develop strategically.

The basic orientation of this research was configurational. Strategies themselves were identified as episodes—patterns in action that sustained themselves for identifiable periods of time. These strategies were then lined up against one another to identify distinct periods in the history of the organization. Such periods were labeled in various ways (growth, flux, continuity) and were then used to develop general theoretical conclusions, the thrust of which was also configurational—for example, concerning life cycles in the development of strategies.

A number of doctoral students at McGill have written theses that, while not replicating any of our own work, approached the research from a configurational perspective. We have already referred to the theses of Firsirotu (1985) and Rieger (1987), the former on "strategic turnaround as cultural revolution" in a machine bureaucratic organization, the latter linking national cultures with aspects of structure and strategy formation to describe different configurations in airlines around the world. Langley (1987) wrote her thesis at H.E.C. Montreal in conjunction with McGill on the role of analysis in three organizations, categorized as a machine bureaucracy, professional bureaucracy, and adhocracy, as did Taylor (1982) on the strategic adaptation of four organizations in low growth environments. Other work of a configurational nature by colleagues at McGill include Jorgensen (1989) (see also Hafsi et al. 1987) on different configurations in state owned enterprises, and Hardy (1988, 1989) on the configurations of structure and strategy making used by universities in Canada and Brazil. Hardy et al. 1984 also published on "Strategy Formation in the University Setting"—namely, in professional bureaucracy.

Danny Miller, our first doctoral student, has been most prolific in this regard. His doctoral dissertation (Miller 1976; see also 1979) used published articles and cases on organizations to induce archetypes of strategy formation. Miller has produced a steady stream of publications since then, a certain amount of it with McGill management science professor Peter Friesen, most of this closely related to the configurational school (though some, as noted earlier, falls into the environmental school's contingency theory).

Miller's work has been especially ambitious in its integration across attributes; he has had particular success in combining breadth (large samples) with depth (often based on intensive reports[24]) to produce taxonomies. Some of this work has developed "archetypes," by which he means states of organizations, described in terms of strategy, structure, situation, and process (Miller 1979, 1986; Miller and Friesen 1977, 1978). Other work has described "transitions" between such archetypes (Miller and Friesen 1980a), while another body of writing has addressed configurational implications of strategic and structural change in organizations in terms of a "quantum" theory (Miller 1982; Miller and Friesen 1980b, 1982). Miller also coauthored "the case for configuration" (Miller and Mintzberg 1983, 1984), about the benefits of this approach both for conducting research and for developing useful theory. (See Miller and Friesen 1984 for a compendium of much of this work.)

The concept of quantum change goes to the heart of the configurational school. As Miller and Friesen depict it, it stands for the changing of many elements in coalignment, in contrast to piecemeal change—one element at a time. But as depicted in some of the other work of this school, such as Firsirotu's (1985) thesis or our own studies of Steinberg and Volkswagenwerk (Mintzberg and Waters 1982; Mintzberg 1978), or even Miller and Friesen's own references to "revolutionary change" (1984: 217–218, 223–226), quantum change often tends to be not only coaligned but also rapid rather than incremental. Indeed, without revolutionary change it could be argued that configurations would be more difficult to isolate: "the economics of adaptation, as well as some recent empirical evidence, argue for a dramatic quantum approach to organizational change— long periods of the maintenance of a given configuration, punctuated by brief periods of multifaced and concerted transition to a new one" (Miller and Mintzberg 1984: 23).[25]

This debate in strategic management between the revolutionary change of the configurational school and the incremental change of the learning school (especially as in Quinn's writings) is paralleled in the debate in biology between Gould's notion of punctuated equilibrium and Darwin's claims for evolutionary change,[26] also in the philosophy of science between Kuhn's (1970) revolutions and Popper's (1959) evolution. Of course, which it is depends on how closely one looks, and where. Change that looks incremental to one researcher may seem revolutionary to another. Different researchers may be focusing on different types of organizations, or different episodes in their development. Or perhaps, as we believe most likely, the difference is not one of context or time frame as much as of the phenomenon studied. For example, while Quinn interviewed individual executives about their thought processes (namely, their cognitions and intentions), Miller tracked the recorded behaviors of organizations (that is, their actions and realizations). So the two might in fact have been describing two sequential stages in the same process: Strategists learn incrementally and then oversee strategic change in revolutionary fashion. In other words, organizations bide their time until they learn where to go (perhaps also awaiting the opening of the necessary strategic windows) (Abell 1979), and then they leap in revolutionary fashion.

Other Configurational Studies in Strategic Management

There are several other bodies of literature in strategic management that take a configurational approach. One group of writers, linking to organizational theory, considers the relationship between various forms of strategy and structure (Rumelt 1974; Fredrickson 1986; Bart 1986; Daniels et al. 1984), or else the evolution of organizations over time, in stages of strategy and structure (Scott 1971; Greiner 1972; Galbraith and Nathanson 1978; Galbraith 1985).

Another group looks carefully at strategic change, placing strategic behavior in the context of specific types of organizations or of their stages. Firsirotu's (1985) thesis on machine bureaucracy as well as Hardy et al.'s work on professional bureaucracy has already been mentioned in the McGill work. In addition, Ettlie et al. (1984) consider strategy and structure in the cases of radical and incremental innovation; and Grinyer and Spender (1979) focus on "industry recipes" in the context of turnaround.

Still another body of literature is more typological in nature, concerned with the classification of organizational forms based primarily on their strategies.[27] Best known perhaps is the Miles and Snow (1978) typology of prospectors, defenders, analyzers, and reactors,[28] which has spawned a literature of its own (Snow and Hrebiniak 1980; Hambrick 1983; Zahra 1987; Smith et al. 1986; see also Miles 1982: 102-113). Our own initial typology of entrepreneurial, adaptive, and planning modes of strategy making (Mintzberg 1973) stands as a simple precursor of these ten schools. Other three-model typologies are those of Chaffee (1985) and Allison (1971), the latter on three models to interpret the American government's response to the Cuban missile crisis, which although in public policy has been widely cited in the strategic management literature.

In another vein, Hambrick (1984), like Miller (1981, with Friesen 1984), has argued the issues surrounding taxonometric research in strategic management. Hambrick has, in fact, done his share of such research, some of which we see as representing a configurational approach to the positioning school (for example, presenting taxonomies of strategies for mature industrial-product businesses) (1984).[29] In fact, a certain amount of other positioning research is also configurational in nature, especially what we put into our "cluster" cells of figure 5-2, for example, on strategic groups, generic industries, and strategy life cycles. Of course, the notion of configuration has not been absent from some of the other schools as well—for example in stagnation and turnaround as distinct periods in the cultural school or reframing as a stage in the cognitive school. In fact, we have used the configurational approach throughout this discussion, in delineating the types of organizations and the stages of development that seemed most applicable to each of the schools.[30]

Critique, Context, and Contribution of the Configurational School

Because pattern is in the eye of the beholder, all lumping must be considered somewhat artificial. To describe by configuration is to distort, in order to explain. But since all theory distorts by simplifying in one way or another, what really matters is how serious such distortion is compared with other forms. This question can be addressed through empirical research—one can study the extent to which various elements configure into new categories—but at its root it shall always remain a question of perception. The fact is that we need typologies to perceive our world. Like it or not, people prefer to think in terms of categories—envelopes of attributes by which we sort out a complex world (see Miller and Mintzberg 1983).

Thus, we conclude that we need lumping, but that we must also be beware of its distortions. Consider the categorizations of continents by geographers. This has certainly proven useful, yet it is also somewhat arbitrary. Australia certainly sits as a geographically distinct entity; even the character of its people can be distinguished to some extent (at least with regard to language and accent). But these things are even more true of Greenland, which doesn't merit the label continent. (Would that have been true if the Inuit made the categories?) Africa is just as distinct geographically although it is more diverse culturally. But to call Europe a continent, especially with regard to its physical geography, seems arbitrary, more a reflection of *who* categorized than *how.* We need such typologies—categorizing helps us understand our messy world—but we had better beware of their limitations.

The configurational approach should not, therefore, be used to ignore the nuances of our messy world. We need fine-grained work that exposes all the complex interrelationships among attributes— such as the gradualism of some change and the hybrids among types. Karl Weick has quoted Raphael (1976: 5-6) on the fact that the richest forms of life exist on the edges, between sea and land, forest and field. In organizations, too, that is where much of the exciting innovation takes place—outside of the pat categories, "beyond configuration" (Mintzberg 1989). In one sense then, while we cannot specify context for this school—it is, after all, the school *of* contexts—we can draw attention to the contexts it misses: nuanced ones not easily categorized.

Nevertheless, the contribution of the configurational school has been clear in strategic management. It brings order to the messy world of strategy formation—and that includes its huge, diverse literature, for bear in mind what these ten schools of thought constitute: a typology too, ten lumps in these dispersed writings. But if you have read this far, and this long, unless you are a masochist, you must have some appreciation for the configuration school, and we hope for the other nine schools as well!

TOWARD SEEING THE WHOLE BEAST

Since an elephant *is* body and tusk, trunk and legs, and ears and tail, we summarize by drawing together the various schools of the strategy formation beast, in terms of various dimensions that have been present in our presentation. But since an elephant is also more than the simple sum of its parts, we then conclude by discussing a set of issues that cut across the schools, issues that seem central to our understanding of the strategy formation process. Finally, we close this chapter with some brief comments on "where to from here," including ideas for the field in general and plans for ourselves in particular.

Underlying Dimensions of the Schools

Historical Evolution.   This is the first of four dimensions we refer to as *underlying* our discussion. The field of strategic management has come a long way since the early works of the 1960s. A literature that grew slowly at first, then faster but in a one-sided way in the 1970s, took off on a variety of fronts in the 1980s. Today it constitutes a dynamic if disparate field, in full bloom, with much excitement. Figure 5–3 seeks to capture its development since 1965 by plotting activity in its ten schools. These graphs are impressionistic. One could, of course, try to categorize each publication into one or more schools, weigh it, apportion its weight to schools by year, and then plot precisely the activity in each school over time. But we shall leave that exercise to someone with a scale and a great deal of free time. Figure 5–3 presents subjective estimates of the amount of publication in the field of strategic management and business or management policy as well as closely related work.

Overall, the graphs reveal the successive dominance of the three prescriptive schools. The design school perhaps had an early lead. But the planning school soon displaced it with a major surge in volume in the 1970s, only to be displaced by the positioning school in the 1980s. During that time the design school waned, except for a small

Figure 5-3. Historical Evolution of the Ten Schools.

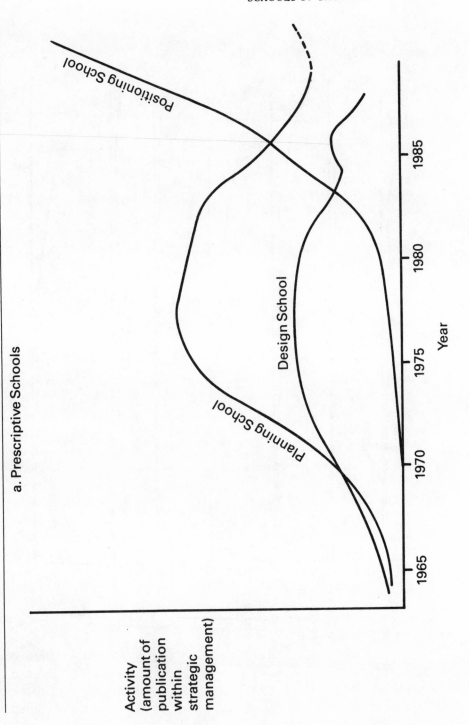

a. Prescriptive Schools

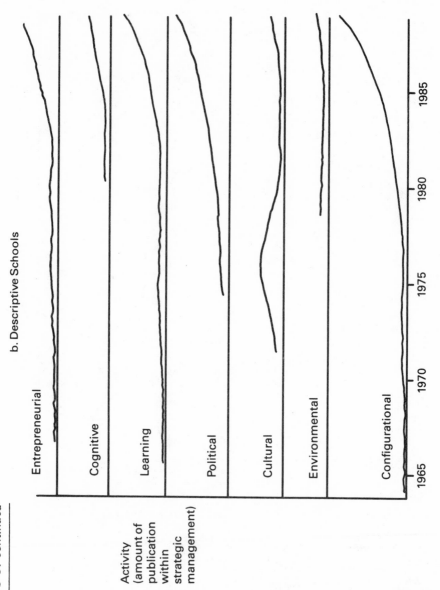

Figure 5-3. *continued*

b. Descriptive Schools

resurgence on the part of planning school practitioners frustrated with their technology.

On the descriptive front, most of the other schools appeared as relatively thin trickles that became thicker streams in the 1980s, sometimes growing exponentially. This is the pattern of the entrepreneurial school from well back, and of the political and cognitive schools somewhat later. The environmental school is shown as remaining a thin trickle, while both the learning and configurational schools (with early work dating way back) are shown as attaining higher levels in the 1980s. The only exception to the pattern is the cultural school, which is shown as having a small surge in the mid-1970s (in its Swedish version) followed by a decline and then another (smaller) surge after the mid-1980s.

Influential Sources. The origins of these ten schools are suggested in the graphs; table 5–1 lists some of the early work within strategic management, or closely related fields, that established the roots of each of the schools or else acted as stimulants to further research. In some cases, for example Ansoff's 1965 book on planning or Chandler's 1965 book on business history, the identification is precise. In others, we merely identify widely cited early work associated with the school.

Base Disciplines. We have already discussed the variety of disciplines on which strategic management has drawn. While economics is currently in vogue due to recent activity in the positioning school, the field has and must continue to draw on a wide range of disciplines, both to maintain its own internal balance and to make use of all relevant theory. Various disciplines are listed by school in table 5–1.

Current and Possible Future Status. Next we consider the current status of each of the schools (as suggested in figure 5–3) within the field of strategic management as well as its likely attention in the short-term future, the latter, of course, our subjective opinion. Table 5–1 summarizes the following comments.

The design school has clearly had its day. It will not likely resurge (although it does remain the foundation for the other prescriptive schools). Planning also has paid the price of its excesses of the 1970s. Its literature remains voluminous (when pushed down in one place, it inevitably reemerges in another, much as PPBS was reincarnated as

Table 5-1.

Underlying Dimensions	Design	Planning	Positioning	Entrepreneurial	Cognitive
Influential Sources	Selznick, 1957 (perhaps earlier work), later Andrews, 1965	Ansoff, 1965	Purdue work (Schendel, Cooper, Hatten) mid-1970s; then notably Porter, 1980	Schumpter, 1934, Cole, 1959, others in economics	Simon, 1945, March and Simon, 1958
Base Disciplines	none (architecture as metaphor)	(some links to urban planning, systems theory, and cybernetics)	economics (industrial organization), military history	none	psychology (Cognitive)
Current and Future Status	as foundation of prescription only	low, unless becomes empirical	very high, likely to remain so	some increased interest	moderate now, leading to frustration?
Champions	case study proponents, believers in rational leadership ("judgment"); especially in America	rationalizers, "professional" managers, MBAs, financial types, staff experts; especially in America, France, communist countries	as in planning school, especially MBAs and analytical staff types	business press, individualists, innovators, small business people; probably randomly distributed	psycho-logically oriented; probably randomly distributed
Contributing Dimensions					
Intended Message	fit	formalize (decompose)	analyze (slot)	envision	cope
Realized Message	think (strategy making as case study)	program (rather than formulate)	calculate (rather than create or commit)	centralize (then hope)	worry (since can't cope or invent)
Vocabulary	distinctive competence, competitive advantage, SWOT (strengths, weaknesses, opportunities, threats), formulation/ implementation	programming, budgeting, scheduling	generic strategy, strategic group, industry and competitive analysis, portfolio, experience curve	vision	map, frame, concept attainment, reframe, mental set, bounded rationality, cognitive style

Table 5-1. *continued*

Underlying Dimensions	Learning	Political	Cultural	Environmental	Configurational
Influential Sources	Lindblom, 1959, 1963; Cyert and March, 1963; Quinn, 1980; Weick, 1969	Allison, 1971 (micro); Perrow, 1970, Pfeffer and Salanick, 1978 (macro)	Rhenmann and Norman, late 1960s in Sweden; no obvious source elsewhere	Hannan and Freeman, 1977; Aldrich and Pfeffer, 1976; contingency theorists	Chandler, 1962, McGill group (Miller, Mintzberg, etc.), late 1970s, Miles and Snow, 1978
Base Disciplines	none (perhaps some peripheral links to learning theory in psychology and education)	political science	anthropology	biology	history (perhaps also catastrophy theory in mathematics and punctuated equilibrium theory in biology)
Current and Future Status	growing interest	growing interest	moderate now, decline likely unless conceptual breakthrough	low now, decline likely	growing interest
Champions	divergent thinkers, demystifiers, frustrated lower managers; especially in Japan, Scandinavia, Canada	power oriented, conspiracy theorists; especially in Latin countries and the U.K. somewhat	mythologists, more socially oriented; especially in Scandinavia	"population ecologists," some organization theorists, splitters and positivists in general; especially in America	lumpers, integrators; probably randomly distributed
Contributing Dimensions					
Intended Message	learn (evolve)	promote	coalesce	react	integrate
Realized Message	play (rather than pursue)	hoard (rather than share or even produce)	perpetuate (rather than change)	capitulate (in pop. ecol.), split (in contingency theory)	lump (rather than nuance)
Vocabulary	incrementalism (disjointed or logical), emergent strategy, sensemaking, revitalization, intrapreneurship, strategic candidate, champion	power, coalition, political games, collective strategy	myth, culture, ideology	selection, environmental dynamism, complexity, niche	configuration, archetype, stage, life cycle, quantum change, strategic revolution

Table 5-1. *continued*

	Design	*Planning*	*Positioning*	*Entrepreneurial*	*Cognitive*
Content Dimension					
Strategy	explicit perspective, unique	explicit plan, decomposed into sub-strategies and programs	explicit generic positions (economic and competitive), also ploys	implicit perspective (vision), personal and unique (niche)	mental perspective (individual concept)
Process Dimensions					
Basic Process	cerebral, simple and informal, judgmental, deliberate (prescriptive)	formal, decomposed, staged, deliberate (prescriptive)	analytical, systematic, deliberate (prescriptive)	visionary, intuitive, largely deliberate (descriptive)	mental, overwhelming (descriptive)
Change	occasional, quantum	periodic, incremental	piecemeal, can be ad hoc	occasional, typically quantum and revolutionary, opportunistic	infrequent (resisted mentally)
Central Actor(s)	chief executive ("architect")	planners	analysts	leader	brain
Environment	expedient (economic, social, technical, etc.), containing mostly opportunities, sometimes threats	acquiescent, checklist of factors to be forecast or preferably controlled	exigent in terms of established competition, but analyzable in economic terms	maneuverable, to find niche	overwhelming for cognition
Organization	ordered, acquiescent (for "implementation"), font of given strengths and weaknesses	structured, decomposed, acquiescent (for programming)	font of competitive advantages, otherwise incidental (implicitly mass producer)	malleable, simple	incidental
Leadership	dominant, judgmental	responsive to procedure	responsive to analysis	dominant, intuitive	source of cognition

Table 5-1. *continued*

	Learning	Political	Cultural	Environmental	Configurational
Content Dimension					
Strategy	implicit patterns, often collective	ploys and positions, overt and covert; subunit (micro) or organizational (macro)	collective perspective, unique and usually implicit	specific position (niche in pop. ecol.)	all those to the left, in context
Process Dimensions					
Basic Process	emergent, informal, messy (descriptive)	conflictive, aggressive, messy; emergent (micro), deliberate (macro) (descriptive)	ideological, constrained, collective, deliberate (descriptive)	passive, emergent (descriptive)	integrative, episodic, sequenced, plus all of those to the left, in context (descriptive)
Change	continual, typically incremental and perhaps piecemeal but with occasional quantum insight	frequent, piecemeal idiosyncratic	infrequent (resisted ideologically)	never or rare and quantum (in pop. ecol.), frequent and piecemeal (in contingency theory)	occasional, quantum and revolutionary
Central Actor(s)	whoever can learn	whoever has power	collectivity	environment	all those to the left, in context
Environment	demanding, difficult	intractable (in micro), malleable (in macro)	incidental	dictatorial (in pop. ecol.), exigent, broad dimensions (in contingency theory)	any, so long as categorical (e.g., those to the left)
Organization	eclectic, flexible, playful	conflictive, disjointed, uncontrollable, disjointed (micro); aggressive, controlling (macro)	cohesive, normative	acquiescent	any, so long as categorical (e.g., those to the left, or contextual structures below)
Leadership	responsive to initiatives or to own learning	weak, at best a player (micro); at helm (macro)	part of collectivity	acquiescent	any, so long as categorical (e.g., those to the left)

Table 5-1. *continued*

	Design	Planning	Positioning	Entrepreneurial	Cognitive
Contextual Dimensions					
Situation (best fit)	simple, stable (and so predictable), integrated	simple, stable (and so predictable), ideally controllable	simple, stable (predictable and preferably controllable), mature and therefore structured (so that data quantified)	dynamic but simple	individual
Structure (implicitly favored)	machine bureaucracy (centralized, formalized)	large machine bureaucracy (centralized, formalized), also divisionalized form	large machine bureaucracy in commodity or mass production (centralized, formalized), also divisionalized form	simple structure (centralized, organic)	not specified
Period (most likely)	reconception	strategic programming	recalculation	start-up, turnaround, sustained small size	original conception, reconception, clinging

Table 5-1. *continued*

	Learning	Political	Cultural	Environmental	Configurational
Contextual Dimensions					
Situation (best fit)	complex, dynamic (and so unpredictable), ideally novel	divisive, malevolent (in micro), controllable (in macro)	passive	uniform, set, competitive (in pop. ecol.); any (in contingency theory)	any, so long as categorical (e.g., those to the left)
Structure (implicitly favored)	adhocracy, professional bureaucracy (decentralized)	often adhocracy or professional bureaucracy (in micro), closed system machine bureaucracy or divisionalized form (in macro)	missionary organization, sometimes stagnant bureaucracy	passive, so likely bureaucratic (in pop. ecology); any (in contingency theory)	any, so long as configurational (e.g., those to the left)
Period (most likely)	dramatic, unprecedented, or evolving change	major change, blockage, flux	reinforcement, resistance to change (reframing and cultural revolution)	life cycle stages (e.g., birth, niche, death)	any, so long as isolatable (e.g., those to the left)

zero-based budgeting in government and contingency planning as scenario planning in business). Nonetheless, should the planning school become more empirical, focusing not on the glories of procedure and technique but on what these have truly accomplished, and have to offer in specific contexts, then this literature could again grow in influence (represented by the dotted line in figure 5-3). The positioning school is riding high right now for good reason, although it is not without its problems (as already discussed). This school now gets far more attention than any other school, and it will likely continue to do so for some time, although we would make a plea for more balance.

Of the descriptive schools, all are attracting a reasonable amount of attention now, some more (learning, political, configurational, perhaps entrepreneurial) and some less (cognitive, cultural, environmental). We believe interest will grow most rapidly in the configurational school, as more integrative and intense research takes place (a phenomenon that can already be seen within the positioning school, in its cluster-type research). Interest will also likely increase in the learning, political, and perhaps entrepreneurial schools, as increased efforts may be made to probe the darker side of the strategy formation process. Our suspicion is that frustration will increase in the cognitive school, as the poverty of cognitive psychology becomes evident. Similarly, the cultural school will likely decline if it continues to harp on the difficulties of changing cultural and strategic perspectives, although a conceptual breakthrough could regenerate interest in this school. As for the environmental school, we believe that little will be made in strategic management of the population ecology work, although work on the dimensions of the environment will likely retain some interest, especially if these can be made more tangible and nuanced.

Champions. Table 5-1 lists the groups that tend to champion the various schools, when evident. In some cases these are by nationality, in others by academic or personal orientation.

Contributing Dimensions of the Schools

Intended Message. Listed next in table 5-1, as the first of three contributing dimensions, is the overall message that each of the schools seeks to convey. In fact, starting with a blank sheet, it was rather easy to fill in this line of the table with one key verb (sometimes with a backup one) for each school.

Realized Message. This row of the table lists the message we believe is *actually* conveyed by each of the schools, also in a brief verb or two. This, too, is based on personal opinion, except here with a touch of cynicism. Like strategy, the message realized is not always consistent with the message intended.

Vocabulary. Next in table 5-1 are listed some of the main concepts or terms of vocabulary that each school has contributed to the field of strategic management. We do not mean to cover all the important terms here but rather to convey the flavor of each school.

Content Dimensions of the Schools

At the heart of the issue are three fundamental sets of *dimensions: content* dimensions (strategy itself), *process* dimensions (how strategy gets formed), and *contextual* dimensions (what conditions surround strategy formation, especially of situation, structure, and stage).

Content Dimensions. Here we consider how each of the schools considers strategy itself. We draw on our own typology of 5 Ps— strategy as plan, pattern, position, perspective, and ploy (Mintzberg 1987a)—but also include in table 5-1 other adjectives to describe strategy (for example, as unique or generic, individual or collective).

Process Dimensions
Basic process. We delineate six process dimensions concerning the nature of the process itself, the nature of the strategic change assumed, the central actor in the process, and the specific roles of environment, organization, and leadership. On the first, we use a series of adjectives in table 5-1 to describe how each of the schools views the basic process of strategy formation—how conscious, formal, stable, and so on. In addition, where possible we categorize each school as deliberate or emergent in its orientation and as prescriptive or descriptive in its approach (although it should be noted that the prescriptive schools have made important descriptive contributions,

for example, in concepts introduced,[31] while the schools labeled descriptive, by exposing exemplary strategic behavior, have made major contributions to prescription).

Change. Next we isolate in table 5-1 the dimension of change as viewed in each school. Is strategy formation piecemeal or quantum, incremental or revolutionary, a process of gradual learning or one of rapid insight? Does it happen hardly ever, occasionally, often, or regularly?

Central actor. The schools vary perhaps most clearly in who each identifies as the central actor in the strategy formation process, as shown in table 5-1. In some cases, this is associated with one individual (that is, by rooting the process in personalized entrepreneurship or individual cognition), in others, with the collectivity (by depicting the process as collective learning or the interplay of power). Two schools fall in between (by identifying small groups of planners or analysts), while one identifies the central actor as the abstraction of the "environment."

Environment, Organization, and Leadership. Next, we delineate in three rows of table 5-1 what we believe to be the natural influence of the three basic elements of the strategy formation process. Each school has its own view of the environment, of the organization itself, and of the leadership in the process of strategy making.

Contextual Dimensions

Situations. We conclude with the *contextual* dimensions, which specify the types of contexts most appropriate for each of the ten schools. First we discuss external situations, then structures, and finally periods, as discussed in the contents sections of the text on each school. The first of those listed in table 5-1 concerns situation, or the types of environments most likely to support the approaches of the various schools, as already discussed (characterized mainly in the terms of the environmental school).

Structures. Again we list the types of organizations most likely to favor the approaches of the various schools, as described in the text (here in the spirit of the configurational school, drawing on our own typologies of organizations) (Mintzberg 1979, 1983).

Periods. Finally, we list in table 5-1 the types of stages or periods during which the different approaches of the various schools would likely be present, again as discussed in the text (and again in the spirit of the configurational school).

Emergent Issues in Strategy Formation

Moving ever closer to the whole beast, if never quite arriving there, we now leave the schools per se and consider issues that cut across them. These issues are raised by the schools (really by the contradictions between them) but cannot be resolved by them. We believe all are fundamental to our understanding of the strategy formation process.

Eight issues are introduced, first under a label, then by a question, and finally as a dilemma. But in each case we reject the extreme answers—the "whether's"—in favor of the "when's" and the "where's." In other words, ultimately these issues should not be considered dilemmas because the answers lie not consistently at one extreme or another but in how the contradictary positions are reconciled in practice—where each is used and to what degree.

Thus, an issue can sometimes be resolved by lumping—as long as different lumps are recognized as viable (that is, sometimes strategies are best treated as generic, sometimes as unique)—but other times there is a need to resort to splitting (not voluntarism or determinism, but what extent of strategic choice under different circumstances). It makes no sense to debate whether an elephant has four legs or a trunk (or, in the spirit of the configurational school, whether mammals have trunks). What we must do is describe all the real beasts in the strategy formation jungle—which have trunks, how thick are their legs, and so on. Thus, each of our schools is both right and wrong: We need to find out when and where. The first three issues relate to strategy content; the other five to the strategy formation process.

Complexity Issue. How complex should a good strategy be? On one hand, we are directed by Ashby's (1956: 11/8) "Law of Requisite Variety" to ensure that the controlling system is as complex, as capable of variety, as the system being controlled. Strategies (at least intended ones) are surely controlling systems, and organizations subject to that control can be awfully complex beasts. So strategies must be complex, nuanced. On the other hand is the equally plausible KISS imperative ("Keep It Simple, Stupid," as in Peters and Waterman 1982). Thus, Andrews argues in the design school for strategies as simple, informing ideas (in Christensen et al. 1982: 12, 554, 835), while in the learning school Pascale (1982) criticizes Americans for "getting off" on simplistic notions of strategy the way the Japanese get off on sumo wrestling. Kenneth Boulding addresses this dilemma well: "Somewhere . . . between the specific that has no meaning and the general that has no content, there must be, for each purpose and each level of abstraction, an optimum degree of generality" (1956: 197-198). The issue has scarcely been addressed in strategic management: How elaborate, how nuanced, how comprehensible, how general do we want our strategies to be, when and where?

Integration Issue.   How tightly integrated should a good strategy be? In much of the positioning school, especially its second wave and its more recent work on shareholder value, the impression is given that strategy is a portfolio, just a loosely coupled collection of components. This notion is also present in the planning school, earlier in capital budgeting (strategic choice as a collection of independent decisions), later in the decomposition of strategies into corporate, business, and functional forms. Indeed, the same view is evident in much of Burgelman's work in the learning school and, of course, in much of the political school—strategy as a collection of independent strategic initiatives. Others, however, make a case for strategy as the integration of components—for example, in Porter's (1985) positioning school work on "horizontal strategy" (to knit diversified businesses together)—while still others do not recognize components at all, only strategy as a fully integrated perspective (notably the entrepreneurial, cultural, and design schools). Various mechanisms have been proposed to integrate strategies: plans to integrate formally, cognition or vision to integrate mentally, culture to integrate normatively, mutual adjustment to integrate collectively, and so on. How much integration is desirable, of what kind, when, and where?

Generic Issue.   How unique or novel should a good strategy be? Is the number of available strategies infinite, or is there a "generic" set from which organizations should chose? Correspondingly, do organizations succeed by respecting the rules or by breaking them? The positioning school tells us that strategies are generic (as does the political school in its macro form), that they exist a priori and are well defined (the environmental school suggesting that the defining is done by established niches). No doubt there are, to use Grinyer and Spender's (1979) term, many "industry recipes" out there, and no shortage of "mainline" strategies and "me too" strategy-making behaviors. But the entrepreneurial and cultural schools tell us, in contrast, that strategies are unique—perspectives particular to the vision of one person or the culture of one organization. No two can be alike.[32] The learning school adds that all strategies are the products of idiosyncratic learning processes. And the design school links this issue to process, differentiating itself from its sister prescriptive schools by arguing that strategies are unique because they are created in a personalized process of design.[33] Here the question concerns not only which is it, when, and where, but how the two interrelate. For example, when and how do novel strategies become generic, and how do strategic groups (as clusters of generic strategies) form?

Working toward the perception of whole beasts, note how our three content issues combine: generic strategies would seem to be simpler, less integrated (portfolios of components), and looking ahead to one of our process issues, more flexible and easier to articulate. In contrast, novel strategies seem likely to be more complex, more integrated (as perspectives), and therefore less flexible (because if you change any one part of an integrated strategy, you risk *dis*integrating it) and less easy to articulate. In fact, these two combinations (configurations?) suggest conditions under which researchers might focus on content or process. When strategies tend to be generic, then they can be delineated and so studied. But when they are novel, their variety is effectively infinite and so the study of content becomes more difficult; researchers and strategists alike cannot then concern themselves with *selection* as much as with *conception*, which is process. Let us now turn to the issues of process.

Control Issue. How deliberate or emergent should an effective strategy formation process be, how predetermined, cerebral, and centralized, as opposed to evolved, actionable, and eclectic? To what extent is there a need for a priori control and to what extent a posteriori learning? We discuss this as the first of the process issues because it is also one of content—concerning strategies as intended plans versus realized patterns. (Indeed the more emergent a strategy, the more a central management must treat content as process—in other words, manage people and structures in the hope that they will come up with desirable content.) The three prescriptive schools aggressively promote deliberateness, as does the entrepreneurial school (although less formally). The cognitive school raises doubts about the power of the strategist's mind over strategic matter, while the learning school dismisses the deliberate bias in favor of an emergent one. (The political school, in its macro form promotes deliberateness; in its micro form, it dismisses collective deliberateness while promoting individual deliberateness.) Although we may be responsible for proposing the terms in the literature, we have also argued (Mintzberg and Waters 1984) that no strategy can be purely deliberate or purely emergent. One precludes learning while the other precludes control. Clearly, no real-world strategy can be completely devoid of either, even though many logically tilt one way or the other. The question then becomes: what degree of each, where, and when?

Associated with this is the question of "strategic control." What should the term mean? And how should organizations exercise it? Each school can, of course, have its own interpretation of the phenomenon. For example, to the cultural school, it may mean protecting the ideology, to the environmental school, sustaining the niche, and to the configurational school, maintaining a state or shifting as quickly as possible to a necessary new one. To the entrepreneurial school, strategic control may mean close, personalized supervision by the leader of the application of his or her vision to correct problems en route and to seize new opportunities.

But it is the view of the planning school that has tended to dominate here. It considers the concept traditionally, in terms of the use of objectives, budgets, schedules, and the like to keep the implementation of intended strategy on track. But from the perspective of the learning school, this is an overly narrow interpretation of the concept: Strategic control must focus on behavior as well as performance. In other words, it is the performance of the organization that matters, not the performance of the plans!

Thus the starting point for strategic control would be what strategies have, in fact, been realized, as patterns in action. These could then be compared with intended strategies to determine their degree of deliberateness, but more important would be to ascertain how effective they are, no matter how deliberate. With this information, management could decide what to do with its realized strategies—for example, in the case of a relatively emergent one, to stop it as ineffective, to render it deliberate as effective, or to ignore it for a while longer until its consequences more clearly manifest themselves. (See

Mintzberg 1990 for an elaboration of these notions of strategic control.)

Collective Issue. Who is the strategist? How do we read the "organization's mind"? What is collective cognition? We listed the candidates for the job of strategist in table 5-1: Each school has its own. At one extreme, the strategist is the *him* or *her* of the design and entrepreneurial schools, at the other extreme, the *them* of the learning, political, and cultural schools. Or perhaps the strategist is the *it* of the environmental, planning, positioning, and cognitive schools—the world out there, technique and analysis, or the biological brain. To put all this another way, is strategy formation fundamentally a personal process, a technical process, a physiological process, a clandestine process, a collective process, or even a nonprocess? Clearly, it may be all of the above, but which, or how much of each, when, and where?

Change Issue. A number of issues relate to strategic change—its nature, its pattern, and its source. First, how do strategists reconcile the conflicting forces for change and for stability? How do they maintain alignment and promote order, efficiency, pattern, and control, while having to reconfigure and adapt, respond, innovate, and learn? The impression conveyed in most of the literature notwithstanding, strategy is a concept rooted in stability, not change. Organizations pursue strategies for purposes of consistency, whether as intentions to set future directions or as patterns that reflect the directions they have felt necessary to take in the past. But organizations, of course, sometimes need strategic change too. In other words, they must discard their established or intended directions in response to a changed environment.

The planning school, as noted, pretends that organizations can have stability and change concurrently: Planned strategies set course, coordinate activities, are made explicit and implemented through intricate systems of procedures, yet change every year, on schedule. Very convenient. But very naive. The dilemma is never addressed. Other schools avoid the dilemma by coming down clearly in favor of one side or the other: Organizations are either changing all the time or else hardly ever change. To the political school (micro), strategies change frequently, whenever new challenges arise; indeed change can be so prevalent that strategies never get a chance to form (as patterns in behavior or collectively shared intentions). The learning school comes out in a similar place: Strategic learning is an ever-unfolding process; patterns may form but since initiatives are always forthcoming, strategies can never fully settle down. To the environmental and cultural schools, also perhaps the cognitive school, strategies change rarely if ever—the organization slots into a niche, settles on a culture, slips into a mental frame, and then holds on for dear life. (In the environmental school they would rather die than switch.) But surely real-world behavior must fall largely between these extreme.

When considered in terms of the pattern or pace of change, rather than the very existence of change, the views of certain schools become more operational. The configurational school makes a strong case for strategic change that is quantum and revolutionary in nature. In other words, organizations prefer continuity but must submit occasionally to change that is dramatic, as long as it is integrated. The design and entrepreneurial schools imply a similar pattern of change, as do the cognitive and cultural schools due to their forces that resist change. In contrast, the learning school permits change that is incremental, as strategists over time come to know a complex situation through experimentation (though they can sometimes leap in a more revolutionary way when struck by a sudden insight). The planning school also tends to promote incremental change, though perhaps inadvertently, as we noted earlier, while the political school (micro) tends to favor the disjointed, piecemeal change that arises from conflict.

All of these views seem plausible. Indeed, there is empirical evidence in support of various ones of them. For example, Miller and Friesen (1980a) in their quantum theory find that organizations usually change incrementally in the direction of their established strategies but occasionally shift direction in revolutionary fashion. In other words, they either do more of the same, perfecting a given strategic perspective (including elaborating strategic positions within it), or else they change dramatically, doing new things (and shifting strategic perspective). In our tracking strategy studies, we found this to be especially true of entrepreneurial and mass production (machine bureaucratic) organizations (Mintzberg and Waters 1982, 1984; Mintzberg 1978; Mintzberg, Brunet, and Waters 1987). More innovative organizations (labeled "adhocracies"), in contrast, may tend to alternate more balanced cycles of convergence and divergence

(Mintzberg and McHugh 1985), implying that experimental change is more habitual and quantum shifts more frequent in this context. Thus a variety of patterns of change are possible; questions remain as to which, when, where, and why.

A last issue of change concerns its source. Where do new strategies come from? Extending the concept of learning beyond just one school, do organizations learn by doing (learning school), by thinking (design or entrepreneurial school), by programming (planning school), by calculating (positioning school), or by disputing (political school)? While the learning school suggests that organizations learn with ease, the cognitive and cultural schools claim that they learn only with great difficulty. And the environmental school suggests that organizations don't learn at all. How much, then, do organizations learn, how easily, and how, when, and where?

Choice Issue. We have discussed this issue at some length already: The question is not whether there exists strategic choice out there, but how much? We have, therefore, rejected the pure determinism of the environmental school and the closely related worlds of the cognitive and cultural schools that overwhelm strategists. Likewise, we have rejected the easy voluntarism of the design and entrepreneurial schools, in which the "great man" can do almost anything. As for the assumed voluntarism of the planning and positioning schools—a world ripe for plucking by the clever analyst—on closer examination we found the planning school terrified by unexpected change, the positioning school wary of real choice, with determinism parading under the guise of free will. Perhaps it is the macro side of the political school that achieves the right balance here, with its notion that the power of an organization reflects its resource dependency on its environment. Some organizations must largely acquiesce, at least some of the time, while others can sometimes dominate (and some acquiesce while believing they dominate, like that king in *The Little Prince* who could order the sun to set, but only at a certain time of the day). A balance is also struck in the learning school, which suggests that strategists cope with a difficult world by learning over time, even occasionally achieving leaps of insight that belie their supposed cognitive limitations. The question then becomes: What is the power of proactive leadership, personalized intuition, even collective learning, against the forces of environmental demand, organizational inertia, and cognitive limitation, when and where?

Thinking Issue. Finally, we come to perhaps the most intriguing issue of all, related also to deliberate control. Pascale (1984) poses it as how much strategic thinking do we want anyway, implying that organizations obsessed with the strategy formation process lose control of it. Coming from the learning school, he believes they should get on with acting. But again, the issue need not be so dichotomized. Certainly, we need to think—we are cerebral animals—and even sometimes to formalize. Yet as we critiqued the design school, we can become too mentally conscious at the expense of our ability to act ("paralysis by analysis"). Indeed, conscious thought did not fare so well in the cognitive school, although ironically, it did get redeemed somewhat in the learning school (through its acknowledgment of insight and inspiration). Perhaps Karl Weick strikes the right balance here by arguing that we need to act but then we need to make sense of our actions. Given that this long chapter has, we hope, encouraged a good deal of thinking about strategy formation, perhaps we should convert Pascale's point into the following question, which is largely unaddressed in the literature of strategic management: What is "strategic thinking" anyway? And what forms of it—what "strategic styles"—work most effectively? How is thought best coupled with action in strategy making? How is the specific made to inform the general and the general brought to bear on the specific? When and where?

SAFARIS FOR STRATEGIC MANAGEMENT

It is time to leave our academic offices and plunge into the tangled jungle of real beasts, to observe them with clear vision. We certainly encourage people in the field of strategic management to continue probing the important issues of each school: We need to know more about tusks and trunks and legs. But more important, we need to get beyond the narrowness of each school; we need to know how this beast called strategy formation, which combines all of these schools and more, really lives its life. Specifically, we believe the starting point for research should increasingly be case and context as opposed to concept. We need to ask more questions and generate fewer hypotheses—to allow ourselves to be pulled by the concerns out there rather than pushed by the concepts in here. And more often we need to be comprehensive—to concern ourselves with process *and* content, statics *and* dynamics, constraint *and* inspiration, the cognitive *and* the collective, the planned *and* the learned, the economic *and* the political.

We know our own course in this regard: As indefatigable lumpers (assuming we have any energy left after the ten schools of Volume I are fully written), we intend to devote Volume II, on *Strategy Formation: Toward a General Theory*, to integration in the spirit of the configurational school. Using the available intensive studies of particular organizations, we wish to delineate common sequences (life cycles) of strategic periods in different types of organizations. In other words, we wish to describe configurations of strategy process and strategy content, related to configurations of organizational structure, environmental context, and leadership style, as they unfold in distinct periods, arrayed over time. But this is only one approach among the many that are possible. Our point is that, in addition to probing its parts, we must give more attention to the whole strategy formation beast. We shall never find it, never really see it all. But we can certainly see it better. And so (forgive me):

> It was the gang from strategy
> Who went to see their beast,
> To learn by observation:
> No blind man the true strategist[34]
> Cried they, "The wonder of this process
> Is very like a feast!"

NOTES

1. Actually, Miller argues for a limit of this order to the number of "bits" we can handle in what he refers to as "absolute judgment" and the number of "chunks"—combinations of these bits—in "intermediate memory."

2. This chapter outlines the first of a two-volume work in process, entitled *Strategy Formation*, to be published by Prentice-Hall as the fourth of my "Theory of Management Policy" series. This volume, entitled *Schools of Thought*, will present a chapter on each of the ten schools as well as an introductory chapter on various definitions of strategy (summarized in Mintzberg 1987b) and a final, integrative chapter. Volume II, entitled *Toward a General Theory*, will seek to synthesize the empirical research (more on that at the end).

3. Several writers have categorized the literature of strategy formation in ways compatible with some of these schools. Lindgren and Spangberg (1981: 25-28) have discussed the "planning school," the "fit school" (our

design school), the "muddling through" school (our learning school, with aspects of our political school as well), and the "entrepreneurial school." Hambrick (1980: 569) discussed "strategy as a situational art" (design school), and use of "one or a few key variables to position strategic behavior," "strategy as a quantifiable interaction of a broad set of variables" (both of which we cover in our positioning school), and "strategic typologies" (our configuration school). Bower and Doz (1979: 159) have distinguished cognitive, political, and social and organizational processes of strategy formation (the latter relating perhaps to our learning and cultural schools). Lenz and Engledow (1983) have proposed as models for analyzing environments, industry structure (our positioning school), cognitive, organizational field (our environmental school), ecological and resource dependence (the former our environmental school, the latter in our political school), strategic issues, and era (both our configurational school). Bourgeois and Brodwin (1984) present five approaches to "strategic implementation": a Commander model with the CEO as rational actor (our positioning school), a Change model with the CEO as architect (our design school), a Collaborative model with the CEO as coordinator (likely between our design and learning schools, perhaps closest to the Quinn approach discussed in the latter), a Cultural model with the CEO as coach (in fact our entrepreneurial school, but as described leading to our cultural school), and a Crescive model with the CEO as premise-setter and judge (our learning school). A broader typology from another sphere is the set of "models" Kirlin and Erie (1972: 176) present from the study of urban governance: institutional (our planning school), power and cleavages (both internal aspects of our political school), culture, resource (in some ways, our positioning school), and symbolic (the external aspect of our political school). Finally, some years ago we published an article entitled "Strategy Making in Three Modes" (Mintzberg 1972); this chapter may be seen as an extension of that work, which discussed only the planning, entrepreneurial, and learning schools (really one limited aspect of the latter under the label "adaptive mode"). In fact, as we shall see, with the exception of the design school, these were the three most developed schools up to the time of that article.

4. It should be noted that detailed work on these ten schools has been only partially completed, and so the descriptions provided here may seem somewhat unbalanced. In particular, work on the design school exists as an eighty-four page chapter, to be published shortly in abbreviated form (Mintzberg 1990a). Likewise, the planning school has been written up; that "chapter" will be published in book form (Mintzberg 1990b). Work is about half completed on the positioning school, which is also emerging as book length. The other chapters have not been started. We go into print with this review at this time because there appears to be interest in the

idea of the ten schools now, although the entire volume will take several years to complete. It should also be noted that Chapter 1 of that first volume has been published (Mintzberg 1987); the five definitions of strategy that it presents—as plan, pattern, position, perspective, and ploy—will be used in the following discussion of the ten different schools.

5. Porter (1981: 610; 1983: 173), for example, a coauthor in the 1982 edition of the Harvard textbook, writes of how the ideas in the original text (the "LCAG *paradigm*," after the names of the four original authors) were "subsequent[ly]" translated and extended by others, citing in particular Igor Ansoff's book *Corporate Strategy*. In fact, Ansoff went to press with very similar ideas in the same year (1965) as Porter's coauthors originally did, and neither book references any work by authors of the other (although Edmund Learned, the senior author of the first edition of the Harvard textbook, did note the similarities in a book published with Sproat one year later: "Significantly, [Ansoff's] work offers numerous parallels with Harvard thinking that should not be obscured by differences in terminology, definitions, emphasis, and coverage" [1966: 94]). In the preface to the first edition of the Harvard book, the authors write that the content of the book "is the outcome of about ten years of case and course development" (Learned et al. 1965: vii), although in the 1982 version they refer to the core idea having developed in the early 1960s (Christensen et al. 1982: viii). Coauthor Bower is more precise in a 1986 publication: "The problem of corporate strategy was first phrased as a research question in 1959 when Kenneth Andrews reported his study of the Swiss watch industry in a note and a series of cases" (p. vi). Ansoff published a rough version of his approach in an article two years before his book (Ansoff 1963), although he referred there to an initial unpublished paper of 1957.

6. Andrews qualifies each of these premises in one place or another, but the tone and organization of his overall discussion make his belief in them quite clear (for example, dividing his 1982 text into two "books," one on determining, the second on implementing corporate strategy). See Mintzberg (1990a) for details on this.

7. In reference to a comment in the 1982 edition, that the references in this book's footnotes "comprise a relevant but incidental source of knowledge" (1982: 6), it is instructive to consider their source: Thirty-one of the thirty-nine references to theoretical works in the text are by doctoral students or faculty members of the Harvard Business School. Even some theory by coauthor Michael Porter (as we shall see, a proponent of the positioning school) that was allowed into the 1982 text was literally spliced in between two sentences that appear next to each other in the previous edition (Christensen et al. 1982: 167 and 179; 1978: 251), while Andrews' own text questions assumptions fundamental to Porter's work (see 1982: 5).

8. Cases can, of course, be taught from a different perspective—for example, to reveal different forms of strategic behavior rather than to elicit superficial strategic choices from the students. But that would require case writing to be based on more than the design school model (that is, focusing attention beyond the chief executive because that person may not be the "architect" of strategy).

9. "Decentralized planning" may be another oxymoron, since a major purpose of planning is to coordinate activities, which it does by bringing control over many decisions to a central place (see especially Devons 1950: 14).

10. See references below.

11. The industrial organization approach supposedly relied on the

    Structure ⟶ Conduct ⟶ Performance

    relationship, but the literature has, in fact, been far more concerned with the relationship between industry structure and performance, bypassing conduct (strategy). Indicative of this is, for example, its treatment of differentiation, one of Porter's key strategies, as a dimension of context. Of course, every dimension of strategy is, in the aggregate, a dimension of context, since the strategic behavior of all competitors makes up an industry context. But this indicates the different orientation of the two fields. Indeed, from the strategist's perspective, a focus on the aggregate renders much of the research useless for application. An industrial organization article entitled "The Market for Lemons" (Akerlof 1970) explains the phenomenon of the sudden drop in the price of a newly purchased automobile in terms of statistical uncertainty—the buyer of the week-old used car cannot distinguish a "lemon" from an automobile whose owner was simply forced into a quick sale. By the same token, the industrial organization research is a lemon for the business strategist: He or she has no way to know whether or not his or her firm fits into the aggregated sample. (Remember that person who drowned in a lake whose average depth was only six inches.) It is also interesting to note in this regard that one of the generally recognized fathers of this field, Edward Mason, began his career by calling for in-depth studies on the strategy and context of the industrial firm, but after several decades of watching the field being pulled (especially by his star student, Joe Bain), in the opposite direction, toward aggregated studies that emphasized market context, Mason ended his career by applauding the rigor of its statistical samples (see Phillips and Stevenson 1974).

12. Missing from this school is a comprehensive typology of generic strategies, as well as one of generic conditions. Popular lists of generic strategies tend to be either confusing mixtures (see, for example, the Arthur D. Little list in Hax and Majluf 1984: 23) or narrowly focused (as in Porter's triad of

cost leadership, differentiation, and focus, or scope). See Mintzberg (1988) for one effort at a comprehensive typology of generic strategies.

13. See Mintzberg (1981) for an elaboration of these four forms of positioning school research.

14. As he himself noted with reference to "formal strategy formulation models" (namely the prescriptive schools) as well as "the political or power-behavioral approaches to . . . decision making, logical incrementalism does not become subservient to any one model" (1980: 58).

15. Since this chapter is on strategy formation, we shall not probe into the literature of strategic management that deals with the making of individual strategic decisions. Strategy formation is more concerned with the interaction of decisions over time. Nonetheless, the relationship between decision and strategy does merit mention at this point. In the conventional literature of the three prescriptive schools, deliberate strategies are thought to lead decisions, which in turn evoke actions. In other words, the general concept (strategy) drives the specific commitments (decisions) in deductive fashion. In the learning school, however, actions and/or decisions converge into patterns that become strategies. In other words, the specific experience evokes the general concept, in inductive fashion. While there are substantial literatures on strategic decision making and on strategy formation, there is a need for more research on the relationship between the two—for example, on the precedent-setting decision that evokes a strategy, as opposed to decisions that elaborate or reinforce existing strategies; also on decisions that are not clear in their relationship to strategy (as in certain capital budgeting proposals).

16. In preparing this chapter, I reviewed the articles I had collected since I did my initial reading in 1984, each coded in terms of one or more of the schools. I was struck by the appearance for the first time of a number of articles by Japanese authors, almost all of which I had coded in the learning school (for example, Takeuchi and Nonaka 1986; Nonaka and Johansson 1985; and Kogono et al. 1985). There must be a message in that.

17. Staw titles his article "Knee Deep in the Big Muddy" in reference to the Vietnam experience. But could he have done so if the United States emerged victorious? Or can the label "escalating commitment" be applied to Pilkington Glass's excursion into the float glass process: It took seven years of development before the process became operational, and subsequently changed the fortunes of that company (Quinn et al. 1988: 781–799). Needed is a theory that helps to distinguish doomed incrementalism from that with a reasonable chance of success.

18. Including these under the political school not only reflects the noncompetitive and possible not-strictly-economic nature of these strategies, but also draws attention to the ease with which they can become collusive and exclusive—in other words, actively political.

19. Mention must also be made here of the work of Bengt Stymne, a professor at the Stockholm School of Economics, whose thesis of 1970, published by SIAR in English in 1972, was acknowledged by Rhenman alongside Normann's thesis of 1969 to "have probably been my greatest single source of inspiration" (1973: v).

20. In 1972, John Child published an article entitled "Organizational Structure, Environment and Performance: The Role of Strategic Choice." While most people in strategic management shrugged their shoulders—they hardly needed someone to discover that organizations could make decisions—the article elicited a great deal of attention in organization theory. To this day, one can often distinguish membership in these two groups (whether by formal affiliation or informal identification) by the presence or absence of citation to this article in papers dealing with strategy as a function of context. In fact, an interesting bit of research might be to tabulate the extent to which these two groups, when writing on strategy, cross-reference each other's works. As one example, we find that citations to quantum or revolutionary change, to be discussed later, tend to be to Miller and Friesen (1982; Miller and Friesen 1980a, 1982, 1984) in the strategic management literature, to Tushman and Romanelli (1985) in organization theory.

21. Gould makes the intriguing point that "dinosaurs dominated the land for 100 million years, yet a species that measures its own life in but tens of thousands of years has branded dinosaurs as a symbol of failure"! (1982: 12).

22. Thus, ironically, the increasingly popular positioning school can be criticized on similar grounds, notably its tendency to slight the more creative, nuanced, and intuitive forms of strategy making.

23. Anthropology is another, although perhaps less with regard to using configuration than in a predisposition to describe in qualitative terms. Anthropologists may be splitters of another kind.

24. Miller has pointed the way to using the in-depth reports of others (such as book histories, detailed case studies, and *Fortune* articles, tested for reliability) as a data base to attain large samples without huge investment of research resources.

25. On revolutionary change, see also Tushman and Romanelli (1985) and Hoskissan and Galbraith (1985). Those interested in theoretical elegance may also find justification for it in catastrophy theory—the mathematical study of sudden effects (Zeeman 1977).

26. See also Astley (1983), who links the literature of biology with change in organizations. The following might also be added as the opening words of the first article I published (Mintzberg 1967: 31):

   Man's beginnings were described in the Bible in terms of conscious planning and grand strategy. The opposing theory, developed by Darwin, suggested that no such grand design existed but that environmental forces gradually shaped man's evolution. The disagreement between the biblical and Darwinian theorists is paralleled on a more mundane level in the study of strategy-making. There are those who envision grand calculated designs for the corporate entity, and there are those who cite current practice to argue that organizational strategy evolves, shaped less by man than by his environment.

27. Of course, there has been a strong tradition of developing such typologies based on structure alone in some of the literature of organizational theory, including Burns and Stalker (1964), Woodward (1965), Lawrence and Lorsch (1967), and Mintzberg (1979).

28. We see this as a dichotomy of prospectors and defenders, with analyzers as a hybrid of the two and reactors as a catch-all category for all kinds of ineffective behaviors.

29. Hambrick's research has, in fact, ranged widely; he, like Miller, is one of the few in strategic management to have done highly regarded empirical research of both the "lumping" and the "splitting" variety.

30. In passing, it is of interest to note how different schools of strategy formation have implicitly favored particular types of organizations (leaving aside which seemed most appropriate). In the positioning school, for example, we already drew attention to its bias toward the large industrial enterprise; "global" industries are also very popular there now, although the term is used rather loosely (Mintzberg 1990a). The planning school has exhibited an implicit bias, as suggested, toward the stable mature organization (the machine bureaucracy), and the learning school toward the adhocracy-type organization (ones in high technology). These biases have to be understood if the conclusions and prescriptions of the various schools are not to be misapplied.

31. For example, my own assessment of Ansoff's more recent, rather complex work (1979, 1984) is that he has identified important problems and supplied interesting concepts (such as "strategic surprise" and "weak signals") in the process of developing questionable procedures.

32. Note that a school's view of the novelty of strategy corresponds to its view of competition. Where competition is considered direct, strategies tend to be viewed in more generic terms—as structured, zero sum games. This is generally evident in the literature of military strategy, much of which sought to delineate standard strategies, although it is true too that writers such as Sun Tzu (1971) described how to beat competitors by resorting to surprise—that is, to unexpected, novel strategies that break the rules. The schools that promote novel strategies tend to view strategy formation as a process of finding niches protected from direct competition. (Note that niche to the environmental school is not a place protected from competition so much as one in which to compete with like entities. What this school means by *niche* is what economists mean by *market*.)

33. Andrews is, however, ambiguous on this point by repeatedly discussing the "choice" of strategy and the process as one of "decision" from among given alternatives (see Mintzberg 1989). In our own research on decision making (Mintzberg, Raisinghani, and Theorêt 1976), we found that while "choice" generally came from a set of "ready-made" alternatives, "design" generally involved the development of only a single "custom-made" solution.

34. No poet either.

REFERENCES

Abell, D. F., and J. S. Hammond. 1979. *Strategic Market Planning.* Englewood Cliffs, N. J.: Prentice-Hall.

Akerlof, G. A. 1970. "The Market for Lemons: Qualitative Uncertainty and the Market Mechanism." *Quarterly Journal of Economics* 84 (August): 488–500.

Aldrich, H. E. 1979. *Organizations and Environments.* Englewood Cliffs, N. J.: Prentice-Hall.

Aldrich, H. E., and J. Pfeffer. 1976. "Environments of Organizations." In *Annual Review of Sociology*, Vol. 2, edited by A. Inkeles, Palo Alto: Annual Reviews Inc.

Allaire, Y., and M. Firsirotu. 1985. "How to Implement Radical Strategies in Large Organizations." *Sloan Management Review* 26 (Spring): 19–33.

Allison, G. T. 1971. *Essence of Decision: Explaining the Cuban Missile Crisis.* Boston: Little, Brown.

Andrews, K. R. 1980. "Director's Responsibility for Corporate Strategy." *Harvard Business Review* (November–December): 30–44.

———. 1987. *The Concept of Corporate Strategy*, 3d ed. Homewood, Ill.: Irwin.

Ansoff, H. I. 1965. *Corporate Strategy.* New York: McGraw-Hill.

———. 1975. "Managing Strategic Surprise by Response to Weak Signals." *California Management Review* 18, no. 2: 21–33.

———. 1979. *Strategic Management.* New York: Macmillan.

———. 1984. *Implementing Strategic Management.* Englewood Cliffs, N. J.: Prentice-Hall.

Argyris, C. 1976. *Increasing Leadership Effectiveness.* New York: Wiley.

Ashby, W. R. 1956. *An Introduction to Cybernetics.* New York: Wiley.

Astley, W. G. 1983. "The Dynamics of Organizational Evolution: Critical Reflections on the Variation-Selection-Retention Model." Working paper, Department of Management, The Wharton School, University of Pennsylvania.

———. 1984. "Toward an Appreciation of Collective Strategy." *Academy of Management Review* 9, no. 3: 526–535.

Astley, W. G., and C. J. Fombrun. 1983. "Collective Strategy: Social Ecology of Organizational Environments." *Academy of Management Review* 8, no. 4: 576–587.

Axelrod, R. 1976. *Structure of Decision: The Cognitive Maps of Political Beliefs.* Princeton: Princeton University Press.

Bain, J. S. 1956. *Barriers to New Competition.* Cambridge, Mass.: Harvard University Press.

Barney, J. B. 1986. "Organizational Culture: Can It Be a Source of Sustained Competitive Advantage?" *Academy of Management Review* 11, no. 3: 656–665.

Bart, C. K. 1986. "Product Strategy and Formal Structure." *Strategic Management Journal* 7, no. 4: 293–312.

Bauer, R. A., and K. J. Gergen, eds. 1968. *The Study of Policy Formation.* New York: Free Press.

Baumol, W. J. 1968. "Entrepreneurship in Economic Theory." *American Economic Review* 58 (May): 64–71.

Berg, P. -O. 1979. *Emotional Structure in Organizations: A Study of the Process of Change in a Swedish Company.* Lund: Studentlitteratur.

Berle, A. A., Jr., and G. C. Means. 1968. *The Modern Corporation and Private Property*, rev. ed. New York: Harcourt, Brace and World.

Birnbaum, P. H. 1985. "Political Strategies of Regulated Organizations as Functions of Contest and Fear." *Strategic Management Journal* 6, no. 2: 135–150.

The Boston Consulting Group, Inc. 1975. *Strategies Alternatives for the British Motorcycle Industry.* A report prepared for the Secretary of State for Industry. London: Her Majesty's Stationery Office.

Boulding, K. E. 1956. "General Systems Theory: The Skeleton of Science." *Management Science* 2, no. 3: 197–208.

Bourgeois, L. J., III, and D. R. Brodwin. 1984. "Strategic Implementation: Five Approaches to an Elusive Phenomenon." *Strategic Management Journal* 5: 241–264.

Bower, J. L. 1970. *Managing the Resource Allocation Process.* Boston: Division of Research, Harvard Business School.

——. 1986. *Managing the Resource Allocation Process: A Study of Corporate Planning and Investment*, rev. ed. Boston: Harvard Business School.

Bower, J. L., and Y. Doz. 1979. "Strategy Formulation: A Social and Political Process." In *Strategic Management*, edited by D. E. Schendel and C. W. Hofer, pp. 152–166. Boston: Little, Brown.

Braybrooke, D., and C. E. Lindblom. 1963. *A Strategy of Decision.* New York: Free Press.

Bresser, R. K., and R. C. Bishop. 1983. "Dysfunctional Effects of Formal Planning: Two Theoretical Explanations." *Academy of Management Review* 8, no. 4: 588–599.

Brinton, C. 1938. *The Anatomy of Revolution.* New York: Vintage Books.

Bruner, J. S., J. J. Goodnow, and G. A. Austin. 1956. *A Study of Thinking.* New York: John Wiley.

Brunet, J.-P. 1986. "Strategic Groups: An Emergent Taxonomy." Ph.D. dissertation, Ecole des Hautes Etudes Commerciales, Montreal.

Brunsson, N. 1976. *Propensity to Change: An Empirical Study of Decisions on Reorientations.* Goteborg, Sweden: BAS.

_____. 1982. "The Irrationality of Action and Action Rationality: Decisions, Ideologies, and Organizational Actions." *Journal of Management Studies* 19: 29-44.

Burgelman, R. A. 1980. "Managing Innovating Systems: A Study of the Process of Internal Corporate Venturing." Ph.D. dissertation, Graduate School of Business, Columbia University.

_____. 1983a. "A Model of the Interaction of Strategic Behavior, Corporate Context, and the Concept of Strategy." *Academy of Management Review* 8, no. 1: 61-70.

_____. 1983b. "A Process Model of Internal Corporate Venturing in the Diversified Major Firm." *Administrative Science Quarterly* 28: 223-244.

_____. 1983c. "Corporate Entrepreneurship and Strategic Management: Insights from a Process Study." *Management Science* 29, no. 12: 1349-1364.

Burgelman, R. A., and L. R. Sayles. 1986. *Inside Corporate Innovation: Strategy, Structure, and Managerial Skills.* New York: Free Press.

Burns, T., and G. M. Stalker. 1966. *The Management of Innovation,* 2nd ed. London: Tavistock.

Business Week. 1984. "The New Breed of Strategic Planner." (September 17): 62-66, 68.

Buzzell, R. D., T. G. Bradley, and R. G. M. Sultan. 1975. "Market Share: A Key to Profitability." *Harvard Business Review* (January-February): 97-111.

Carland, J. W., F. Hoy, W. R. Boulton, and J. C. Carland. 1984. "Differentiating Entrepreneurs from Small Business Owners: A Conceptualization." *Academy of Management Review* 9, no. 2: 354-359.

Caves, R. E. 1974. "Industrial Organization." In *Economic Analysis and Multilateral Enterprise,* edited by J. H. Dunning, ch. 5. London: Allen and Unwin.

_____. 1980. "Industrial Organization, Corporate Strategy, and Structure." *Journal of Economic Literature* 18 (March): 64-92.

Caves, R. E., and M. E. Porter. 1980. "The Dynamics of Changing Seller Concentration." *Journal of Industrial Economics* 29, no. 1: 1-15.

Caves, R. E., M. E. Porter, A. M. Spence, and J. J. Scott. 1980. *Competition in the Open Economy: A Model Applied to Canada.* Cambridge, Mass.: Harvard University Press.

Chaffee, E. E. 1985. "Three Models of Strategy." *Academy of Management Review* 10, no. 1: 89-98.

Chamberlain, E. H. 1933. *The Theory of Monopolistic Competition*. Cambridge, Mass.: Harvard University Press.

Chandler, A. D., Jr. 1962. *Strategy and Structure: Chapters in the History of the Industrial Enterprise*. Cambridge, Mass.: MIT Press.

Channon, D. F. 1977. "Strategy Formulation as an Analytical Process." *International Studies of Management and Organization* 7, no. 2: 41–57.

Child, J. 1972. "Organizational Structure, Environment and Performance: The Role of Strategic Choice." *Sociology* (January): 2–22.

Christensen, C. R., K. R. Andrews, J. L. Bower, R. G. Hamermesh, and M. E. Porter. 1987. *Business Policy: Text and Cases*, 6th ed. Homewood, Ill.: Irwin.

Clark, B. R. 1970. *The Distinctive College*. Chicago: Aldine.

_____. 1972. "The Organizational Saga in Higher Education." *Administrative Science Quarterly* 17, no. 2: 178–184.

Clausewitz, C. von. 1968. *On War*. Harmondsworth, Middlesex: Penguin.

Cole, A. H. 1959. *Business Enterprise in Its Social Setting*. Cambridge, Mass.: Harvard University Press.

Collins, O., and D. G. Moore. 1970. *The Organization Makers: A Behavioral Study of Independent Entrepreneurs*. New York: Appleton-Century-Crofts.

Collomb, B., and J. P. Ponsard. 1982. "Creative Management in Mature Capital Intensive Industries." Conference on Creative and Innovative Management, Austin, Texas, October 5–6.

Connolly, T. 1982. "On Taking Action Seriously: Cognitive Fixation in Behavioral Decision Theory." In *Decision-Making: An Interdisciplinary Inquiry*, edited by G. R. Ungson and D. N. Braunstein, pp. 42-47. Boston: Kent.

Cool, K. O., and D. Schendel. 1986. "Strategic Group Formation and Performance: The Case of the U.S. Pharmaceutical Industry, 1963–1982." Working paper, Krannert Graduate School of Management, Purdue University, West Lafayette, Indiana.

Cooper, A. C., and W. C. Dunkelberg. 1986. "Entrepreneurship and Paths to Business Ownership." *Strategic Management Journal* 7, no. 1: 53–68.

Cooper, A. C., and W. R. Soukup. 1983. "Strategic Responses to Technological Change in the Electronic Components Industry." *R&D Management* 13, no. 4: 219–230.

Cooper, A. C., G. E. Willard, and C. Woo. 1984. "A Re-examination of the Niche Concept: The Direct Challenge." Working paper, Krannert Graduate School of Management, Purdue University, West Lafayette, Indiana.

Cyert, R. M., and J. G. March. 1963. *A Behavioral Theory of the Firm*. Englewood Cliffs, N. J.: Prentice-Hall.

Daniels, J. D., R. A. Pitts, and M. J. Tretter. 1984. "Strategy and Structure of U.S. Multinationals: An Exploratory Study." *Academy of Management Journal* 27, no. 2: 292–307.

Darwin, F., ed. 1887. *The Life and Letters of Charles Darwin, Including an Autobiographical Chapter.* 3 vols. London: John Murray.

Demers, C. 1987. "La Diffusion strategique dans les organisations complexes: Outil de conversion ou lieu privilegie de gestation de la strategie." Rapport theorique no. 1, Programme conjoint de doctorat en administration, Ecole des Hautes Etudes, Montréal.

Devons, E. 1950. *Planning in Practice: Essays in Aircraft Planning in Wartime.* Cambridge, Eng.: Cambridge University Press.

Drucker, P. F. 1970. "Entrepreneurship in Business Enterprise." *Journal of Business Policy* 1, no. 1: 3–12.

———. 1985. "Entrepreneurial Strategies." *California Management Review* 27, no. 2: 9–25.

Dubé, C. 1973. "The Department of National Defence and the Defence Strategies from 1945 to 1970." MBA thesis, Faculty of Management, McGill University.

Duhaime, I. M., and C. R. Schwenke. 1983. "Cognitive Simplification Processes in Acquisition and Divestment Decision-Making." Proceedings of the National Conference of the Academy of Management, pp. 12–16.

Dunbar, R. L. M., J. M. Dutton, and W. R. Torbert. 1982. "Crossing Mother: Ideological Constraints on Organizational Improvements." *Journal of Management Studies* 19, no. 1: 91–108.

Duncker, K. 1945. "On Problem Solving." In *Psychological Monographs*, edited by John F. Dashiell, 58, no. 5. L. S. Lees (translator). Washington, D.C.: American Psychological Association.

Dutton, J. M., and R. D. Freedman. 1985. "External Environment and Internal Strategies: Calculating, Experimenting, and Imitating in Organizations." In *Advances in Strategic Management*, Vol. 3, edited by R. Lamb and P. Shrivastava, pp. 39–67. Greenwich, Conn.: JAI Press.

Ebert, D. G., and R. Wehrell. 1984. "Historical Analysis: A Strategic Planning Tool." Working paper, Mount Allison University.

Edwards, J. P. 1977. "Strategy Formulation as a Stylistic Process." *International Studies of Management and Organizations* 7, no. 2 (Summer): 13–27.

Ettlie, J. E., W. P. Bridges, and R. D. O'Keefe. 1984. "Organization Strategy and Structural Differences for Radical versus Incremental Innovation." *Management Science* 30, no. 6: 682–695.

Evered, R. 1983. "So What Is Strategy?" *Long Range Planning* 16, no. 3: 57–72.

Feldman, S. P. 1986. "Management in Context: An Essay on the Relevance of Culture to the Understanding of Organizational Change." *Journal of Management Studies* 23, no. 6: 587–607.

Fiol, C. M., and M. A. Lyles. 1985. "Organizational Learning." *Academy of Management Review* 10, no. 4: 803–813.

Firsirotu, M. 1985. "Strategic Turnaround as Cultural Revolution." Ph.D. dissertation, Faculty of Management, McGill University.

Fredrickson, J. W. 1986. "The Strategic Decision Process and Organizational Structure." *Academy of Management Review* 11, no. 2: 280–297.

Freeman, J., and W. Boeker. 1984. "The Ecological Analysis of Business Strategy." *California Management Review* 26, no. 3: 73–86.

Freeman, R. E. 1984. *Strategic Management: A Stakeholder Approach.* Marshfield, Mass.: Pitman.

Galbraith, C. S., and C. H. Stiles. 1984. "Merger Strategies as a Response to Bilateral Market Power." *Academy of Management Journal* 27, no. 3: 511–524.

Galbraith, J. K. 1967. *The New Industrial State.* Boston: Houghton Mifflin.

Galbraith, J. R. 1985. "Types of Strategic Changes." Working paper. Denver, Colorado.

Galbraith, J. R., and D. A. Nathanson. 1978. *Strategy Implementation: The Role of Structure and Process.* St. Paul: West.

Gerhard, D. 1956. "Periodization in European History." *American Historical Review* 61: 900–913.

Gluck, F. W., S. P. Kaufman, and S. P. Walleck. 1980. "Strategic Management for Competitive Advantage." *Harvard Business Review* (July-August): 154–161.

Gomer, H. 1973. "Corporate Planning in Action." Working paper, Institut d'Administration des Entreprises, Université de Grenoble.

_____. 1974. "L'Utilization des systèmes formels de planification d'entreprise face à la 'crise petrolière.'" Thèse doctorat troisième cycle, Institut d'Administration des Entreprises, Université de Grenoble.

_____. 1976. "The Functions of Formal Planning Systems in Response to Sudden Change in the Environment." D.B.A. dissertation, Harvard University, Graduate School of Business Administration.

Gould, S. J. 1980. *The Panda's Thumb.* New York: W. W. Norton.

_____. 1982. "Free to Be Extinct." *Natural History* (August): 12–16.

Gram, H. A., and R. L. Crawford. 1985. "Strategies in Firms with Undifferentiated Products." Proceedings of the ASAC Conference, Université de Montréal.

Gray, B., and S. S. Ariss. 1985. "Politics and Strategic Change across Organizational Life Cycles." *Academy of Management Review* 10, no. 4: 707–723.

Greiner, L. E. 1972. "Evolution and Revolution as Organizations Grow." *Harvard Business Review* (July-August): 37–46.

Grinyer, P. H., and J. -C. Spender. 1979a. "Recipes, Crises, and Adaptation in Mature Business." *International Studies of Management and Organization* 9, no. 3: 113–133.

_____. 1979b. *Turnaround: Managerial Recipes for Strategic Success (The Fall and Rise of the Newton Chambers Group).* London: Associated Business Press.

Hadamard, J. 1945. *The Psychology of Invention in the Mathematical Field.* New York: Dover Press.

Hafsi, T., M. N. Kiggunda, and J. J. Jorgensen. 1987. "Strategic Apex Configurations in State-Owned Enterprises." *Academy of Management Review* 12, no. 4: 714–730.

Hafsi, T., and H. Thomas. 1985. "Planning under Uncertain and Ambiguous Conditions: The Case of Air France." Working paper, Ecole des Hautes Etudes Commerciales, Montreal.

Hage, D. J. 1976. "Choosing Constraints and Constraining Choice." Paper for Anglo-French Conference at the Tavistock Institute, London.

Hall, D. J., and M. A. Saias. 1980. "Strategy Follows Structure!" *Strategic Management Journal* 1: 149–163.

Hambrick, D. C. 1980. "Operationalizing the Concept of Business-Level Strategy in Research." *Academy of Management Review* 5, no. 4: 567–575.

———. 1983a. "Some Tests of the Effectiveness and Functional Attributes of Miles and Snow's Strategic Types." *Academy of Management Journal* 26, no. 1: 5–26.

———. 1983b. "An Empirical Typology of Mature Industrial-Product Environments." *Academy of Management Journal* 26, no. 1: 213–230.

———. 1984. "Taxonomic Approaches to Studying Strategy: Some Conceptual and Methodological Issues." *Journal of Management* 10, no. 1: 27–41.

Hambrick, D. C., and S. M. Schecter. 1983. "Turnaround Strategies for Mature Industrial-Product Business Units." *Academy of Management Journal* 26, no. 2: 231–248.

Hamermesh, R. G. 1986. *Making Strategy Work.* New York: Wiley.

Hannan, M. T., and J. Freeman. 1977. "The Population Ecology of Organizations." *American Journal of Sociology* 82, no. 5: 929–964.

———. 1984. "Structural Inertia and Organizational Change." *American Sociological Review* 49 (April): 149–164.

Hardy, C. 1983. "Is Strategy-Making a Political Process? The Example of Retrenchment." Working paper, Faculty of Management, McGill University.

———. 1988. "Managing the Interest Groups in University Structures." In *Academy of Management Best Paper Proceedings, 48th Annual Meeting,* edited by F. Hoy. Anaheim, Calif.: Academy of Management.

———. 1989. "Leadership Strategy and University Culture." Paper presented at the fourth International Conference on Organizational Symbolism and Corporate Culture, Fontainebleau, France.

Hardy, C., A. Langley, H. Mintzberg, and J. Rose. 1984. "Strategy Formation in the University Setting." In *College and University Organization: Insights from the Behavioral Sciences,* edited by J. L. Bess, pp. 169–210. New York: New York University Press.

Harrigan, K. R. 1984. "Formulating Vertical Integration Strategies." *Academy of Management Review* 9, no. 4: 638–652.

———. 1985. "Vertical Integration and Corporate Strategy." *Academy of Management Journal* 28, no. 2: 397–425.

Hatten, K. J., and D. E. Schendel. 1977. "Heterogeneity within an Industry: Firm Conduct in the U.S. Brewing Industry, 1952–1971." *Journal of Industrial Economics* 26: 97–113.

Hax, A. C., and N. S. Majluf. 1984. *Strategic Management: An Integrated Perspective.* Englewood Cliffs, N. J.: Prentice-Hall.

Hay, D. A., and D. J. Morris. 1979. *Industrial Economics: Theory and Evidence.* Oxford, Eng.; New York: Oxford University Press.

Hayes, R. H. 1985. "Strategic Planning: Forward in Reverse?" *Harvard Business Review* (November-December): 111–119.

Hedberg, B. 1973. "Organizational Stagnation and Choice of Strategy: Observations from Case Studies." Working paper, International Institute of Management, Berlin.

_____. 1974. "Reframing as a Way to Cope with Organizational Stagnation: A Case Study." International Institute of Management, Berlin.

_____. 1981. "How Organizations Learn and Unlearn." In *Handbook of Organizational Design. Vol. 1, Adapting Organizations to Their Environments,* edited by P. C. Nystrom and W. H. Starbuck, pp. 3–27. New York: Oxford University Press.

Hedberg, B., and S. A. Jonsson. 1977. "Strategy Formation as a Discontinuous Process." *International Studies of Management and Organization* (Summer): 88–109.

Hedberg, B., and A. Targama. 1973. "Organizational Stagnation, a Behavioral Approach." Proceedings of the Conference, TIMS XX, pp. 635–641.

Henderson, B. D. 1979. *On Corporate Strategy.* Cambridge, Mass.: Abt Books.

Hilsman, R. 1969. "Policy-Making Is Politics." In *International Politics and Foreign Policy,* edited by J. N. Rosenau, pp. 232–238. New York: Free Press.

Hirsch, P. M. 1975. "Organizational Effectiveness and the Institutional Environment." *Administration Science Quarterly* 20 (September): 327–344.

Hofer, C. W. 1980. "Turnaround Strategies." *Journal of Business Strategy* (Summer): 19–31.

Hofer, C. W., and D. Schendel. 1978. *Strategy Formulation: Analytical Concepts.* St. Paul: West.

Hogarth, R. M., and S. Makridakis. 1981. "Forecasting and Planning: An Evaluation." *Management Science* 27, no. 2: 115–138.

Holsti, O. R. 1976. "Foreign Policy Formation Viewed Cognitively." In *Structure of Decision: The Cognitive Maps of Political Elites,* edited by R. Axelrod, pp. 18–54. Princeton: Princeton University Press.

_____. 1978. "Limitations of Cognitive Abilities in the Face of Crisis." *Journal of Business Administration* 9, no. 2: 35–55.

Hoskisson, R. E., and C. S. Galbraith. 1985. "The Effect of Quantum versus M-form Reorganization on Performance: A Time-Series Exploration of Intervention Dynamics." *Journal of Management* 11, no. 3: 55–70.

Hrebiniak, L. G., and W. F. Joyce. 1984. *Implementing Strategy.* New York: Macmillan.

_____. 1985. "Organizational Adaptation: Strategic Choice and Environmental Determinism." *Administrative Science Quarterly* 30: 336–349.

Jauch, L. R., and K. L. Kraft. 1986. "Strategic Management of Uncertainty." *Academy of Management Review* 11, no. 4: 777–790.

Jelinek, M. 1979. *Institutionalizing Innovation.* New York: Praeger.

Jelinek, M., L. Smircich, and P. Hirsch. 1983. "Introduction: A Code of Many Colors." *Administrative Science Quarterly* 28, no. 3: 331–338.

Jervis, R. 1969. "Hypotheses on Misperception." In *International Politics and Foreign Policy,* edited by J. N. Rosenau, pp. 239–254. New York: Free Press.

Jonsson, S. n.d. "A City Administration Facing Stagnation: Political Organization and Action in Goteborg." Goteborg: Swedish Council for Building Research.

Jonsson, S., and R. A. Lundin. 1977. "Myths and Wishful Thinking as Management Tools." In *Prescriptive Models of Organizations,* edited by P. C. Nystrom and W. H. Starbuck, pp. 157–170. Amsterdam: North-Holland.

Jonsson, S. A., R. A. Lundin, and L. Sjoberg. 1977–78. "Frustration in Decision Processes: A Tentative Frame of Reference." *International Studies of Management and Organization* (Fall-Winter): 6–19.

Jorgensen, J. J. 1989. "Managing Three Levels of Culture in State-Controlled Enterprises." In *Strategic Issues in State-Controlled Organizations,* edited by T. Hafsi. Greenwich, Conn.: JAI Press.

Kagono, T., I. Nonaka, K. Sakakibara, and A. Okumura. 1985. *Strategic versus Evolutionary Management: A U.S.-Japan Comparison of Strategy and Organization.* Advanced Series in Management, Vol. 10. Amsterdam: North-Holland.

Kaplan, R. 1987. "Entrepreneurship Reconsidered: The Antimanagement Bias." *Harvard Business Review* (May-June): 84–89.

Katz, R. L. 1970. *Cases and Concepts in Corporate Strategy.* Englewood Cliffs, N. J.: Prentice-Hall.

Keim, G. D., C. P. Zeithaml, and B. D. Baysinger. 1984. "SMR Forum: New Directions for Corporate Political Strategy." *Sloan Management Review* 25, no. 3: 53–62.

Kets de Vries, M. F. R. 1977. "The Entrepreneurial Personality: A Person at the Crossroads." *Journal of Management Studies* (February): 34–57.

_____. 1985. "The Dark Side of Entrepreneurship." *Harvard Business Review* 6: 160–167.

Kets de Vries, M. F. R., and D. Miller. 1986. "Personality, Culture, and Organization." *Academy of Management Review* 11: 266–279.

Khandwalla, P. N. 1970. "The Effect of the Environment on the Organizational Structure of Firm." Ph.D. dissertation, Carnegie-Mellon University.

_____. 1977. *The Design of Organizations.* New York: Harcourt, Brace, Jovanovich.

Kiechel, W., III. 1984. "Sniping at Strategic Planning (Interview with Himself)." *Planning Review* (May): 8-11.

Kiesler, C. A. 1971. *The Psychology of Commitment: Experiments Linking Behaviour to Belief.* New York: Academic Press.

Kiesler, S., and L. Sproull. 1982. "Managerial Response to Changing Environments: Perspectives on Problem Sensing from Social Cognition." *Administrative Science Quarterly* 27: 548-570.

Kirlin, J. J., and S. P. Eric. 1972. "The Study of City Governance and Public Policy Making: A Critical Appraisal." *Public Administration Review* 32 (March-April): 173-184.

Knight, K. E. 1967. "A Descriptive Model of the Intra-Firm Innovation Process." *Journal of Business* 40: 478-496.

Kobrin, S. J. 1984. "Strategic Integration in Fragmented Environments: Social and Political Assessment by Subsidiaries of Multinational Firms." Prince Bertil Symposium on Strategies in Global Competition, Institute of International Business, Stockholm School of Economics, November 7-10.

Koch, S. J. 1976. "Nondemocratic Nonplanning: The French Experience." *Policy Sciences* 7: 371-385.

Kohler, W. 1925. *The Mentality of Apes.* New York: Humanitarian Press.

Kress, G., G. Koehler, and J. F. Springer. 1980. "Policy Drift: An Evaluation of the California Business Enterprise Program." *Policy Studies Journal* 111 (Special Issue): 1101-1108.

Kuhn, T. S. 1970. *The Structure of Scientific Revolutions*, 2nd ed. Chicago: University of Chicago Press.

Kylen, B. J. 1982. "Explaining the Double Shock." Paper for the JMS Conference.

Lampel, J., and H. Mintzberg. 1987. "Customizing Strategies . . . and Strategic Management." Working paper, Faculty of Management, McGill University.

Langley, A. 1987. "The Role of Formal Analysis in Organizations." Ph.D. dissertation, Ecole des Hautes Etudes, Montréal.

Lapierre, R. 1980. "Le Changement Stratégique: Un rêve en quête du réel." Doctoral course paper, Faculty of Management, McGill University.

Lawrence, P. R., and J. W. Lorsch. 1967. *Organization and Environment.* Homewood, Ill.: Irwin.

Learned, E. P., C. R. Christensen, K. R. Andrews, and W. D. Guth. 1965. *Business Policy: Text and Cases.* Homewood, Ill.: Irwin.

Learned, E. P., and A. T. Sproat. 1966. *Organization Theory and Policy: Notes for Analysis.* Homewood, Ill.: Irwin.

Lenz, R. T. 1980. "Strategic Capability: A Concept and Framework for Analysis." *Academy of Management Review* 5, no. 2: 225-234.

Lenz, R. T., and J. L. Engledow. 1983. "Alternative 'Models' for Analyzing Organizational Environments: Theoretical Issues and Administrative Implications." Working paper, Columbia University, New York.

Liddell-Hart, B. H. 1967. *Strategy*, 2nd ed. New York: Praeger.

Lindblom, C. E. 1959. "The Science of 'Muddling Through.'" *Public Administration Review* 19, no. 2: 79–88.

_____. 1968. *The Policy Making Process*. Englewood Cliffs, N. J.: Prentice-Hall.

Lindgren, U., and K. Spangberg. 1981. "Corporate Acquisitions and Divestments: The Strategic Decision-Making Process." *International Studies of Management and Organization* 11, no. 2: 24–47.

Lipsky, M. 1978. "Standing the Study of Public Policy Implementation on Its Head." In *American Politics and Public Policy*, edited by W. D. Burnham and M. W. Weinberg, pp. 391–402. Cambridge, Mass.: MIT Press.

Lorange, P. 1979. "Formal Planning Systems: Their Role in Strategy Formulation and Implementation." In *Strategic Management*, edited by D. E. Schendel and C. W. Hofer, pp. 226–241. Boston: Little, Brown.

Lorange, P., I. S. Gordon, and R. Smith. 1979. "The Management of Adaption and Integration." *Journal of General Management* 4 (Summer): 31–41.

MacMillan, I. C. 1978. *Strategy Formulation: Political Concepts*. St. Paul: West.

MacMillan, I. C., and W. D. Guth. 1985. "Strategy Implementation and Middle Management Coalitions." In *Advances in Strategic Management*, Vol. 3, edited by R. Lamb and P. Shrivastava, pp. 233–254. Greenwich, Conn.: JAI Press.

MacMillan, I. C., and P. E. Jones. 1986. *Strategy Formulation: Power and Politics*, 2nd ed. St. Paul: West.

Majone, G., and A. Wildavsky. 1978. "Implementation as Evolution." *Policy Studies Review Annual* 2: 103–117.

Makridakis, S. 1990. *Management in the Twenty-first Century: Facing the New Challenges*. New York: Free Press. Forthcoming.

Makridakis, S., C. Faucheux, and D. Heau. 1982. "What Is Strategy?" Paper presented at INSEAD, Fontainebleau, France.

Malmlow, E. G. 1972. "Corporate Strategic Planning in Practice." *Long Range Planning* 5 (September): 2–9.

March, J. G., and H. A. Simon. 1958. *Organizations*. New York: Wiley.

McClelland, D. C. 1961. *The Achieving Society*. New York: Van Nostrand.

McKelvey, B., and H. Aldrich. 1983. "Populations, Natural Selection, and Applied Organizational Science." *Administrative Science Quarterly* 28: 101–128.

Meindl, J. R., S. B. Ehrlich, and J. M. Dukerich. 1985. "The Romance of Leadership." *Administrative Science Quarterly* 30 (March): 78–102.

Melin, L. 1982. "Structure, Strategy and Organization: A Case of Decline." Paper for an EIASM-workshop, Strategic Management under Limited Growth and Decline, Brussels.

_____. 1983. "Implementation of New Strategies and Structures." Paper for the Third Annual Strategic Management Society Conference, Paris.

_____. 1985. "Strategies in Managing Turnaround." *Long Range Planning* 18, no. 1: 80–86.

Miles, R. H. 1982. *Coffin Nails and Corporate Strategies.* Englewood Cliffs, N. J.: Prentice-Hall.

Miles, R. E., and C. C. Snow. 1978. *Organizational Strategy, Structure, and Process.* New York: Mc Graw-Hill.

Miller, D. 1976. "Strategy Making in Context: Ten Empirical Archetypes." Ph.D. dissertation, Faculty of Management, Mc Gill University, Montreal.

_____. 1979. "Strategy, Structure and Environment: Context Influences upon Some Bivariate Associations." *Journal of Management Studies* 16 (October): 294–316.

_____. 1981. "Toward a New Contingency Approach: The Search for Organizational Gestalts." *Journal of Management Studies* 18: 1–26.

_____. 1982. "Evolution and Revolution: A Quantum View of Structural Change in Organizations." *Journal of Management Studies* 19: 131–151.

_____. 1983. "The Correlates of Entrepreneurship in Three Types of Firms." *Management Science* 29: 770–791.

_____. 1986. "Configurations of Strategy and Structure: Towards a Synthesis." *Strategic Management Journal* 7: 233–249.

_____. 1987. "The Structural and Environmental Correlates of Business Strategy." *Strategic Management Journal* 8: 55–76.

Miller, D., and P. H. Friesen. 1977. "Strategy-Making in Context: Ten Empirical Archetypes." *Journal of Management Studies* 14: 253–279.

_____. 1978. "Archetypes of Strategy Formulation." *Management Science* 24, no. 9: 921–933.

_____. 1980a. "Momentum and Revolution in Organizational Adaptation." *Academy of Management Journal* 23: 591–614.

_____. 1980b. "Archetypes of Organizational Transition." *Administrative Science Quarterly* 25: 268–299.

_____. 1982. "Structural Change and Performance: Quantum vs. Piecemeal-Incremental Approaches." *Academy of Management Journal* 25: 867–892.

_____. 1983. "Strategy-Making and Environment: The Third Link." *Strategic Management Journal* 3: 221–235.

_____. 1984. *Organizations: A Quantum View.* Englewood Cliffs, N. J.: Prentice-Hall.

Miller, D., and H. Mintzberg. 1983. "The Case for Configuration." In *Beyond Method,* edited by G. Morgan, pp. 57–73. Beverly Hills: Sage. Reprinted in *The Strategy Process,* edited by H. Mintzberg, J. B. Quinn, and R. M. James, pp. 518–524. New York: Prentice-Hall.

_____. 1984. "The Case for Configuration." In *Organizations: A Quantum View,* edited by D. Miller and P. H. Friesen. Englewood Cliffs, N. J.: Prentice-Hall.

Miller, G. A. 1956. "The Magical Number Seven, Plus or Minus Two: Some Limits on Our Capacity for Processing Information." *Psychological Review* 63, no. 2: 81–107.

Minsky, M. 1975. "A Framework for Representing Knowledge." In *The Psychology of Computer Vision*, edited by P. Winston. New York: McGraw-Hill.

Mintzberg, H. 1967. "The Science of Strategy-Making." *Industrial Management Review* 8, no. 2: 71–81.

———. 1972. "Research on Strategy-Making." *Proceedings of the 32nd Annual Meeting of the Academy of Management.* Minneapolis.

———. 1973. "Strategy-Making in Three Modes." *California Management Review* 16, no. 2: 44–53.

———. 1975. *Impediments to the Use of Management Information.* New York: National Association of Accountants.

———. 1978. "Patterns in Strategy Formation." *Management Science* 24, no. 9: 934–948.

———. 1979. *The Structuring of Organizations.* Englewood Cliffs, N.J.: Prentice-Hall.

———. 1982. "If You're Not Serving Bill and Barbara, Then You're Not Serving Leadership." In *Leadership: Beyond Establishment Views*, edited by J. G. Hunt, U. Sekaran, and C. A. Schriesheim, pp. 239–259. Carbondale: Southern Illinois University.

———. 1983. *Power in and Around Organizations.* Englewood Cliffs, N.J.: Prentice-Hall.

———. 1987a. "Crafting Strategy." *Harvard Business Review* (July–August): 66–75.

———. 1987b. "The Strategy Concept I: Five P's for Strategy." *California Management Review* 30, no. 1: 11–24.

———. 1988. "Strategy Content Research in Perspective." Working paper, McGill University.

———. 1989. "Beyond Configuration: Forces and Forms in Effective Organizations." In *Mintzberg on Management: Inside Our Strange World of Organizations*, ch. 14. New York: Free Press.

———. 1990a. *"Strategic" Planning: In Search of Roles for Planning, Plans, Planners.* Forthcoming.

———. 1990b. "The Design School: Reconsidering the Basic Premises of Strategic Management." *Strategic Management Journal* (Forthcoming).

———. 1990c. "Globalization: Separating the Fad from the Fact." In *International Management Research: Looking to the Future*, edited by D. Wong-Rieger and F. Rieger. London: Routledge. Forthcoming.

Mintzberg, H., J. P. Brunet, and J. A. Waters. 1986. "Does Planning Impede Strategic Thinking? Tracking the Strategies of Air Canada from 1937 to 1976." In *Advances in Strategic Management*, Vol. 4, edited by R. Lamb and P. Shrivastava. Greenwich, Conn.: JAI Press.

Mintzberg, H., and A. McHugh. 1985. "Strategy Formation in an Adhocracy." *Administrative Science Quarterly* 30: 160–197.

Mintzberg, H., S. Otis, J. Shamsie, and J. A. Waters. 1988. "Strategy of Design: A Study of 'Architects in Co-Partnership.'" In *Strategic Management Frontiers*, edited by J. Grant, pp. 311–359. Greenwich, Conn. JAI Press.

Mintzberg, H., D. Raisinghani, and A. Théorêt. 1976. "The Structure of 'Unstructured' Decision Processes." *Administrative Science Quarterly* 21: 246–275.

Mintzberg, H., W. D. Taylor, and J. A. Waters. 1984. "Tracking Strategies in the Birthplace of Canadian Tycoons: The Sherbrooke Record 1946–1976." *ASAC Journal* 1, no. 1: 11–28.

Mintzberg, H., and J. A. Waters. 1982. "Tracking Strategy in an Entrepreneurial Firm." *Academy of Management Journal* 25, no. 3: 465–499.

———. 1983. "The Mind of the Strategist(s)." In *The Executive Mind*, edited by Suresh Srivastva and Associates, pp. 58–63. San Francisco: Jossey-Bass.

———. 1984. "Researching the Formation of Strategies: The History of Canadian Lady 1939–1976." In *Competitive Strategy Management*, edited by R. B. Lamb, pp. 62–93. Englewood Cliffs, N. J.: Prentice-Hall.

———. 1985. "Of Strategies, Deliberate and Emergent." *Strategic Management Journal* 6: 257–272.

Montgomery, C. A. 1982. "The Measurement of Firm Diversification: Some New Empirical Evidence." *Academy of Management Review* 25: 299–307.

Moulton, W. N., and H. Thomas. 1987. "Bankruptcy as a Deliberate Strategy by Troubled Firms." Paper presented at the Annual Conference of the Strategic Management Society, Boston.

Murray, E. A., Jr. 1978. "Strategic Choice as a Negotiated Outcome." *Management Science* 24, no. 9: 960–972.

Murray, J. A. 1984. "A Concept of Entrepreneurial Strategy." *Strategic Management Journal* 5, no. 1: 1–13.

Narayanan, V. K., and L. Fahey. 1982. "The Politics of Strategy Formulation." *Academy of Management Review* 7, no. 1: 25–34.

Neisser, U. 1976. *Cognition and Reality: Principles and Implications of Cognitive Psychology*. New York: Freeman.

Newman, W. H. 1951. *Administrative Action: The Techniques of Organization and Management*. Englewood Cliffs, N. J.: Prentice-Hall.

Newman, W. H., C. E. Summer, and E. K. Warren. 1967. *The Process of Management: Concepts, Behaviour and Practice*, 2nd ed. Englewood Cliffs, N. J.: Prentice-Hall.

Newman, W. H., E. K. Warren, and J. E. Schee. 1982. *The Process of Management: Concepts, Behaviour and Practice*, 5th ed. Englewood Cliffs, N. J.: Prentice-Hall.

Noel, A. 1989. "Strategic Cores and Magnificent Obsessions: Discovering Strategy Formulation Through Daily Activities of CEOs." *Strategic Management Journal* 10 (Special Issue, Summer): 33–49.

230 PERSPECTIVES ON STRATEGIC MANAGEMENT

Nonaka, I., and J. K. Johansson. 1985. "Japanese Management: What about the 'Hard' Skills?" *Academy of Management Review* 10, no. 2: 181–191.

Normann, R. 1971. "Organizational Innovativeness: Product Variation and Reorientation." *Administration Science Quarterly* 16, no. 2: 203–215.

_____. 1977. *Management for Growth.* Chichester: Wiley.

Nystrom, H. 1979. *Creativity and Innovation.* New York: Wiley.

Ohmae, K. 1982. *The Mind of the Strategist.* New York: McGraw-Hill.

Ornstein, R. F. 1972. *The Psychology of Consciousness.* San Francisco: Freeman.

Ouchi, W. G. 1981. *Theory Z: How American Business Can Meet the Japanese Challenge.* Reading, Mass.: Addison-Wesley.

Papandreou, A. G. 1952. "Some Basic Problems in the Theory of the Firm." In *A Survey of Contemporary Economics*, Vol. 2, edited by B. F. Haley. Homewood, Ill.: Irwin. For the American Economics Association.

Pascale, R. T. 1982. "Our Curious Addition to Corporate Grand Strategy." *Fortune* (January): 115–116.

_____. 1984. "Perspectives on Strategy: The Real Story Behind Honda's Success." *California Management Review* (Spring): 47–72.

Pascale, R. T., and A. G. Athos. 1981. *The Art of Japanese Management: Applications for American Executives.* New York: Simon and Schuster.

Pennington, M. W. 1972. "Why Has Planning Failed?" *Long Range Planning* 5, no. 1: 2–9.

Perrow, C. 1970. *Organizational Analysis: A Sociological View.* Belmont, Calif.: Wadsworth.

_____. 1972. *Complex Organizations: A Critical Essay.* Glenview, Ill.: Scott, Foresman.

Peters, T. H., and R. H. Waterman, Jr. 1982. *In Search of Excellence.* New York: Harper & Row.

Peterson, R. A. 1981. "Entrepreneurship and Organization." In *Handbook of Organizational Design*, Vol. I, edited by P. C. Nystrom and W. H. Starbuck, pp. 65–83. Oxford: Oxford University Press.

Pettigrew, A. M. 1977. "Strategy Formulation as a Political Process." *International Studies of Management and Organization* (Summer): 78–87.

_____. 1985. *The Awakening Giant: Continuity and Change in Imperial Chemical Industries.* Oxford: Basil Blackwell.

Pfeffer, J., and G. R. Salancik. 1978. *The External Control of Organizations: A Resource Dependence Perspective.* New York: Harper & Row.

Phillips, A., and R. E. Stevenson. 1974. "The Historical Development of Industrial Organization." *Journal of Political Economy* 6: 323–342.

Pokora, T. 1966. "A Theory of the Periodization of World History." *Archiv Orientalni* 34: 602–605.

Polanyi, M. 1983. *The Tacit Dimension.* Gloucester, Mass.: Peter Smith.

Pondy, L. R., and A. S. Huff. 1985. "Achieving Routine in Organizational Change." *Journal of Management* 11, no. 2: 102–116.

Popescu, O. 1965. "Periodization in the History of Economic Thought." *International Social Science Journal* 17, no. 4: 607–634.

Popper, K. 1959. *The Logic of Scientific Discovery*. London: Hutchinson.

Porter, M. E. 1974. "Consumer Behavior, Retailer Power, and Market Performance in Consumer Group Industries." *Review of Economics and Statistics* 56, no. 4: 419–436.

_____. 1979. "The Structure within Industries and Companies Performance." *Review of Economics and Statistics* 61: 214–227.

_____. 1980. *Competitive Strategy: Techniques for Analyzing Industries and Competitors*. New York: Free Press.

_____. 1981. "The Contributions of Industrial Organizations to Strategic Management." *Academy of Management Review* 6, no. 4: 609–620.

_____. 1983. "Industrial Organization and the Evolution of Concept for Strategic Planning: The New Learning." *Managerial and Decision Economics* 4, no. 3: 172–180.

_____. 1985. *Competitive Advantage: Creating and Sustaining Superior Performance*. New York: Free Press.

Prescott, J. E. 1986. "Environments as Moderators of the Relationship between Strategy and Performance." *Academy of Management Journal* 29, no. 2: 329–346.

Quinn, J. B. 1980. *Strategies for Change: Logical Incrementalism*. Homewood, Ill.: Irwin.

Quinn, J. B., H. Mintzberg, and R. B. James. 1988. *The Strategy Process: Concepts, Contexts, and Cases*. Englewood Cliffs, N. J.: Prentice-Hall.

Radosevich, R. 1974. "A Critique of 'Comprehensive Managerial Planning.'" In *Contemporary Management*, edited by J. W. McLuin, pp. 356–361. Englewood Cliffs, N. J.: Prentice-Hall.

Raphael, R. 1976. *Edges*. New York: Knopf.

Rhenman, E. 1973. *Organization Theory for Long-Range Planning*. London: Wiley.

Rieger, F. 1987. "The Influence of National Culture on Organizational Structure, Process, and Strategic Decision Making: A Study of International Airlines." Ph.D. dissertation, Faculty of Management, McGill University, Montreal.

Ringbakk, K. A. 1971. "Why Planning Fails." *European Business* 29 (Spring): 15–241.

Rokeach, M., and F. Restle. 1960. *The Open and Closed Mind*. New York: Basic Books.

Rosenau, J. N., ed. 1969. *International Politics and Foreign Policy*, rev. ed. New York: Free Press.

Rostow, W. W. 1971. *The Stages of Economic Growth*, 2nd ed. Cambridge, Eng.: Cambridge University Press.

Rumelt, R. P. 1974. *Strategy, Structure, and Economic Performance.* Division of Research, Graduate School of Business Administration, Harvard University.

_____. 1982. "Diversification Strategy and Profitability." *Strategic Management Journal* 3: 359–369.

_____. 1984. "Towards a Strategic Theory of the Firm." In *Competitive Strategic Management*, edited by R. B. Lamb, pp. 556–570. Englewood Cliffs, N. J.: Prentice-Hall.

Saint-Exupéry, A. 1943. *Le Petit Prince.* New York: Harcourt, Brace, Jovanovich.

Sarrazin, J. 1975. "Le role des processus de planification dans les grandes entreprises francaises: un essai d'interpretation." Doctorat troisième cycle, Université de droit, d'economie et des sciences d'Aix-en-Province.

_____. 1977–78. "Decentralized Planning in a Large French Company: An Interpretive Study." *International Studies of Management and Organization* (Fall-Winter): 37–59.

Schein, E. H. 1985. *Organizational Culture and Leadership.* San Francisco: Jossey-Bass.

Scherer, F. M. 1980. *Industrial Market Structure and Market Performance*, 2nd ed. Boston: Houghton Mifflin.

Schmalensee, R. 1978. "Entry Deterence in the Ready-to-Eat Breakfast Cereal Industry." *Bell Journal of Economics* 9: 305–327.

Schnaars, S. P. 1986. "When Entering Growth Markets, Are Pioneers Better Than Poachers?" *Business Horizons* (March-April): 27–36.

Schoeffler, S. 1980. "Nine Basic Findings on Business Strategy." *Strategic Planning Institute* 1, Boston.

Schoeffler, S., R. D. Buzzell, and D. F. Heany. 1974. "Impact of Strategic Planning on Profit Performance." *Harvard Business Review* (March-April): 137–145.

Schoettle, N. C. B. 1968. "The State of the Art in Policy Studies." In *The Study of Policy Formation*, edited by R. A. Bauer and K. J. Gergen, pp. 149–179. New York: Free Press.

Schroder, H. M., M. J. Driver, and S. Streufert. 1967. *Human Information Processing: Individuals and Groups Functioning in Complex Social Situations.* New York: Holt, Rinehart, and Winston.

Schumpeter, J. A. 1934. *Theory of Economic Development: An Inquiry into Profit, Capital, Credit Interest, and Business Cycle.* Cambridge, Mass.: Harvard University Press.

_____. 1947. "The Creative Response in Economic History." *Journal of Economic History* (November): 149–159.

Schwartz, H., and S. M. Davis. 1981. "Matching Corporate Culture and Business Strategy." *Organizational Dynamics* (Summer): 30–48.

Schwenk, C. R. 1984. "Cognitive Simplification Processes in Strategic Decision-Making." *Strategic Management Journal* 5: 111–128.

Scott, B. R. 1971. "Stages of Corporate Development, Part 1." Working paper, Graduate School of Business Administration, Harvard University.

Selznick, P. 1957. *Leadership in Administration: A Sociological Interpretation.* New York: Harper & Row.

Shrader, C. B., L. Taylor, and D. R. Dalton. 1984. "Strategic Planning and Organizational Performance: A Critical Appraisal." *Journal of Management* 10, no. 2: 149–171.

Shrivastava, P. 1983. "A Typology of Organizational Learning Systems." *Journal of Management Studies* 20, no. 1: 7–28.

Simon, H. A. 1957. *Administrative Behavior,* 2nd ed. New York: Macmillan.

Singh, J. V., R. J. House, and D. J. Tucker. 1986. "Organizational Change and Organizational Mortality." *Administrative Science Quarterly* 31: 587–611.

Smircich, L., and C. Stubbart. 1985. "Strategic Management in an Enacted World." *Academy of Management Review* 10, no. 4: 724–736.

Smith, C. G., and A. C. Cooper. 1986. "Established Companies Diversifying into Young Industries: A Comparison of Firms with Different Levels of Performance." Working paper, Krannert Graduate School of Management, Purdue University, West Lafayette, Indiana.

Snow, C. C., and L. G. Hrebiniak. 1980. "Strategy, Distinctive Competence, and Organizational Performance." *Administrative Science Quarterly* 25: 317–336.

Sperry, R. 1974. "Messages from the Laboratory." *Engineering and Science*: 29–32.

Starbuck, W. H. 1965. "Organizational Growth and Development." In *Handbook of Organizations,* edited by J. G. March, pp. 451–533. Chicago: Rand-McNally.

———. 1976. "Organizations and Their Environments." In *Handbook of Industrial and Organizational Psychology,* edited by M. D. Dunnett, pp. 1069–1123. Chicago: Rand-McNally.

Starbuck, W. H., A. Greve, and B. L. T. Hedberg. 1978. "Responding to Crises." *Journal of Business Administration*: 111–138.

Starbuck, W. H., and B. L. T. Hedberg. 1977. "Saving an Organization from a Stagnating Environment." In *Strategy + Structure = Performance: The Strategic Planning Imperative,* edited by H. B. Thorelli, pp. 249–258. Bloomington: Indiana University Press.

Staw, B. M. 1976. "Knee Deep in the Big Muddy: A Study of Escalating Commitment to a Chosen Course of Action." *Organizational Behavior and Human Performance* 16: 27–44.

———. 1981. "The Escalation of Commitment to a Course of Action." *Academy of Management Review* 6, no. 4: 577–587.

Steinbruner, J. D. 1974. *The Cybernetic Theory of Decision: New Dimensions of Political Analysis.* Princeton, N. J.: Princeton University Press.

Steiner, G. A. 1979. *Strategic Planning: What Every Manager Must Know.* New York: Free Press.

———. 1983. "Formal Strategic Planning in the United States Today." *Long Range Planning* 16, no. 3: 12–17.

Stevenson, H. H. 1976. "Defining Corporate Strengths and Weaknesses." *Sloan Management Review* 17, no. 3: 51–68.

Strauss, J. H. 1944. "The Entrepreneur: The Firm." *Journal of Political Economy* (June): 112–127.

Stubbart, C. I. 1987. "Cognitive Science and Strategic Management: Theoretical and Methodological Issues." Proceedings of the Academy of Management Review.

Stymme, B. 1972. *Values and Processes: A System Study of Effectiveness in Three Organizations.* Scandinavian Institutes for Administrative Research.

Sun, Tzu. 1971. *The Art of War,* S. G. Griffith, translator. London: Oxford University Press.

Takeuchi, H., and I. Nonaka. 1986. "The New Product Development Game." *Harvard Business Review* 64, no. 1: 137–146.

Taylor, W. D. 1982. "Strategic Adaptation in Low Growth Environments." Ph.D. dissertation, Ecole des Hautes Etudes Commerciales, Montreal.

Thietart, R. A., and R. Vivas. 1984. "An Empirical Investigation of Success Strategies for Businesses along the Product Life-Cycle." *Management Science* 30, no. 12: 1405–1423.

Toynbee, A. 1946-57. *Study of History.* Abridgement of Vol. I–X. New York: Oxford University Press.

Tregoe, B. B., and J. W. Zimmerman. 1980. *Top Management Strategy.* New York: Simon and Schuster.

Tushman, M., and E. Romanelli. 1985. "Organizational Evolution: A Metamorphosis Model of Convergence and Reorientation." In *Research in Organizational Behavior,* Vol. 7, edited by L. Cummings and B. Shaw, pp. 355–389. Greenwich, Conn.: JAI Press.

Tversky, A., and D. Kahneman. 1974. "Judgment under Uncertainty: Heuristics and Biases." *Science* 185: 1124–1131.

Uttal, B. 1983. "The Corporate Culture Vultures." *Fortune* (October): 66–72.

Utterback, J. M., and W. J. Abernathy. 1975. "A Dynamic Model of Process and Product Innovation." *Omega: The International Journal of Management Science* 3, no. 6: 639–656.

Van de Ven, A. H. 1979. "Review of H. Aldrich's Organizations and Environments." *Administrative Science Quarterly* 24: 320–326.

Van de Ven, A. H., R. Hudson, and D. M. Schoeder. 1984. "Designing New Business Startups: Entrepreneurial, Organizational, and Ecological Considerations." *Journal of Management* 10, no. 1: 87–107.

Vickers, G. 1965. *The Art of Judgment: A Study of Policy Making.* New York: Basic Books.

Weick, K. E. 1979. *The Social Psychology of Organizing*, 2nd ed. Reading, Mass.: Addison-Wesley.

_____. 1983. "Managerial Thought in the Context of Action." In *The Executive Mind*, edited by S. Srivastva and Associates, pp. 221–242. San Francisco: Jossey-Bass.

Wernerfelt, J. M. 1985. "The Dynamics of Prices and Market Shares over the Product Life-Cycle." *Management Science* 31, no. 8: 928–939.

Westley, F. 1983. "Harnessing a Vision: The Role of Images in Strategy-Making." Working paper, McGill University.

Westley, F., and H. Mintzberg. 1988. "Profiles of Strategic Vision: Levesque and Iacocca." In *Charismatic Leadership: The Elusive Factor in Organizational Effectiveness*, edited by J. Conger, R. N. Kanungo, and Associates, pp. 161–212. San Francisco: Jossey-Bass.

_____. 1989. "Visionary Leadership and Strategic Management." *Strategic Management Journal*. Forthcoming.

Wholey, D. R., and J. W. Brittain. 1983–84. "Organizational Ecology and Strategy: A Theoretical Assessment." Working paper, University of Texas at Austin.

Wildavsky, A. 1965. "Budgeting as a Political Process." *International Encyclopedia of the Social Sciences* 2: 192–199.

_____. 1974. *The Politics of the Budgeting Process*, 2nd ed. Boston: Little, Brown.

_____. 1979. *Speaking Truth to Power: The Act and Craft of Policy Analysis.* Boston: Little, Brown.

Wissema, J. G., H. W. Van Der Pol; and H. M. Messer. 1980. "Strategic Management Archetypes." *Strategic Management Journal* 1: 37–47.

Witkin, H. A. et al. 1974. *Psychological Differentiation: Studies of Development.* Potomac, Md.: Erlbaum.

Woo, C. Y., and A. C. Cooper. 1981. "Strategies of Effective Low Share Businesses." *Strategic Management Journal* 2: 301–318.

Woodward, J. 1965. *Industrial Organization: Theory and Practice.* London: Oxford University Press.

Wrapp, H. E. 1967. "Good Managers Don't Make Policy Decisions." *Harvard Business Review* (September–October): 91–99.

Zahra, S. A. 1987. "Research on the Miles-Snow (1978) Typology of Strategic Orientation: Review, Critique and Future Directions." *Proceedings of the Academy of Management Meeting.*

Zand, D. E. 1981. *Information, Organization, and Power.* New York: McGraw-Hill.

Zeeman, E. C. 1977. *Catastrophe Theory: Selected Papers, 1972–1977.* Reading, Mass.: Addison-Wesley.

6

THE ADOLESCENCE OF STRATEGIC MANAGEMENT, 1980–1985
Critical Perceptions and Reality

Donald C. Hambrick

In 1980, the field of strategy was at a crossroads. The Schendel and Hofer (1979) volume, summarizing the views of many of the leading figures of the field, had just the year before called for rechristening "business policy" as "strategic management." And 1980 was also the year two new journals—*Strategic Management Journal (SMJ)* and *Journal of Business Strategy (JBS)*—dealing exclusively with the topic of strategy were created, which greatly multiplied the printed pages available for the field's work.

The distance traveled since 1980 has been substantial. For instance, possibly twice as much strategy research has been done in the past five years as in the preceding twenty. But we still seem to be at a crossroads: not fully sure of where we've been, much less where we're headed; not sure we always like what we see in our research, much less that we can expect others to like it. Many of the weaknesses do not lie in individual pieces of research. Each is typically competent and contributes in its own way. Rather, our problem lies in our general inability or hesitance to reflect broadly upon our field—its context, its purpose, its comparative advantages, its rocky adolescence. This lack of introspection is what makes volumes such as this one so important.

Chandrasekaran Rajam, of Pennsylvania State University, deserves great credit for his help in several phases of this project.

When Jim Fredrickson asked me to participate in the symposium that spawned this book, my immediate reaction was to pull out a notepad and start thinking of all of my general impressions and pet peeves about what had been going on in the field of strategy for the last several years. But then my dyed-in-the-wool empiricist tendencies took over.

Why not study it? So that is what I did, along with Chandru Rajam, a doctoral student at Penn State, where I was on sabbatical. We conducted a large-scale, systematic study of strategy research published between 1980 and 1985. We chose 1980 as the starting year because, as noted above, it is a relatively clean point of demarcation in our field: the start of two new journals; publication of Mike Porter's (1980) immensely important book; and a year following the publication of the Schendel and Hofer (1979) book rechristening the field. We closed with 1985 because we were doing the project in early 1986.

It is useful now to discuss how the study was conducted. Then we will turn to our analyses and findings, many of which I leave to the reader to interpret.

DESCRIPTION OF THE STUDY

So much was written in the field between 1980 and 1985 that there was no way that we could study everything. Nor did we choose to study a random sample, since such a sample would not be very meaningful. We decided instead to identify and study the fifty works, among those published between 1980 and 1985, that were most cited by other works published during the same period. To do this, we conducted an exhaustive analysis of all of the reference lists of all strategy-oriented and top management–oriented articles in *Academy of Management Journal (AMJ), Academy of Management Review (AMR), Administrative Science Quarterly (ASQ),* and *Harvard Business Review (HBR)*, and of all articles in *JBS* and *SMJ*. In total, the reference lists of 479 articles were studied to determine the post–1980 works they cited most often. We used a weighting system (described in appendix 6–1) to adjust for publication date since, of course, more recent works have inherently less opportunity to be cited. The list of fifty most noted works is reported in appendix 6–2.

Two legitimate concerns can be raised about the time frame of the study. First, it can be argued that six years is a very thin slice of the field's existence to study. This is true; however, earlier eras of the field have been analyzed elsewhere (Hofer 1976; Saunders and Thompson 1980; Jauch 1983). As noted above, the six years we focus on appear to be a somewhat well-defined "adolescent" period for the field; obviously, we encourage studies of this type to examine strategy research for the second half of the 1980s.

The second timing concern is whether the list of the fifty most-noted works would hold together if a longer citation period were allowed. Fortunately, the two years that have lapsed between the initial analysis and this writing allow us to address this concern systematically. Namely, we examined all the strategy-oriented articles appearing during 1986 and 1987 (a total of 146) in the six journals listed above in order to observe the degree to which they, too, cited the fifty "most-noted" works from 1980–1985. The results were striking. The Pearson correlation between the original recency-adjusted scores (as reported in appendix 6-2) and the number of citations in 1986–1987 articles was .76 (p < .001). Appendix 6–3 reports the number of 1986–1987 citations for the first ten works in the list, the second ten, and so on, clearly confirming that the composition of the list, and even its general order, is stable over time.

A final caveat should be expressed about this list: *It is not a "hit parade."* By identifying the "fifty most-noted works," one has done just that: identified the fifty most-noted works. Works are just as often cited for their limitations and weaknesses as they are for their contributions. Moreover, the tendency for a work to be cited is a function of its topic, particularly whether the topic is of central concern to the field or highly specialized. Therefore, this list should not be taken as any sort of popularity index.

THE ISSUES ADDRESSED

There are many things that these fifty works might tell us about the recent development of the field of strategy. However, we must limit our discussion to some manageable scope. Therefore, this analysis will focus on a handful of concerns—six to be exact—that people both within and outside the field seem to be voicing more and more.

I do not have definitive proof that these are the most burning issues among us; but as I visit colleagues around the country, these are the concerns that come out, time and again, about the field of strategy in the eighties:

- "We have broken too sharply from our past; we've discarded our legacy."
- "We are using increasingly sterile data that lack organizational richness and texture."
- "We are doing too much number-crunching, often without any theoretical aim."
- "Our models and methods are too static."
- "Our research is based on restrictive and naive assumptions about managerial roles."
- "Our research is overly concerned with performance and pre-scription."

In the sections that follow, I will use data from our study to shed light on the validity of each of these concerns. As noted earlier, I will concentrate on reporting the findings and will leave much of the interpretation to the reader.

Broken from Our Past?

A concern I often hear voiced is that the field of strategy has dis-carded its legacy. In its quest for legitimacy and maturity, and with an influx of newly trained researchers, the field is accused of scrap-ping its origins, ignoring a substantial theoretical, methodological, and practical tradition. To the extent that this continual reinvention and redefinition is occurring, it no doubt aggravates any identity crisis the field may have.

An approach to studying this issue is to examine continuity in researchers and exemplars in the field. Chuck Hofer's 1976 paper, in which he examined essentially everything that had been written in the field at the time, serves as one basis for comparison. In fact, it is hard to identify anything then in the field of strategy that was excluded from that article's reference list. The reference list cites works by 105 different authors; that is, 105 different people after accounting for multiple and joint authorships. In turn, our set of fifty works from the early eighties had fifty-eight different authors. What is the overlap between the two lists? Seven people. This signals a radical demarcation between who did research in the sixties and seventies, and who did it in the early eighties.

If one uses the Schendel and Hofer (1979) book as another basis for comparison, the conclusion is the same. The book had forty-two contributors, carefully selected as the field's leading thinkers. The overlap with our list is five people. This small, hence extraordinary, group consists of Arnold Cooper, John Grant, Ian MacMillan, Henry Mintzberg, and Ian Mitroff. Although needing verification, I would guess that few other fields, in any two nearly adjacent five-year periods, would have such radical changes in their principal figures.

Another way of looking at continuity is in terms of the field's exemplars, or the kinds of works that the field draws upon. Evered (1980) tallied the most commonly cited works by contributors to the Schendel and Hofer volume. In order of frequency, they were Chandler (1962), Ansoff (1965), Boston Consulting Group (1968), Rumelt (1974), Andrews (1971), Allison (1971), and Hofer's (1975) contingency article. By comparison, if one looks at the reference lists of our fifty early 1980s works, the most common entries were Porter (1980), Miles and Snow (1978), Child (1972), Thompson (1967), Andrews (1971), and Chandler (1962). So, there is some overlap. Interestingly, by their vintage, Lawrence and Lorsch, Child, and Thompson could have been more prominent in the Schendel and Hofer volume. Their recent emergence adds evidence of a shift in the paradigms and the literature bases the field of strategy has tended to draw upon.

Sterile Data?

The next concern often heard is that strategy researchers are using increasingly sterile data that lacks richness and texture and is detached from the phenomena being studied. Others writing in this volume—Ned Bowman, Dick Daft, and Vicki Buenger—have echoed this criticism. Judging the "richness" of data is, of course, a matter of taste. However, knowing the means of data collection is helpful to anyone making that judgment.

Among our fifty early 1980s works, twenty-three were empirical. Table 6-1 reports their data sources. (Some used more than one kind of data.) Fifteen were archival (six of which were based on the PIMS

Table 6-1. Data Sources for Twenty-three Empirical Projects.*

Archival	15
Survey	9
Interview/observation	10
Laboratory	0

*Adds to more than twenty-three owing to multiple data sources.

data set), nine used survey data, ten used interview and observation data, and none used laboratory data. Thus, there appears to be a reasonable spread. If we assume that laboratory studies are most remote from organizational reality, the criticism of sterility seems ill founded. Conversely, if we assume that only interview and observation data can qualify as textured, then over 40 percent (ten of the twenty-three) of the empirical studies qualify. Eclecticism seems to exist. Strategy researchers appear not to have abandoned talking to managers or getting inside organizations.

In a related vein, Ned Bowman raises concern in this book about the lack of recent empirical books in the field. Such projects, which Ned appropriately contends often carry the most texture and richness, were indeed in short supply among our fifty works. In fact, there were only three: Harrigan's (1980) book on decline, Quinn's (1980) book on logical incrementalism, and the Peters and Waterman (1982) book. (I consider Peters and Waterman not only to be an unequivocally empirical project but also, in major ways, to be literature-based and theory-based. For instance, it is often forgotten that the first nearly 100 pages present a very substantial literature review.) All the other books, of which there were eight, were texts or quasi-texts. So, it seems Ned Bowman is right: there has not been much in the way of research-oriented empirical books recently.

Too Much Aimless Number-Crunching?

The next concern often heard is that strategy researchers are doing too much atheoretical number-crunching. The critics say that, in their attempt to escape being labeled "soft," strategists will factor, cluster, regress, and LOGIT everything in sight.

Have we really fallen into a "numbers mentality"? Dare I now say, "Let's look at the numbers?" Adapting a system set forth by Dick Daft (1980) in a review of *ASQ* works, we can classify the twenty-three early 1980s empirical projects according to how they present their data, or by what Dick would call "the richness of the language." The results are as follows (these will add up to more than twenty-three because data can be presented in multiple ways): four were qualitative, three were quantitative with no significance tests, seven were bivariate with significant tests, and eleven were multivariate. There is a clear tendency toward multivariate number-crunching, the kind of reporting that Dick Daft would call "low-variety language." I know my own research has made me a party to this trend, but I have to share Dick and Ned's concern about it.

We now turn to the other part of the criticism—that a great deal of strategy research is without any theoretical focus. To start an examination of this issue, we need to first identify whether the twenty-three empirical projects in our study were primarily inductive or deductive in their intent. As figure 6–1 indicates, seven were induc-

Figure 6–1. Theoretical Focus of Twenty-three Empirical Projects.

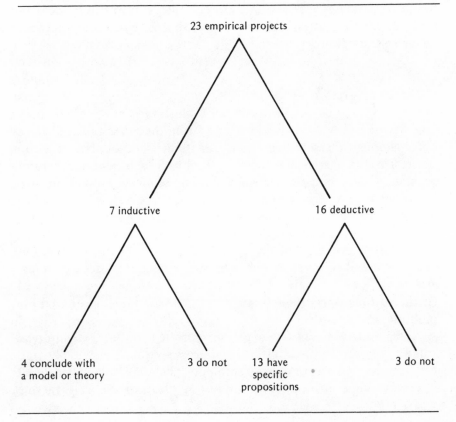

tive and sixteen were deductive. Proponents of inductive research might be troubled by this lopsidedness. However, I am not at all sure the proportions are amiss. For instance, any halfway promising theory ought to be tested at least three to five times with different types of samples, different control variables, and so on. Thus, we might expect the general proportion of emphasis on theory generation as opposed to theory testing to be about one to four. The fact that the ratio is one to two supports my own concern that we have far too many untested or undertested ideas in our field.

Of the seven inductive projects, four conclude by articulating a model, theory, or propositions. The other three present data and demonstrate some general patterns, but never do achieve a theoretical statement of what the data mean. As for the sixteen deductive projects, critics would anticipate that many would be without any guiding hypotheses—that they would just be descriptive data exploration. In actuality, thirteen had very specific propositions. This is heartening—and certainly not the sort of pattern we would have found a decade ago. More and more, strategy researchers seem to have concise theoretical frameworks and specific hypotheses they are trying to work from.

Too Static?

The next concern we hear a lot about, from the other authors in this book, among others, is that the field's models and methods are too static. This is an especially crippling weakness for a field that focuses on managerial problems, for which timing, sequence, and change are key elements. As figure 6–2 indicates, there are two ways in which we can examine the dynamism embedded in a research project. One has to do with the model or theory, the other has to do with the data. Models can be thought of as either static or dynamic. A dynamic model involves flows—growth, stages, sequence, decay, timing, and so on. In turn, data can be categorized as either cross-sectional (gathered for a specific point of time) or longitudinal (gathered for multiple time periods).

As figure 6–2 portrays, the majority of the twenty-three empirical studies we examined were static and cross-sectional, essentially running counter to the essence of strategy. The static longitudinal cell is empty, since no one would undertake the expense of gathering

Figure 6–2. Treatment of Time in Twenty-three Empirical Projects.

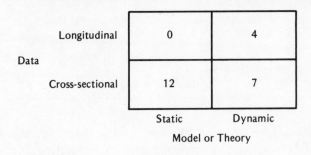

		Static	Dynamic
Data	Longitudinal	0	4
	Cross-sectional	12	7

Model or Theory

longitudinal data to test a static model. The two dynamic-model cells are somewhat represented. However, the ideal for the field of strategy—the dynamic model with longitudinal data—is, as the critics would predict, now a very scant cell.

Naive Assumptions?

Dick Daft and Vicki Buenger, in their chapter, express concern with the field's assumptions about managerial work. Particularly to the extent that researchers assume managers to be rational maximizers, they are laboring under a very restrictive and naive view.

We explored the underlying assumptions about managerial work in the fifty early 1980s works, classifying the dominant assumption of each work as follows:

Strategic Rationality: The general management task is to identify techno-economic opportunities and problems, systematically search for and weigh alternatives, and make choices that maximize organizational performance.

Bounded Rationality: Organizations and individuals within them have bounded rationality. The management task is to accommodate these limitations or develop ways to minimize them (improved information flows, staffing, and so on).

Political: The general management task is to maintain the organizational coalition by acquiring, using, allocating, and channeling power (both externally and internally).

Table 6-2. Dominant Underlying Assumptions About Managerial Work.

Strategic Rationality	26
Bounded Rationality	9
Political	5
Symbolic	2
Garbage Can	0
No Single Dominant Assumption	8

Symbolic: The general management task is to maintain the organizational coalition by creating and manipulating symbols (for both internal and external consumption).

Garbage Can: Since organizations are "garbage cans" into which problems, solutions, and people are thrown together, the general management task is either (a) futile, (b) a matter of dealing with chaos, or (c) not amenable to coherent description and analysis.

This list is in order of the restrictiveness or naivete of the assumption, with strategic rationality being most restrictive and naive, and the garbage can assumption probably the least.

As table 6-2 indicates, and as Dick and Vicki speculate, the field is enamored with the underlying assumption of strategic rationality. Collectively, strategy researchers seem unwilling to cater to the humanly flawed organization—the bundle of incomplete cognitions, cliques, biases, distorted sensors and information channels, boredom, and distractions that typify the real firm. Unfortunately, if our assumptions outstrip and defy reality, our contributions to managerial practice are destined to be modest.

Too Concerned with Prescription?

The final concern to be addressed—and here again, one that Dick and Vicki address in their chapter—is that the field of strategy is overly concerned with performance and prescription. My own view is that an emphasis on prescription is a central part of the mission and distinctive competence of the field of strategy. It is part of what sets us apart from, say, organization theory or economics. However, I agree it would be a mistake to focus solely on prescription without

Figure 6-3. Conceptual Elements in Strategy Research.

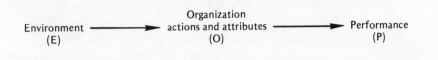

Environment ———————▶ Organization actions and attributes ———————▶ Performance
(E)   (O)   (P)

an understanding of the inner workings of the phenomena that lead to the prescriptions.

To examine the question of whether the field is overly prescriptive, we built a simple, concise framework for classifying all the conceptual elements that strategy researchers examine. As figure 6-3 portrays, there are three broad classes of conceptual elements: (E) environment, or phenomena existing outside the organization; (O) the organization's actions and attributes, including strategy, policies, people, information flows, and so on; and (P) performance, or effectiveness.

Using this three-element framework, the fifty works we examined can be classified according to whether they are prescriptive or not, where a prescriptive work is defined as having performance as a dependent construct. As table 6-3 reports, the primary emphases of the fifty works are about evenly divided between description and prescription.

We can start by looking at the tallies of descriptive studies—those that do not attempt to relate aspects of environment or organization to performance. One work—my own on an empirical typology of industrial-product environments (Hambrick 1983)—examined only aspects of environments (E). There were seven works that focus on identifying and elaborating upon some single organizational phenom-

Table 6-3. Dominant Conceptual Focus of Fifty Projects.

Descriptive		Prescriptive	
E	1	O,P	5
O	7	E,P	1
P	1	E,O,P	16
O_1,O_2	7		
E,O	5		

enon (O), be it slack, structure, executive behavior, or whatever. One—Ed Freeman's (1984) book on stakeholder analysis—focused exclusively on performance (P), asking such questions as: What constitutes performance? What do we need to know about performance? Seven works examined the associations or links between two or more different aspects of organizations (O_1, O_2). Five dwelt on relationships between environmental and organizational phenomena (E,O).

The remaining works (excluding seven that had no dominant assumption or discernible correspondence to our framework) were prescriptive. That is, they included performance as an explicit or implicit dependent construct. Five works focused on the links between certain organization characteristics and performance (O,P), usually implicitly arguing for universal prescriptions. One work— Scherer (1980)—focuses predominantly on the link between environmental (or industry) attributes and performance (E,P). Finally, a heartening sixteen—the largest number for any single category—took essentially contingency views, in which environment was posited as moderating the links between organizational characteristics or actions and performance (E,O,P).

This seems a very encouraging spread, highlighting that the field is not single-minded in its concern with prescription. A significant body of researchers have focused on the theoretical description of phenomena apart from their implications for performance. If I had one pet idea, however, it would be that we need more studies and theories that, like Ed Freeman's book, look strictly at performance. What constitutes performance? How should it change over time? What are the connections among various aspects of performance? Prescription should be our ultimate aim, but we must learn more about what really qualifies as an improved state for the organization.

NEEDED DIRECTIONS: PREPARING
FOR THE NINETIES

This chapter has focused on where we have been as a field. It makes sense now to discuss where we ought to go from here. Some of my preferences already will have been apparent in the above analysis, but now I would like to discuss five specific hopes for future strategy research. These will not deal with topical areas of study or specific methodologies. Those choices depend on trends unfolding in the business environment around us, theoretical breakthroughs, and dead ends none of us can possibly foresee, as well as researcher tastes and repertoires. Instead, my emphasis will be on relatively broad themes that I hope will define the essential character of the strategy field in the 1990s.

Continuing Commitment to Generalism

As a field matures, there is a natural tendency for specialization to occur. However, this trend is eventually destructive, leading to microscopic inquiries, lack of integration, and divisiveness. The field of strategy is falling victim to this trend, and we must somehow countervail it. Our researchers—particularly the younger researchers—are increasingly specialized, constrained in their theoretical and methodological range, and dogmatic about their preferred perspectives. At national meetings, I see more and more intolerant eye-rolling during paper presentations. As a member of several editorial review boards, I observe more and more fellow reviewers engaged in knee-jerk criticisms, not of black-and-white matters but of matters on which no one really knows what perspective will eventually prove most informative.

Aggravating the problem is the increasing tendency for strategy departments at different schools to pursue "niche" strategies, some focusing on behavioral perspectives, others on industrial organization, institutional economics, or game theory. These specializations carry through to the doctoral programs of these schools, and the spiral of parochialism tightens all the more.

The phenomena with which we are concerned—issues facing general managers—inherently require a generalist perspective. The use of various frameworks, methods, and levels of analysis will provide us our best chance for moving knowledge forward.

As already noted, it is only realistic to expect researchers in a burgeoning field to specialize. However, the ideal is that they also will stay open-minded, engage in constructive give-and-take with those holding different interests, read widely, and be alert to deficiencies in their own approaches. We should promote these qualities in our professional societies and journals, in our schools and departments, and particularly in the training and socialization of our students.

Multiple Methods

After the above plea for diversity of perspective, it will not be surprising that I also hope to see diversity of research methods over the years ahead. Our field grew out of a clinical research tradition. This method took a great deal of abuse in the late seventies and early eighties; as our data showed above, the trend has been toward much heavier reliance on archival and survey data. Fortunately, the data also show a reasonable spread of methods used in our recent research. This diversity needs to continue, since every research question needs to be explored from different vantages. Some of those vantages incorporate great richness and texture; some provide tests of generalizability; some (lab experiments) provide stringent controls. Research will progress only with an interweaving of these methods. Researchers not only should be tolerant and encouraging of others in the use of various methods but should expand their own methodological repertoires in pursuit of their research questions.

Theory Testing

The strategy field has a tradition of idea generation with relatively little follow-up testing. It is, as the old wag goes, an area in which far more has been written than is known. In the recent past, as our data above show, researchers have done a somewhat higher number of deductive, theory-testing projects. This type of research is very important. Ironically, it often goes unsung and is even criticized as derivative or incremental.

In the academic business, ideas are a dime a dozen; in contrast, good ideas are exceedingly rare. However, in order to know whether an idea is good or not, it must be tested and retested. It may be the original theorist who earns the most eventual acclaim for a great idea. However, it is the testers—those who painstakingly design studies, operationalize complex constructs, and undertake the expense and frustrations of securing data—who ultimately inform us of the worth of different ideas. We need to keep the importance of theory testing squarely in front of us and bestow credit on those who do it well, each of us striving to do our fair share of testing—of both our own and others' ideas.

Dynamic Models and Data

Strategy and all other aspects of top management work are dynamic—involving timing, sequencing, ebbs and flows, and responses and counter-responses. Yet, as our data above show, research in the field scarcely acknowledges the role of time. We must correct this problem. More of our models need to be dynamic, and our data need to be longitudinal.

Without necessarily embracing their assumptions about limits on managerial discretion, strategists stand to learn a great deal from population ecologists. They incorporate the flow of time into almost every model they build; similarly, they collect longitudinal data for all their empirical projects. These models and methods often require more ingenuity, money, and analytical sophistication than static models and cross-sectional data. However, adoption of these is essential to the future of strategy.

Realistic Assumptions About Managers and Organizations

Our data revealed that the vast preponderence of recent strategy research has labored under an assumption of strategic rationality in organizations. Top managers may intend to be rational maximizers (and they can be counted on to tell researchers of those intentions), but the reality is that they are finite individuals like the rest of us. When put together in a social context—complete with information distortions, division of labor, status seeking, and imprecise control systems—managers can be expected to deviate from techno-economic rationality all the more. The strategy field needs more models and methods that account for and examine departures from strategic rationality. This invariably will require more input from behavioral disciplines—particularly psychology, sociology, and political science—and proportionately less from economics and traditional management thought. Until our assumptions square with reality, we have little chance to influence managerial practice.

CONCLUSION

I close by emphasizing that we, as a field of inquiry, must build into our efforts a capacity to be reflective and self-critical. We need the courage and patience to step back and see if we are on track and comfortable with where we are headed. Conversely, we must avoid yo-yoing around each time a critic claims the wisdom of a new path or perspective. We must be true to our charter: the study of general management problems from the point of view of the general manager. That is our distinctive competence, and it is a realm of great theoretical and practical promise.

REFERENCES

Allison, G. T. 1971. *Essence of Decision: Explaining the Cuban Missile Crisis.* Boston: Little, Brown and Company.

Andrews, K. R. 1971. *The Concept of Corporate Strategy.* Homewood, Ill.: Dow Jones-Irwin.

Ansoff, H. I. 1965. *Corporate Strategy.* New York: McGraw-Hill Book Company.

Boston Consulting Group. 1968. *Perspectives on Experience.* Boston: Boston Consulting Group.

Chandler, A. D., Jr. 1962. *Strategy and Structure: Chapters in the History of the American Enterprise.* Cambridge, Mass.: MIT Press.

Child, J. 1972. "Organizational Structure, Environment and Performance." *Sociology* 6: 1–22.

Daft, R. L. 1980. "The Evolution of Organizational Analysis in *ASQ*, 1959–1979." *Administrative Science Quarterly* 25, no. 3 (September): 623–636.

Evered, R. 1980. Review of *Strategic Management: A New View of Business Policy and Planning*, edited by D. E. Schendel and C. W. Hofer. *Administrative Science Quarterly* 25, no. 3 (September): 536–542.

Freeman, R. E. 1984. *Strategic Management: A Stakeholder Approach.* Marshfield, Mass.: Pitman.

Hambrick, D. C. 1983. "An Empirical Typology of Mature Industrial-Product Environment." *Academy of Management Journal* 26, no. 2: 213–230.

Harrigan, K. R. 1980. *Strategies for Declining Businesses.* Lexington, Mass.: D. C. Heath and Company.

Hofer, C. W. 1975. "Toward a Contingency Theory of Business Strategy." *Academy of Management Journal* 18: 784–810.

_____. 1976. "Research on Strategic Planning: A Summary of Past Studies and Suggestions for Future Efforts." *Journal of Economics and Business* 28: 261–286.

Jauch, L. R. 1983. "An Inventory of Selected Academic Research in Strategic Management." In *Advances in Strategic Management*, edited by R. Lamb, pp. 141–175. Greenwich, Conn.: JAI Press.

Miles, R. E., and C. C Snow. 1978. *Organizational Strategy, Structure, and Process.* New York: McGraw-Hill Book Company.

Peters, T. J., and R. H. Waterman. 1982. *In Search of Excellence: Lessons from America's Best-Run Companies.* New York: Harper & Row.

Porter, M. E. 1980. *Competitive Strategy.* New York: Free Press.

Quinn, J. B. 1980. *Strategies for Change: Logical Incrementalism.* Homewood, Ill.: Richard D. Irwin.

Rumelt, R. P. 1974. *Strategy, Structure and Economic Performance.* Cambridge, Mass.: Harvard University Press.

Saunders, C. B., and J. C. Thompson. 1980. "A Survey of the Current State of Business Policy Research." *Strategic Management Journal* 1: 119–130.

Schendel, D. E., and C. W. Hofer, eds. 1979. *Strategic Management: A New View of Business Policy and Planning.* Boston: Little, Brown and Company.

Scherer, F. M. 1980. *Industrial Market Structure and Economic Performance.* Chicago: Rand McNally and Company.

Thompson, J. C. 1967. *Organizations in Actions.* New York: McGraw-Hill Book Company.

APPENDIX 6-1:
RECENCY-ADJUSTED SCORING SYSTEM

The number of times a work is cited is partly a function of when it was published. For instance, a 1980 work simply has more chance to be cited than, say, a 1984 work. To adjust for this effect, the raw citation counts were weighted by a measure of the opportunity for citation. The opportunity for citation is equal to the total number of strategy articles surveyed that were published in years subsequent to the focal work.

For example, Porter (1980) was cited 63 times in the 479 articles examined. However, 76 of those articles were published in 1980, when there would be essentially no chance that Porter's book could be cited. Therefore, the weighted score for Porter (1980) is: 63/403 × 10,000 = 1,563; where 63 is the number of cites, 403 is the number of articles surveyed subsequent to the focal work's year of publication, and 10,000 is a constant multiplier to scale all the numbers up to integer values.

A more precise weighting scheme would have been to consider the exact issue (within a year) of publication as a bench mark for gauging opportunity for citation. However, such a refined scheme would have led, at most, to a minor rearrangement of the list of fifty, but not to any appreciable changes in its membership.

APPENDIX 6-2:
THE FIFTY MOST-NOTED STRATEGY WORKS OF 1980-1985
(using a recency-adjusted scoring system)

Rank	Score	Citation
1	1563	Porter, M. E. *Competitive Strategy.* New York: Free Press, 1980.
2	875	Gupta, A. K., and V. Govindarajan. "Business Unit Strategy, Managerial Characteristics and Business Unit Effectiveness at Strategy Implementation." *Academy of Management Journal* 27, no. 1 (1984): 25-41.
3	875	Hambrick, D. C., and P. A. Mason. "Upper Echelons: The Organization as a Reflection of Its Top Managers." *Academy of Management Review* 9, no. 2 (1984): 193-206.
4	625	Anderson, C. A., and C. P. Zeithaml. "Stage of the Product Life Cycle, Business Strategy, and Business Performance." *Academy of Management Journal* 27, no. 1 (1984): 5-24.
5	595	Quinn, J. B. *Strategies for Change: Logical Incrementalism.* Homewood, Ill.: Richard D. Irwin, 1980.
6	564	Hambrick, D. C., I. C. MacMillan, and D. L. Day. "Strategic Attributes and Performance in the BCG Matrix—A PIMS-based Analysis of Industrial-Product Businesses." *Academy of Management Journal* 25, no. 3 (1982): 510-531.
7	564	Peters, T. J., and R. H. Waterman. *In Search of Excellence: Lessons from America's Best-Run Companies.* New York: Harper & Row, 1982.
8	545	Bourgeois, L. J., III. "Strategy and Environment: A Conceptual Integration." *Academy of Management Review* 5, no. 1 (1980): 25-39.
9	523	Hambrick, D. C. "Some Tests of the Effectiveness and Functional Attributes of Miles and Snow's Strategic Types." *Academy of Management Journal* 26, no. 1 (1983): 5-26.
10	500	Fredrickson, J. W. "The Comprehensiveness of Strategic Decision Processes: Extension, Observations, Future Directions." *Academy of Management Journal* 27, no. 3 (1984): 445-466.
11	500	Ramanujam, V., and N. Vankatraman. "An Inventory and Critique of Strategy Research Using the PIMS Database." *Academy of Management Review* 9, no. 1 (1984): 138-151.

Appendix 6-2. *continued*

Rank	Score	Citation
12	446	Snow, C. C., and D. C. Hambrick. "Measuring Organizational Strategies: Some Theoretical and Methodological Problems." *Academy of Management Review* 5, no. 4 (1980): 527–538.
13	444	MacMillan, I. C., D. C. Hambrick, and D. L. Day. "The Product Portfolio and Profitability—A PIMS-based Analysis of Industrial-Product Businesses." *Academy of Management Journal* 25, no. 4 (1982): 733–755.
14	422	Hall, W. K. "Survival Strategies in a Hostile Environment." *Harvard Business Review* (September-October 1980): 75–85.
15	422	Harrigan, K. R. *Strategies for Declining Businesses.* Lexington, Mass.: D. C. Heath and Company, 1980.
16	397	Hayes, R. H., and W. J. Abernathy. "Managing Our Way to Economic Decline." *Harvard Business Review* (July-August 1980): 67–77.
17	393	Hambrick, D. C. "Environment, Strategy and Power within Top Management Teams." *Administrative Science Quarterly* 26, no. 2 (1981): 253–276.
18	375	Freeman, R. E. *Strategic Management: A Stakeholder Approach.* Marshfield, Mass.: Pitman, 1984.
19	363	Mason, R. O., and I. I. Mitroff. *Challenging Strategic Planning Assumptions.* New York: John Wiley & Sons, 1981.
20	347	Bourgeois, L. J., III. "Performance and Consensus." *Strategic Management Journal* 1, no. 2 (July-August 1980): 227–248.
21	322	Haspeslagh, P. "Portfolio Planning: Uses and Limits." *Harvard Business Review* (January-February 1982): 58–73.
22	322	Snow, C. C., and L. G. Hrebiniak. "Strategy, Distinctive Competence, and Organizational Performance." *Administrative Science Quarterly* 25, no. 2 (1980): 317–336.
23	303	Cosier, R. A. "Dialectical Inquiry in Strategic Planning: A Case of Premature Acceptance?" *Academy of Management Review* 6, no. 4 (1981): 643–648.
24	302	Jemison, D. B. "The Contributions of Administrative Behavior to Strategic Management." *Academy of Management Review* 6, no. 4 (1981): 633–642.
25	298	Scherer, F. M. *Industrial Market Structure and Economic Performance.* Chicago: Rand McNally and Company, 1980.
26	291	Hambrick, D. C. "An Empirical Typology of Mature Industrial-Product Environments." *Academy of Management Journal* 26, no. 2 (1983): 213–230.

Appendix 6–2. *continued*

Rank	Score	Citation
27	291	Mintzberg, H. *Power in and Around Organizations.* Englewood Cliffs, N. J.: Prentice-Hall, 1980.
28	282	Grant, J. H., and W. R. King. *The Logic of Strategic Planning.* Boston: Little, Brown and Company, 1982.
29	272	Miller, D. "Toward a New Contingency Approach: The Search for Organizational Gestalts." *Journal of Management Studies* 18, no. 1 (1981): 1–26.
30	272	Woo, C. Y. Y., and A. C. Cooper. "Strategies of Effective Low Share Businesses." *Strategic Management Journal* 2, no. 3 (July–September 1981): 301–318.
31	248	Hambrick, D. C. "Operationalizing the Concept of Business-Level Strategy in Research." *Academy of Management Review* 5, no. 4 (1980): 567–575.
32	248	Kudla, R. J. "The Effects of Strategic Planning on Common Stock Returns." *Academy of Management Journal* 23, no. 1 (1980): 5–20.
33	248	Miller, D., and P. H. Friesen. "Archetypes of Organizational Transition." *Administrative Science Quarterly* 25, no. 2 (1980): 268–299.
34	242	Bourgeois, L. J., III. "On the Measurement of Organizational Slack." *Academy of Management Review* 6, no. 1 (1981): 29–39.
35	242	Deal, T. E., and A. A. Kennedy. *Corporate Cultures: The Rites and Rituals of Corporate Life.* Reading, Mass.: Addison-Wesley Publishing Company, 1982.
36	242	Miller, D., M. F. R. Kets De Vries, and J. M. Toulouse. "Top Executive Locus of Control and Its Relationship to Strategy-Making, Structure, and Environment." *Academy of Management Journal* 25, no. 2 (1982): 237–253.
37	242	Pfeffer, J. "Management as Symbolic Action: The Creation and Maintenance of Organizational Paradigms." In *Research in Organizational Behavior*, edited by L. L. Cummings and B. M. Staw, ch. 2, pp. 1–52. Greenwich, Conn.: JAI Press, 1981.
38	242	Pfeffer, J. *Power in Organizations.* Marshfield, Mass.: Pitman, 1981.
39	241	Hitt, M. A., R. D. Ireland, and K. A. Palia. "Industrial Firms' Grand Strategy and Functional Importance: Moderating Effects of Technology and Uncertainty." *Academy of Management Journal* 25, no. 2 (1982): 265–298.

Appendix 6–2. *continued*

Rank	Score	Citation
40	232	Astley, G. W., and A. H. Van de Ven. "Central Perspectives and Debates in Organization Theory." *Administrative Science Quarterly* 28, no. 2 (1983): 245–273.
41	232	Burgelman, R. A. "A Process Model of Internal Corporate Venturing in the Diversified Major Firm." *Administrative Science Quarterly* 28, no. 2 (1983): 223–244.
42	223	Abell, D. F. *Defining the Business: The Starting Point of Strategic Planning.* Englewood Cliffs, N. J.: Prentice-Hall, 1980.
43	212	Jemison, D. B. "The Importance of an Integrative Approach to Strategic Management Research." *Academy of Management Review* 6, no. 4 (1981): 601–608.
44	212	Mitroff, I. I., and R. O. Mason. "The Metaphysics of Policy and Planning: A Reply to Cosier." *Academy of Management Review* 6, no. 4 (1981): 649–651.
45	212	Porter, M. E. "The Contributions of Industrial Organization to Strategic Management." *Academy of Management Review* 6, no. 4 (1981): 609–620.
46	212	White, R. E., and R. G. Hamermesh. "Toward a Model of Business Unit Performance: An Integrative Approach." *Academy of Management Review* 6, no. 2 (1981): 213–223.
47	202	Narayanan, V. K., and L. Fahey. "The Micro-Politics of Strategy Formulation." *Academy of Management Review* 7, no. 1 (1982): 25–34.
48	198	Lindsay, W. L., and L. W. Rue. "Impact of the Organization Environment on the Long-Range Planning Process: A Contingency View." *Academy of Management Journal* 23, no. 3 (1980): 385–404.
49	198	Miller, D., and P. H. Friesen. "Momentum and Revolution in Organizational Adaptation." *Academy of Management Journal* 23, no. 4 (1980): 591–614.
50	198	Wissema, J. G., H. W. Van Der Pol, and H. M. Messer. "Strategic Management Archetypes." *Strategic Management Journal* 1, no. 1 (1980): 37–47.

APPENDIX 6-3: ANALYSIS OF 1986–1987 CITATIONS
OF MOST-NOTED EARLY 1980s WORKS

	Rank Based upon 1980–1985 Analysis _(grouped by tens)_					
	_1–10_	_11–20_	_21–30_	_31–40_	_41–50_	_51–60*_
Number of Cities by 146 1986–1987 Articles	127	64	52	40	31	13

*The works that ranked 51–60 in the original analysis were examined in order to confirm that not only the order of the top fifty was relatively stable but also that the overall membership was stable.